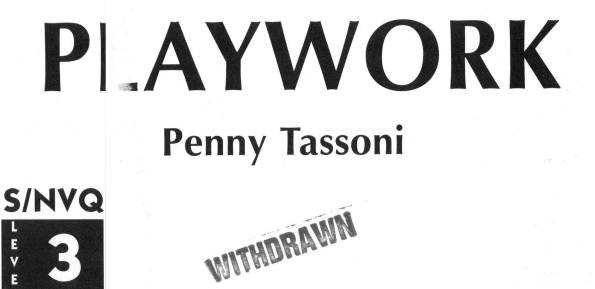

# PLAYWORK

**Penny Tassoni**

**S/NVQ**

**LEVEL 3**

WITHDRAWN

Candidate Handbook

Heinemann Educational Publishers,
Halley Court, Jordan Hill, Oxford OX2 8EJ
A division of Reed Educational & Professional Publishing Ltd

Heinemann is a registered trademark of Reed Educational & Professional Publishing Limited

OXFORD   MELBOURNE   AUCKLAND   JOHANNESBURG
BLANTYRE   GABORONE   IBADAN   PORTSMOUTH NH (USA)
CHICAGO

First published 2001
2005   2004   2003   2002   2001
10  9   8   7   6   5   4   3   2   1

A catalogue record for this book is available from the British Library on request.

ISBN 0 435 44914 1

Designed by Wendi Watson
Cover photograph by Tony Stone Images
Typeset by Techset Ltd, Gateshead
Printed and bound in Great Britain by The Bath Press Ltd, Bath

## Acknowledgements

I would like to start by thanking my family and friends once more for their continued
support, especially the Tassoni Team – Jean-Michel, Anne-Marie, Marie-Lise and Jess the cat.

Many people have helped me research or lent their support for this project. I would
particularly like to thank Tracy Reading, Out of School Manager for Kinderquest, Christine
Banks, Hastings and Rother District Trust along with Deanna Gabb, Schools Out Manager
and Fellowship of St. Nicholas, St. Leonards.

The author and publishers would like to thank the following for permission to reproduce
photographs: Actionplus (page 182), Collections/Anthea Sieveking (page 138), Format/
Joanne O'Brien (page 278), Format Ulrike Preuss (pages 41, 166, 247, 254 and 306),
Sheena Verdun (pages 59 and 84), John Walmsley (pages 18 and 96).

I would also like to thank my publisher Mary James, who once again has skilfully guided
me through this project as well as Gillian Burrell who has successfully and patiently co-
ordinated the editing stages.

## Dedication

In memory of David, my brother

# Contents

# Foreword

*Kids' Clubs Network* welcomes this new publication.

National Vocational Qualifications (NVQs) in Playwork will form the backbone of new developments in childcare for school age children. Level 3 in particular has an importance as it underpins the new Day Care Regulations implemented by OFSTED. Playworkers all over the UK are working towards and gaining this qualification and running projects within communities that are offering quality provision for children and families.

*Kids' Clubs Network* are promoting playwork qualifications and working with local Early Years Development Childcare Partnerships to recruit and train more playwork staff. This publication will be invaluable in that quest for playwork trainers, lead officers, development workers and playworkers themselves.

Playworkers need hands-on experience, either on placement or by being employed in a playwork setting; a kids' club, an adventure playground or a play project. However, they also need theoretical information, inspiration and practical guidance. This publication provides the latter and will go a long way in supporting playworkers in their staff training and development.

The future is exciting for all those involved in developing childcare at local level. There are more opportunities for playwork at local level and more childcare providers are setting up projects. Quality, well-trained playworkers are the key to their success.

Penny Tassoni is a well-known advocate of playwork. Many congratulations on the publication, it will be of great benefit to the playwork profession.

***Maggie Walker***
**Head of Operations**
**Kids' Clubs Network**

# Introduction

Welcome to this handbook for the National Vocational Qualification (NVQ) or Scottish Vocational Qualification (SVQ) Level 3 in Playwork. It is an exciting time to enter the field of Playwork as there are increasing opportunities for qualified playworkers at all levels.

## Understanding the structure of your S/NVQs

There are now S/NVQs for nearly every job sector. Every S/NVQ has formally approved nationally set standards. In order to gain your S/NVQ, you will need to collect evidence which will show that you are working competently and have the knowledge behind what you are doing. The national standards guide you to collecting the evidence.

## How the standards work

The standards are divided into **units** of competence. These are like the mini-job descriptions as they outline particular aspects of playwork. Each unit is given a letter and a number. The units are then subdivided into **elements**. These break down further the skills that the playworker will need to demonstrate (referred to as **performance criteria**) and identify the range of situations that playworkers may have to work in (referred to as the **range**). Finally at the end of each unit, is a list of the **knowledge, understanding, values and skills** that you are expected to have in order to be able to do an aspect of the job well.

To achieve an award at Level 3, candidates must complete nine mandatory units and two optional units chosen from ten.

## Using this book to help you with your S/NVQ

This book can help you in the following ways:

- The book gives unit by unit coverage of each of the mandatory and four of the optional units
- At the end of each chapter there are **short unit tests**. These are questions that will help you to check your knowledge and understanding. These can be used to provide knowledge, understanding and skills evidence and your assessor will guide you on this.
- Within each of the chapters there are also features such as '**Active knowledge**' and '**Consolidation**'. These are a good way of helping you to reflect upon your learning. These can also be used as a way of providing evidence for your portfolio. Your assessor should be able to give you some guidance as to the best use of these.

## Assumptions and values

Playworkers have a special role in working with children as they are able to create safe and exciting opportunities for children to play. This is reflected in the assumptions and values of this sector and in turn underpins the occupational standards for S/NVQs. It is important to make sure that you have read and understood the value statement before starting your course of study.

### Assumptions

The first assumption is that:

- Children's play is freely chosen, personally directed behaviour, motivated from within; through play, the child explores the world and her or his relationship with it, elaborating all the while a flexible range of responses to the challenges she or he encounters; by playing, the child learns and develops as an individual.

The second is that:

- Whereas children may play without encouragement or help, adults can, through the provision of an appropriate human and physical environment, significantly enhance opportunities for the child to play creatively and thus develop through play.

In this way the component Playworker always aims to provide opportunities for the individual child to achieve her or his full potential while being careful **not to control** the child's direction or choice.

# Values

Play opportunities are provided in a number of settings (for example, Local Authority, Voluntary or Commercial) for children with a variety of needs, in a complex society diverse in culture and belief; nevertheless, competent Playwork always has the following underlying *values*:

- The child must be at the centre of the process; the opportunities provided and the organisation which supports, co-ordinates and manages these should always start with the child's needs and offer sufficient flexibility to meet these
- Play should empower children, affirm and support their right to make choices, discover their own solutions, to play and develop at their own pace and in their own way
- Whereas Play may sometimes be enriched by the Playworker's participation, adults should always be sensitive to children's needs and never try to control a child's play so long as it remains within safe and acceptable boundaries
- Every child has the right to a play environment which stimulates and provides opportunities for risk, challenge and the growth of confidence and self-esteem
- The contemporary environment in which many children grow up does not lend itself to safe and creative play; all children have the right to a play environment which is free from hazard, one which ensures physical and personal safety, a setting within which the child ultimately feels physically and personally safe
- Every child is an individual and has the right to be respected as such; each child should feel confident that individuality and diversity are valued by the adults who work and play with them
- A considerate and caring attitude to individual children and their families is essential to competent Playwork and should be displayed at all times
- Prejudice against people with disabilities or who suffer social and economic disadvantage, racism and sexism have no place in an environment which seeks to enhance development through Play; adults involved in Play should always promote equality of opportunity and access for all children, and seek to develop anti-discriminatory practice and positive attitudes to those who are disadvantaged
- Play should offer the child opportunities to extend her or his exploration and understanding of the wider world and therefore physical, social and cultural settings beyond their immediate experience
- Play is essentially a co-operative activity for children both individually and in groups; Playworkers should always encourage children to be sensitive to the needs of others; in providing play opportunities, they should always seek to work together with children, their parents, colleagues and other professionals and, where possible, make their own expertise available to the wider community
- Play opportunities should always be provided within the current legislative framework relevant to children's rights, health, safety and well-being
- Every child has a right to an environment for play, and such environments must be made accessible to children.

Good luck with your S/NVQ in Playwork. I hope that this book will be a helpful tool for you.

*Penny Tassoni*

# Unit A55

# Contribute to improving personal and organisational performance

In order to meet the needs of the children and parents who use your organisation's service, the organisation needs continually to think about what it is doing and consider whether there is a need to make any changes.

The need to think about the 'service' offered means that you have to evaluate your own practice, and that of your organisation. This is not always an easy task, as it involves looking at your own and your organisation's strengths and weaknesses, and considering ways in which performance might be improved.

The elements for this unit are:

A55.1   Contribute to evaluating own and organisational practice
A55.2   Contribute to improving organisational performance
A55.3   Contribute to own personal development

## Element A55.1 | Contribute to evaluating own and organisational practice

Before you can make any improvements, either in your own performance or that of your organisation, you must first evaluate your own strengths and weaknesses. This section looks at the ways in which your own performance and that of your organisation can be measured.

### WHAT YOU NEED TO LEARN

- Monitoring and evaluating your work
- Encouraging feedback from colleagues, parents and children
- Collecting and noting information
- Handling criticism constructively
- Comparing what was achieved with what was planned

## Evaluating your own work

Taking time to consider your own performance and to evaluate your own work is always worthwhile. Doing this allows you to consider how you might handle things differently in the future, as well as helping you to consider why things are working well.

To help you evaluate effectively, it is worth thinking first about what you actually need to do in your job role. Job roles vary enormously from one playworker to another, and most people have several strands to their jobs.

Tasks that playworkers might do include the following:

- liaising with social services
- supervising staff
- working as part of a team
- working with children
- liaising with parents
- checking and putting out equipment
- planning
- keeping registers
- clearing away
- cleaning
- maintaining health and safety
- ordering resources
- marketing.

## Active knowledge ✔

1 Write down the tasks that you carry out in your organisation.
2 Why are these important to the smooth running of the organisation? (You might like to use the list above to help you.)

Your own practice and that of your organisation can be evaluated in three key ways:

- personal observations
- feedback from colleagues
- feedback from children, parents and others.

### Personal observations

One way in which you can evaluate your practice is through your own observations. You might notice that children seem to enjoy talking to you, or that are able to manage squabbles between children effectively. These are *strengths*. In the same way, if you think about all areas of your work, you might be able to identify some *weaknesses* in practice – for example, you might run out of glue, because it was not re-ordered, or you may notice that you find it harder to relate to particular children. To be able to analyse strengths and weaknesses in this way, you need to look carefully at the reactions of others to your work, and to think about the *reasons* for your strengths and weaknesses.

Personal observations can also be used to assess the practice of the whole setting. You may catch the dissatisfied look of a parent, or notice that the number of enquiries about places has increased recently.

Personal observations can therefore be helpful in evaluating both your own and the organisation's practice. You should not rely on them solely, however, because they are individual perceptions – other people's perceptions might be quite different.

## Case study

Hendrick has been working as a playworker for three years. He is keen to gain his NVQ Level 3 in order to start applying for management positions. He tries to reflect on his strengths and weaknesses. He realises that he is particularly good with the older children, who often seem to play for longer periods when he is working with them. He thinks that this is because he has a relaxed approach with them, and is good at acknowledging their ideas. When he considers his weaknesses, he identifies that his organisational skills could be improved – he noticed that a colleague was irritated the other day because he had forgotten to buy some art materials, and this had resulted in one of the promised play activities being abandoned.

## Gaining feedback

Feedback from colleagues, parents and children helps organisations and individuals to be objective in analysing their strengths and weaknesses. Most organisations now recognise that by listening to the people they serve they can improve their service. By encouraging suggestions and comments, you can look more objectively at the way you work and consider whether you should be making any changes. A parent, for example, might suggest that staff wear badges; while a child might comment that the setting needs more footballs! Comments and suggestions such as these are often useful, as they come from the people who actually use your service, who may see things from a slightly different point of view.

There are two types of feedback: *informal* and *formal*.

*Informal feedback can provide valuable insights*

## Informal feedback

*Informal* feedback comes in the form of odd comments and suggestions, often made on the spur of the moment. For example, a parent might comment that his child really enjoyed learning to play a game of cards last week, or a colleague might suggest that it would be a good idea to change the timing of the snack time.

It is important not to 'lose' informal feedback, so it is a good idea to record it, as well as the name of the person who gave it. In some cases, it will be important to act on the feedback immediately, by talking to your line manager or a colleague; in other cases the feedback might form part of a discussion in a staff meeting.

## Case study

Below are some examples of comments made by colleagues, parents and children during a summer's playscheme:

- 'The water in the toilets is very hot today.'
- 'George said that he didn't get a turn on the mini-football last week.'
- 'We're getting low on red paint.'
- 'I like going outside to eat lunch.'
- 'The cost of the trips seems quite high this year.'
- 'The rota for taking children out to the park isn't really working very well.'
- 'I'm worried that the children's lunch boxes aren't being stored in a cool place.'
- 'I wish that you were open a little earlier in the morning – it's such a rush to drop them here and then get to work.'

1 **Explain why these comments are important.**
2 **Which ones need to be acted on immediately?**
3 **Are there any comments that might need following up in a staff meeting?**

## Formal feedback

*Formal* feedback can be collected by using questionnaires, by conducting interviews or by offering a suggestions/comments box. It provides the opportunity to gain different people's opinions about specific subjects, such as opening hours, or the type of activities that children most enjoy.

Information gained from formal feedback must be analysed and used in some way, otherwise the people who gave the information will feel that they wasted their time.

### Using questionnaires and evaluation sheets

Many organisations use written questionnaires or evaluation sheets in order to collect specific information. The advantages of using this method are that people can fill in the forms when they have time and that they can remain anonymous if they wish. This is also a time-effective way of collecting information: it is quicker to distribute 20 sheets than to carry out 20 interviews.

# Keys to good practice

## Devising questionnaires and evaluation sheets

- Choose your questions carefully, to generate the maximum amount of information.
- Make sure that you frame some questions to allow people to make criticisms. For example, 'Were there any activities that you did *not* enjoy?'
- Consider using 'closed' questions, such as 'Which of these activities do you prefer?'
- Use language that is easily understood and clear.
- Make sure your presentation is good.
- Check for spelling errors.
- Make sure that the finished questionnaire or evaluation sheet is not too long.
- Add a 'Comments' section, to allow people to contribute other observations and ideas.
- Try out your questionnaire or evaluation sheet with a colleague.
- Choose a good moment to ask people to fill in your evaluations or questionnaires.

---

Market researchers suggest that to maximise the number that are filled in, you should offer participants a small prize!

## Active knowledge ✔

Choose one area of your work setting's service on which you would like feedback, for example the choice of activities, the opening times, or the cost.

1  *Devise a simple questionnaire, using a maximum of 10 questions.*
2  *Try out the questionnaire on a minimum of 5 people.*
3  *What did you find out from doing this?*

## *Using interviews*

Another way of collecting feedback is by interviewing people, or talking to them. This can be done by having a list of prepared questions which you then ask, noting down the replies. Interview questions can be 'open' ones which allow people to talk generally about particular topics, such as 'What do you think about taking the children out on visits?'

Interviews have the advantage that people will often say more face to face than they are prepared to write down. You can also add supplementary questions if you need clarification. Interviews are useful too in situations in which people might have difficulty in filling in forms.

## Gaining feedback from children

Children should be the main focus of your work, so you need to find ways of gaining feedback from and involving them. Older children might enjoy designing their own evaluation and feedback sheets before filling them in, whereas younger children might prefer just to talk about what they enjoy doing or the equipment that they would like. There is a variety of topics on which you should be gaining feedback from children, as shown in the diagram.

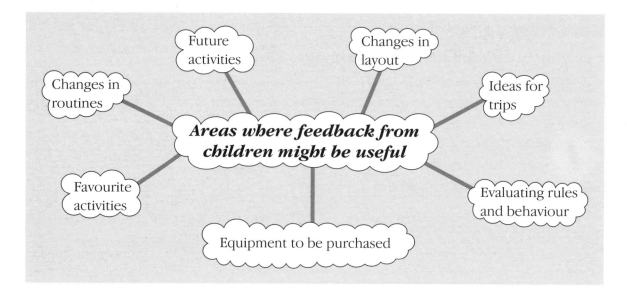

Future activities

Changes in layout

Changes in routines

**Areas where feedback from children might be useful**

Ideas for trips

Favourite activities

Evaluating rules and behaviour

Equipment to be purchased

## Consolidation

Think of a time when you consulted with children in order to help you improve aspects of your own practice or of the organisation's.

◆ *How did you gain the information?*
◆ *How did you record the information?*
◆ *What changes did you make as a result of the children's feedback?*

## Recording information

In order to be able to evaluate practice, it is essential that the information you gain is recorded correctly. This might be in note form, but may need to be in more detail if an important issue has been raised. For example, if a parent has made a strong criticism, it might be a good idea to write down exactly what was said and in what context, and pass this on to your line manager or other members of the team.

## Handling others' criticism constructively

As a result of receiving feedback from others, you might find that some criticisms or comments are linked to work for which you are responsible. A colleague might comment that a rota system does not seem to work, or that she is often not informed of changes that are taking place.

It is never easy to take criticism, especially if you have put 100 per cent effort into your work, but in order to improve your professional practice it is always necessary to listen to what others are saying. Try not to become defensive: instead, see this as a learning process. You might be learning about the way other people perceive situations, or you might be learning about the disadvantages of a certain way of working. One way of coping with criticism is to consider what you can *learn* from criticism. The diagram below shows some questions that you could consider asking yourself.

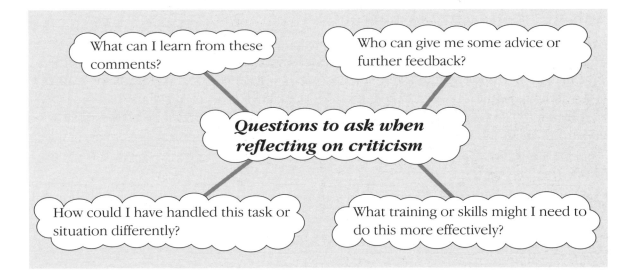

Questions to ask when reflecting on criticism

- What can I learn from these comments?
- Who can give me some advice or further feedback?
- How could I have handled this task or situation differently?
- What training or skills might I need to do this more effectively?

## Comparing what was achieved with what was planned

Most organisations review and monitor their plans. This allows them to see how effective the plans were, and informs future planning. Reviewing can take place on an informal basis or it might take place more formally, for example during staff meetings. In some cases an organisation's funds might be dependent on formal evaluations which monitor the quality of the provision.

There are many ways in which an organisation might monitor and review its plans. Some organisations keep a day-to-day log book in which they evaluate each session's activities, whereas others simply ask staff members to review plans at the end of the week.

**St Nicholas Community Playscheme log book**

| Date | |
|---|---|
| Monday 21st July | Today, we went to the park as the children fancied a picnic outdoors. This was quite a success, although a letter needs to go out to remind parents about sending in sunscreen. Afternoon session went particularly well - a new version of stuck in the mud was invented by one group.<br><br>Jasmina Hurd – Leader |
| Tuesday 22nd July | A wet day meant that the children were unable to go out doors for much of the day. Some tensions in the group at first over the computers until a solution was found. Several children are working on a dance routine and a talent show is being organised for Thursday!<br><br>Jasmina Hurd – Leader |
| Wednesday 23rd July | The children are getting really excited by the talent show and now most of the group is keen to take part in some way. Posters are being designed, competition rules are being drawn up and Michaela's mum has promised to send in a video camera.<br><br>Martin Hargreaves — Deputy |

*A playscheme's log*

## Evaluate events, activities and routines

It is also useful to evaluate our performance on specific tasks. For example, after organising an outing, you could think about how smoothly this went, and what lessons you can draw from this for the future. It is easy to dwell on the weaknesses of any event or activity, but it is also important to consider the positive aspects of events that have been planned – if you can identify the ingredients for success, you will be better able to repeat this on future occasions. It is not always easy to identify the reasons for success, but often some key features can be recognised in each case. Typically these key features will include the following:

- good forward planning
- strong time-management skills
- enthusiasm of staff
- sufficient resources
- children actively involved in planning
- appropriate timing of the activity
- enough time allowed for the activity.

---

### Consolidation

Think about a recent activity or task for which you were responsible.

- ◆ *Explain what you did and why you did it.*
- ◆ *Evaluate your own performance – did the activity go as well as you had planned? Were there any ways in which you could have improved your performance?*
- ◆ *What were your strengths?*
- ◆ *What have you learnt from carrying out the activity or task?*

---

## Element A55.2 Contribute to improving organisational performance

On page 3 we looked at the importance of gaining feedback from others. Feedback and evaluations are only useful, however, if they are acted upon. This section looks at ways in which feedback and evaluations might be used to improve personal or organisational performance.

### WHAT YOU NEED TO LEARN

- Assessing feedback and passing it on to others
- Helping to evaluate information and suggest changes

- Assessing the effect of changes
- Implementing changes
- Monitoring and evaluating changes

## Assessing feedback

There are different ways in which to gain feedback; for example, asking parents and children to fill in evaluation forms or noting down comments that have been made. Other organisations and professionals might also provide feedback – for example inspectors from the local authority, visiting speakers, or assessors. Evaluations and comments are essentially pieces of information: the next stop is to assess this information. This might mean reading through the evaluation sheets or reading through written comments, bearing in mind the context in which comments have been made. In some cases, further information might be needed in order to gain a complete picture – this would be true, for example, if only 6 out of 30 questionnaires have been returned. Gaining a full picture is essential: an organisation is unwise to make changes unnecessarily, based on a single comment. An organisation might therefore decide to follow up a questionnaire by asking some face-to-face questions

### Case study

Joanne, a parent of one of the older children at the after-school club, has decided not to carry on sending her child. The manager is keen to find out whether there is any particular reason why she no longer wants the place, especially as the club is keen to attract older children.

The club has a system of asking parents to fill in a short questionnaire when a child leaves, and the manager asks Joanne if she would mind filling it in. The information gained shows that the main reason for leaving is that there are no facilities for carrying out homework, and that Joanne has decided to take the child to a childminder where some of the homework can be completed.

1 *Why might the manager need to research this issue further?*
2 *In what ways might the manager seek further information about whether facilities for homework are important?*
3 *Why is it a good idea to carry out 'exit' questionnaires when children leave?*

## Passing on feedback to others

It is always a good idea to let colleagues know if you have received any sort of feedback from parents, children or others. Good feedback makes people feel that their work is being valued; negative feedback might need investigating. In some cases, negative feedback might be 'one off', and not representative of the organisation's performance, but it should still be passed on in case the criticism is taken further.

## Case study

One of the children at the playscheme says to Chris, a playworker, that someone has taken the crisps from her lunchbox. Chris smiles and says that the crisps will probably turn up. This same child is always losing things and blaming others – yesterday it was a jumper that was 'stolen', whereas in fact the child had actually left it in the outdoor area.

The next day a very angry parent complains to the manager that her daughter had come home hungry and upset because some of her lunch was missing. The manager does not know what happened, and finds herself in a very awkward position as the parent tells her that this had been reported to a member of staff and nothing had been done.

1  *What should Chris have done?*
2  *Why is it essential that any comments be passed on to others?*

The timing of passing on information to colleagues is also important. Some feedback and comments need to be passed on immediately (as in the case study above), whereas other information should perhaps be presented when there is time to explain or discuss it. If information is going to be presented at team meetings, it is essential that the line manager or colleague responsible has had warning and enough time to look at it carefully before the meeting.

## Assisting others in evaluating information and suggesting changes

If you have been responsible for collecting and collating information, your line manager might find it helpful to have your ideas and comments. In this way, you can help put the information in context and answer any questions that arise. You might also be able to suggest some effective changes to current practice or offer some ideas about how the information might need to be added to or stored.

## Case study

Jo, the deputy manager at an after-school club, feels that homework is a potential issue that might need to be thought about. Several parents have made comments about the difficulty they have in finding time to supervise homework at home, and one parent has withdrawn her child because the club offers no facilities for children to do their homework. Jo asks the manager if they could stay behind one night to talk about the issue of homework. She has the exit questionnaire that was filled in by one parent recently, and she also has noted down the comments of several parents.

Jo realises that many playworkers feel uncomfortable about bringing homework into the club, because they want to create a play environment for the children and are working hard to make the club feel different from school. During the discussion with the manager, Jo puts forwards different points of view regarding homework, and they agree that further information is probably needed before they can make any sort of decision. They agree on the following action plan:

| Action points | By whom? | By when? |
|---|---|---|
| Find out the views of children in the club | Jo | End of March |
| Send out a questionnaire to parents | Jo | End of March |
| Raise the issue of homework with staff during a staff meeting | Manager | 15th March |

1 *Why was it important for Jo to ask for some specific time to talk this through with her manager?*
2 *Why is it a good idea to collect further information before making any decisions?*
3 *Why is it useful to record information on an action plan?*

## Assessing the impact of potential changes

Before implementing any changes, it is essential to assess their potential impact. Most changes will have some disadvantages as well as advantages, so it is a useful skill to be able to consider the effects of changes. The key areas to be thought about before changes can be made include:

- staff support and morale
- staffing requirements
- children's needs
- parents' needs
- the budget
- health and safety
- other organisations.

### Staff support and morale

Most changes that might be made will affect the staff. It is therefore wise to consider the implications of any changes for the morale and work of the staff. For example, it might seem like a good idea to suggest that all staff should sit with the children at lunchtime, but some members of the staff team might prefer to have a break away from the children. As the success of many organisations is reliant on a happy and motivated staff, most managers quickly learn that they have to work *with* their staff in order to implement changes successfully.

### Staffing requirements

In some cases, possible changes will affect the way in which staff are used. For example, parents may comment that they would like longer opening hours: this would have an effect on staffing. Making changes to staffing patterns needs a lot of thought and organisation; staff might need to be approached to change their hours of work or to take on additional hours. In some areas it might be difficult to recruit staff or to find staff willing to work at certain times of the day.

## Case study

Look at the following examples of proposed changes:

- Following a health and safety audit, it has been suggested that during the day all staff, except the manager and deputy, should take it in turns to inspect and where necessary clean the toilets.
- Following a couple of incidents of unwanted behaviour, it has been suggested that staff should plan more structured activities each day.
- It has been suggested that staff should each note down a daily log of their activities.

*Can you work out the likely concerns of staff about these suggestions?*

## Children's needs

Meeting children's needs is paramount. Being with children is the reason why most playworkers love their work. This means that all changes should be thought through to check that they benefit the children. For example, checking that packed lunch boxes are stored in a cool place to avoid food poisoning may seem like a chore, but is essential to children's welfare.

It is good practice to ask children about proposed changes, if these are likely to affect them.

## Parents' needs

In some cases, you need to look at the effect on parents if you make certain changes. You might decide that you would like to increase the number of day trips organised for the children, but you would need to be aware that some parents might not be able to fund these. Parents are important partners in this work: any changes that might affect them should be carefully assessed.

## The budget

Every organisation has to work to some type of budget. Changes might affect the budget of an organisation, so the cost of any change has to be carefully worked out. For example, buying extra equipment might solve one problem, but spending the money in this way might create another. Most managers find that balancing the budget and deciding on priorities is one of the harder aspects of their job. For example, buying a new fridge as a result of a health and safety audit does not seem as attractive as buying some new equipment for the children, but it will have to take priority if the setting is to keep its registration!

## Health and safety

Health and safety must be taken very seriously. If a setting is found to be breaching codes of practice, registration and insurance can be withheld. Suggested changes have to be evaluated carefully with health and safety in mind. For example, changing a layout might affect the ease with which a building could be evacuated in an emergency; and changing a routine might affect the number of staff available to supervise children.

## Other organisations

Some settings have also to consider how any changes will affect organisations with which they work. For example, a setting might be renting premises or using equipment from a school. Similarly, some settings are part of a larger organisation: for example, a playscheme might be based in a workplace or a leisure centre. Settings might also be funded by government grants, or have to work with other partners.

## Implementing changes

As a result of assessing and evaluating feedback, certain changes might be agreed upon. Not everyone finds changes comfortable, and some children and adults can find change quite worrying. If you have responsibility for carrying out changes, you should try to talk to the people who will be affected. This might be colleagues, children or parents. In most cases, when they understand the proposed changes and the reasons for them, those affected are able to adjust happily.

### Active knowledge ✔

Look at the examples below of proposed changes.

- Following several incidents of children losing coats and other items, it has been decided that the cloakroom area should be locked during the day. This means that children who want to get anything will need to ask an adult to accompany them. It also means that if parents want to come and collect their children early, they will need to ask a member of staff to help them collect their children's belongings.
- After a visit from the inspection team, it has been suggested that the setting needs to improve the way in which it is keeping registers of children. A signing-in and -out book has been put at the front door: parents need to sign when they bring or collect their children, and staff must initial each entry.
- Some members of staff have commented that particular people always seem to get out of tidying up at the end of the day, so you have decided that the fairest way would be to design a rota system.

1 *To whom do you need to talk about the changes?*
2 *What would you say about the changes?*

## Keys to good practice

### Implementing changes

- ✎ Avoid making sudden changes, unless there is a good reason for the urgency.
- ✎ Give those concerned ample warning of when changes are taking place.
- ✎ Explain why the changes are necessary.
- ✎ When presenting any changes allow enough time for questions.
- ✎ Think about constructive suggestions.
- ✎ Make sure that you have assessed the effects of any change carefully.
- ✎ Build in opportunities for people to give you feedback after the change has occurred.

*Detailed explanations are necessary when making changes in an organisation*

## Monitoring and evaluating changes

Most changes will need to be monitored in order to see whether they are actually improving the performance of the organisation. There are many ways of monitoring changes. In some cases you will be able to 'see' the change as it will make a visible difference; in others you might need to seek out the views of the children, parents or colleagues. When presenting the change, it is often a good idea to let those concerned know that you will be reviewing its effectiveness later on. This allows everyone to try out the change, knowing that if it does not work they will be able to comment upon it.

## Honeymoon periods

When introducing some changes, you might find that everything seems to go smoothly at first. People may be happy to try out some changes, and enjoy a 'honeymoon' period. Some time later, however, you might find that the changes that have been made are not being carried out, or that those concerned are finding them not effective. You will need to keep monitoring and gathering feedback for some time, and it is not unusual to have to 'tweak' the changes you have made.

### Case study

Carla is responsible for the signing-in and -out book by the front door which has recently been introduced. At first she found that parents were very good about signing in and out, but lately she has noticed that fewer entries are being made. She knows that this system should work well, as she has seen it being used in other settings.

1 *Can you think of any practical reasons why parents might not be signing the register?*

2 *What should Carla do next?*

## Improving performance is a continual cycle

The results of monitoring should mean that the setting develops a cycle of evaluating and improving performance. The most effective and dynamic organisations are always reviewing what they are doing and trying to improve their performance. In contrast, you may be able to think of shops or other services which have a 'tired' or 'sameness' feel to them. This kind of 'tired' feel can sometimes apply in play settings where there have been few changes or attempts to look afresh at what they are doing.

The recipe for a dynamic and successful setting is therefore to develop a positive culture of feedback and improvement. This can be thought of as a continuous cycle, as shown below.

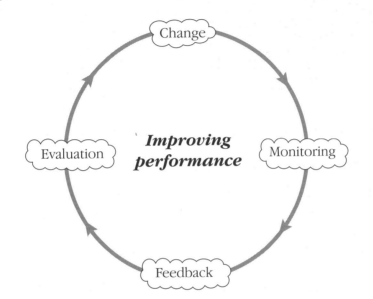

### Consolidation

Think about a change, however small, for which you were responsible.

◆ *Explain how the need for the change was decided upon.*
◆ *How did you present this change to those affected by it?*
◆ *How did you monitor the change?*
◆ *Was the change successful? If so, can you work out why this was?*

## Element A55.3  Contribute to own personal development

Most people in work today realise that continual professional development is essential, not only to safeguard one's job security but also to be able to enjoy and carry out the job effectively. This corresponds with many out-of-school providers, who have realised that staff appraisal is important in developing and retaining motivated and competent staff.

Many employers will offer you the opportunity to have a formal and informal appraisal by your line manager or a responsible colleague. Such appraisals generally result in a personal development plan or action plan which will help you to focus on your strengths and weaknesses. This section looks at how development plans might be used in the workplace, and how you might draw up your own development plan if there is no established staff appraisal system where you work.

## WHAT YOU NEED TO LEARN

- Evaluating work objectively
- Dealing constructively with criticism
- Working out a realistic personal development plan
- Monitoring the development plan

# Evaluating work objectively

## Staff appraisal

When staff appraisal systems were first introduced into organisations, some employees felt very threatened by them. They were often concerned that if any weaknesses were identified they would lose their jobs or their pay. This should not be the case: appraisal is intended to be a two-way process, in which employees are able to talk about what they need in order to carry out their roles more effectively, and what they would like to do to improve their career prospects.

Before staff appraisal systems were introduced, organisations sometimes found that promising employees left them because they were not feeling fulfilled or supported in their jobs. A good staff appraisal system helps both employees and employers. It helps employees because they are able to speak about their jobs and the training they feel they need, and it helps employers because motivated staff work harder.

## Personal development plans

A *personal development plan* can also be known as a *personal action plan* or a *career plan*. Development plans are the end product of a process in which you analyse your strengths, weaknesses and experiences, and consider what the next steps could be for you. The personal development plan is usually drawn up with a line manager, but it could be drawn up with a range of people, providing that they are knowledgeable and objective. If there is no staff appraisal system in your work setting, you could ask a colleague, a careers adviser or an assessor to help you.

Personal development plans vary considerably from individual to individual: some people have a very strong idea of where they want their careers to go and are able to plan for five or more years ahead, whereas many people might look only a year or two ahead.

## Evaluating your current work

The starting point for drawing up a personal development plan is to consider your current role and your work. You will need to consider which parts of your work you carry out effectively, as well as acknowledging any areas in which you could improve your performance. It's also a good idea to reflect upon the areas of work that you most enjoy: these might be areas that you could develop further.

Look at the questions below, and think about your current work.

- What do you enjoy most about your current work, and why?
- What do you least enjoy about your current work, and why?
- Do you have any strengths that you feel are not being used at the moment?
- What areas of your work do you find difficult?

---

## NEWTOWN PLAY CLUB
### Staff Appraisal Form

**Name**    *Simon Mallard*

**Position**   *Deputy Play Leader*

---

1. **Which aspects of your current role do you most enjoy and why?**

   *I enjoy the administrative aspects, particularly record keeping, planning and marketing. I also enjoy the problem solving aspect of my role, for example, organising staff rotas and managing outings.*

2. **Have you identified any areas of work in which you feel you need further training?**

   *I feel that I need further health and safety training so that I can devise the health and safety policy, and carry out risk assessments. I would also like some further computer training so that I can carry out more work on the computer.*

---

*A staff appraisal form*

## Discussing performance and dealing with criticism

You will also need some feedback from your line manager or from a colleague who can be objective about your performance. This can be very helpful: sometimes we are unaware of our own strengths and weaknesses. In order to be able to give you good feedback, your line manager or colleague will probably need to observe you working. This may make you feel quite anxious and self-conscious, but it is actually very useful – by watching you work, the observer will be able to evaluate your performance more effectively and give you more structured feedback.

People who benefit most from appraisals are able to think of feedback, both positive and negative, as a source of information about their performance rather than as critical comments about themselves as people. Try to listen carefully to what is said to you: it is often easy to 'home' in on the negative comments and not hear the full picture.

Remember too that the appraisal process need not be a passive one, in which you simply listen to advice and feedback from the manager. In order to benefit from the process, you should be contributing your own ideas and thoughts, for example explaining how you feel about your current role, and giving you ideas about how the organisation might be able to support you in becoming more effective.

## Case study

Karen has just started her career in playwork, and is keen to progress further. Her organisation runs a staff appraisal system: staff have appraisals every year. Her line manager gave her a form to fill in, and they agreed a date and time when the line manager could watch Karen work. Afterwards the line manager and Karen met together for an hour to carry out the appraisal interview. Karen's line manager used the form that Karen had filled in, and her observation of Karen working, as a basis for the discussion.

Karen's manager started the discussion by saying how well she felt Karen had settled in and how pleased she was that Karen had identified for herself some areas which she still needed to develop. Karen said that she found working with parents difficult and her manager asked if Karen had thought about ways in which she could develop this skill. Karen suggested that she would like some training in working with parents, and also mentioned that the organisation did not really have any policies or guidance to help new staff. The line manager agreed that this was a valid point, and said that she would look at ways in which new staff could be given some induction.

Later in the interview, they looked at ways in which the organisation could help Karen achieve a longer-term career goal: to be a club leader. The line manager asked Karen whether she would be interested in taking on some of the responsibility for ordering stock and marketing, in order to gain some useful experience. Karen said that she would like to do this in a few months' time, but felt that she still needed to get to grips with her current role. They agreed that Karen would come back to her manager when she felt ready to take this on.

1  Why is it important that Karen contributed her own thoughts and ideas?
2  How has the organisation benefited from this appraisal?
3  How has Karen benefited from talking with her line manager?

## Considering areas of potential development

After working out what your strengths and weaknesses are, the next step is to consider which areas you might wish to develop. For instance, you may have realised that you have a talent for working with older children, while also identifying that you never seem to have enough time to keep the paperwork up to date! These might be two areas which you could consider for development, especially if you wish eventually to take on some managerial responsibility where keeping on top of the paperwork will be essential.

*Attending a first aid training course might be a short-term development goal*

Most people find that they have several areas which could be developed, but these then need to be prioritised – it is impossible to work on all areas at once. It is a good idea to decide which areas you feel need to be worked on *immediately*: these will form your short-term development plan, and the others can become part of your medium-term and long-term plans. The case study below shows one playworker's decisions.

## Case study

Asif works in a nursery which also runs a playscheme. The nursery will shortly be opening an after-school club, which Asif is pleased about as he has already started his NVQ in Playwork, working in the holidays on playschemes. Below is a table that he has used to help him identify his areas of development.

| Short term | First-aid training<br>Finish NVQ Level 3 in Playwork<br>Basic computer course |
|---|---|
| Medium term | NVQ Level 4 in Playwork<br>Gain Assessor's Award D32 and D33<br>Apply for positions as deputy manager<br>Book-keeping classes |
| Long term | Manage an after-school club and playscheme |

## Working out how to develop specific areas

Once you have decided which of the areas you wish to prioritise for development, you need to consider how you will do this. In some cases, you might decide that you need some specific training – for example, attending a workshop – or you might feel that you need to gain a qualification. As part of the appraisal interview, your line manager, colleague or assessor should be able to give you some ideas as well. The following list shows some of the ways in which you can help yourself to develop:

- taking on responsibility in the setting, to gain experience
- shadowing a colleague
- a one-day training workshop – in the setting or outside
- a short course of training, such as in first-aid, food hygiene, or basic counselling
- vocational qualifications such as NVQs, an advanced diploma, or management training
- academic qualifications, such as GCSEs, or A-levels
- visiting other settings
- swapping roles with a colleague, for example in another setting
- carrying out research, including reading professional articles
- seeking guidance from a careers adviser.

## Case studies

Look at the following case studies.

- Mary has really enjoyed working with children who have shown difficult behaviour. She wants to find out more about how to work with them. She would like one day to work at the nearby family centre, run by the local authority.
- Simon is new to playwork and feels that he would just like to have a few more ideas for activities, as sometimes the children ask him if he has any ideas for games.
- Jo has worked at the play and family centre for five years and is now a deputy. She already has a qualification in playwork, but feels that she needs some fresh ideas. Eventually she would like to move and take on the position of manager.

1 *Work out what types of development activities might be used for each of these people.*
2 *Explain whether the activities you have chosen might be seen as short-term or medium-term development.*

## Agreeing a realistic personal development plan

There is no point in spending time on drawing up a personal development plan if it is unrealistic. Several factors will affect the success of any plan; they include the following:

- cost
- time
- personal circumstances
- enthusiasm
- support from your organisation.

### Cost

You need to consider the cost of the type of development activity you have chosen. Some development activities, for example shadowing a colleague, should not prove to be expensive; whereas others, such as taking a vocational qualification, might need funding. In some cases the organisation might be able to pay for training, but you might have to fund yourself.

Cost needs to be taken into consideration, but do not let it put you off – by paying for a qualification, you might be able to gain promotion. It is also worth finding out what sources of funding are available: for example, many colleges have bursaries for people on low incomes; and there are government-funded schemes such as Independent Learning Accounts (see Useful addresses on page 325).

## Time

Time is a crucial factor when drawing up your plan. Look at the development activities carefully and consider how much time they will need, and whether you have that time. A two-year course might seem like a good idea, but are you ready to commit yourself to this length of time? It is also a good idea to balance out the development activities so that you have some short-term goals that you can reach quickly, as well as some longer-term ones.

## Personal circumstances

Personal circumstances have a great effect on our working lives. Many people are juggling the needs of their families and friends around their work. It is therefore a good idea to look at the impact of any development activity on your personal life. This is particularly important if you are about to embark on a long-term course of study which will require many extra hours, including the writing of assignments.

If your personal circumstances mean that you cannot take on large-scale development activities, you might decide to focus on small-scale development activities such as shadowing a colleague or setting up an exchange visit with a colleague at another setting.

## Enthusiasm

Your personal development plan will only be useful if *you* want to make a success of it. If you are being 'sent' on training, or if you are only following someone else's suggestions, it is unlikely that you will gain all the benefits.

If you do find that you are unenthusiastic, consider why. Are you lacking in confidence? Are you worried that you will not achieve your goal? Most people have doubts about their abilities, yet taking on development activities tends to make most people feel more confident afterwards.

## Support from your organisation

Although it might not be 100 per cent essential, gaining support from your organisation can be very useful. If you have it, someone will take an interest in what you are doing and may allow you opportunities to gain different experiences. It is also helpful to be able to talk through what you have gained with someone else. Support for development is one sign of a good manager.

## Recording your plan

Most settings have forms on which they record the personal development action plan, although the way that they are used and their style can vary. You can devise your own plan, like the one below. If you design your own form, be sure to consider not just the areas that you intend to develop, but what specific development activities you need, the timescale, and also how you are going to monitor the plan.

# Personal Development Plan

### Area of development – Training

| | Type of training | Reason | Target date | Completed |
|---|---|---|---|---|
| 1. | Appointed persons First Aid course | To gain a basic First Aid qualification | September 2000 | |
| 2. | Behaviour management – workshop | To have some more strategies especially for older children | June 2000 | 15/6/00 |
| 3. | Study skills | To support NVQ work | June 2001 | |
| | | | | |

### Area of development – Work experience

| | Experience | Reason | Target date | Completed |
|---|---|---|---|---|
| 1. | To complete cash book at end of day – shadow Maggie | To have more understanding of running the financial side of the club | September 2000 | |
| 2. | To order stock – see Maggie | To understand how to use the forms – also NVQ evidence | October 2000 | |

*Action plans*

## Getting going!

*You* have to take responsibility for making sure that you can achieve the plan. This might mean finding out about training courses, costs and other development activities yourself. You might also need to be ready to remind colleagues or your line manager that they have agreed to provide you with support. It is a good idea to implement your development plan quickly: most people find that the initial surge of enthusiasm following an appraisal interview fades unless they have actually begun a development activity. This is why you should also include in your plan arrangements for monitoring the plan.

## Monitoring the development plan

For any type of plan to be effective, it is important that you refer to it and chart your progress. You might consider doing this on a weekly or monthly basis. Referring regularly to your plan will help you to remain enthusiastic. It is helpful to do this with your line manager, assessor or colleague, who may have thoughts and ideas.

When you look at your plan, decide what you have achieved and what you could do next. If you see that you have not been able to meet a target, consider the reasons for this. In some cases, you may have been too ambitious, or there may have been circumstances that prevented you from achieving your goal.

Reviewing your plan in this way means that you can set new timescales and decide on any new activities that might be useful. In this way, you should see the whole concept of development plans as an ongoing process, allowing you to build up your experiences and skills.

## Consolidation

Identify one or two areas in your work in which you feel that you might benefit from further training.

◆ **Research the type of training that would be available in your area, including costs.**
◆ **How would your setting benefit if you were to take up this training?**
◆ **What sources of funding might be available for people wishing to take up this type of training?**

*In carrying out this activity, you might find it helpful to contact some of the following:*

- Early Years and Childcare Partnership in your area
- Training and Enterprise Council (from April 2001 this will be called the Learning and Skills Council)
- local colleges of further and higher education
- CACHE, an awarding body for qualifications in playwork
- SPRITO
- National Play Council
- Kids Club Network

## A55 unit test

1 List the three principal ways in which practice can be evaluated.
2 How can questionnaires be used to gain feedback?
3 Why must questionnaires be designed carefully?
4 Why is it important to gain feedback from children?
5 Explain some of the factors to be taken into account before changes can be made to organisational practice.
6 Why is it important to consult with others before making any changes?
7 Why is it important to evaluate any changes once they have been made?
8 What is meant by the term 'staff appraisal'?
9 Why is it a good idea to look for personal development opportunities? What might these include?

# Develop opportunities in the community

Playwork is a relatively new area in the UK, so it is important for everyone working in the field to use opportunities to promote it. In many parts of the country there is very little provision for play activities for older children during holidays and after school. By promoting the benefits of playwork and out-of-school care, you can help stimulate demand for places and thus provide children and parents with more choice and freedom.

This chapter looks at the ways in which you can promote playwork within your local community. The elements for this unit are:

B212.1  Make people aware of benefits and opportunities
B212.2  Establish and maintain effective working relationships with other organisations and individuals
B212.3  Undertake joint initiatives with other organisations and individuals

## Element B212.1  Make people aware of benefits and opportunities

Out-of-school care and playwork have yet to become sustainable and 'embedded' in the UK. For this to happen it is essential that the general public comes to accept its value and be prepared to support it, both by using it and by funding it. For new settings that are receiving financial support from sources such as the local council, local charities and early years partnerships, it is particularly important that they make their community aware of their work and its value. This section looks at the importance of, and ways of, promoting playwork within the local community.

### WHAT YOU NEED TO LEARN

- Promoting your work and your organisation
- Communicating your work's purpose, value and methods
- Emphasising your work's benefits for the community
- Obtaining feedback about its impact

## Understanding the benefits of promoting your work

Some people may find it hard to 'promote' their work or their play setting. They may feel that it is immodest, like 'blowing your own trumpet'. Yet it is essential that playworkers do promote their work, because doing so will:

- help create a demand for places
- help parents and carers to become aware of the setting
- encourage decision-makers to fund the setting
- allow local people to see the benefit of providing play for children
- help to maintain a good reputation
- encourage the general public to see out-of-school care as important.

## Ways of promoting play work and your setting

There are many ways of making your community aware of the work you are doing. It is a good idea to use a variety of methods, although marketing experts say that 'word of mouth' recommendation is always one of the most effective. The diagram below shows some of the methods you could consider.

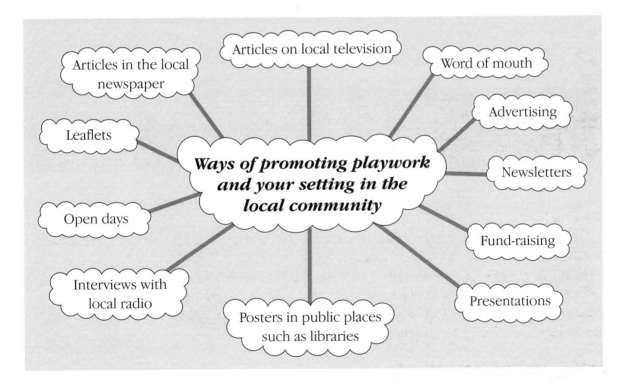

### Using the local media

Television, radio and newspapers are powerful ways of introducing people to the work of your playsetting. Most editors are keen to have local-interest stories, and the coverage of local media can be quite wide.

*Local radio interviews can help to promote the work of your setting*

## How to use the media to get publicity

Editors have to find newsworthy stories whilst working to tight deadlines. Find out when the deadlines are for your local newspaper and radio. Quite often, articles will appear if there is some space to be filled!

## Keys to good practice

### Using the media

- Editors like to tie a local story to a national one. An article about your play setting is more likely to appear if it seems relevant to something happening nationally, or to a debate locally.
- Telephone the organisation to tell them that you have an interesting story.
- Make sure that you write a clear summary of what your setting is doing.
- Make sure that your summary is *concise* – editors will not want to plough through many pages of details.
- Wherever possible, send or fax a typewritten copy – this is easier to read than handwriting.
- Make sure that you give contact details in case the reporter or editor needs further information.
- Be ready to respond straightaway – they may need to go on air quickly, or send a photographer around the next day.
- If an article does not appear, do not give up. Keep sending in 'stories'.

### Word of mouth

Personal contact and recommendation is a powerful way of promoting a setting. There are many ways that this can happen – among parents and carers themselves, or by your talking to parents and carers, other professionals and decision-makers. Personal contact with you will only work well if you are able to communicate sympathetically and effectively.

## Open days

Open days give the whole community an opportunity to come and see a setting in operation. It is important to advertise open days well to ensure a good turn-out. Send personal invitations to neighbours and to people in the community who might not otherwise feel that they should come, such as the local care home, local churches and other places of worship. Providing refreshments for visitors, and competitions and activities for younger children, will help to attract a wide range of people into the setting.

*Open days can show your community the benefit of playwork*

## Keys to good practice

### Organising a successful open day

- Organise the day well in advance.
- Decide on some key people to organise the day.
- Approach other organisations to find out whether they wish to work with you on the day.
- Decide on key organisations and people that you wish to target.
- Advertise and promote the day widely beforehand.
- Write personal invitations to some sections of the community.
- Provide refreshments.
- Consider inviting a well-known person, or having a focus for the day.
- Involve children in the day.
- Make sure that the setting is looking its best.
- Make sure that there are information sheets or leaflets for people to take away.
- Consider giving away badges, pens and other free items. (These could be sponsored by local organisations.)

## Newsletters

Newsletters can help parents, carers and others be more aware of your work. If possible, involve children in the production of the newsletters: this helps them to feel ownership of the setting. The newsletter needs to be interesting and easy to read. If you can, get the newsletter printed professionally – to pay for this, you could consider selling advertising or approaching a sponsor.

## Presentations

Presentations are a useful way of informing a targeted audience of your work. Presentations need to be carefully prepared, and you might need to learn the skills of speaking in public. Wherever possible, make sure that you have plenty of literature about your work for the audience to take away if they wish, for example leaflets, posters and newsletters. Make sure that they know how to make contact with you.

## Keys to good practice

### Preparing presentations

#### Do's

- Prepare notes
- Practise what you are going to say, out loud
- Prepare professional-looking handouts or other materials
- Smile
- Speak slowly and clearly
- Thank your audience for listening to you

#### Don'ts

- Don't apologise for your presence
- Don't talk beyond the time slot you have been allocated
- Don't talk too fast
- Don't talk with your head down
- Don't *read* your 'speech'
- Don't take material that looks amateurish

## Leaflets

Carefully designed leaflets can be very useful. They can be distributed at presentations and during open days, or sent with letters. They can be very economical if they are produced in bulk. It is best to have the leaflets professionally produced: the look of the leaflet may influence people's perceptions of the play setting.

# Keys to good practice

## Designing and producing leaflets

- Try to get them designed and printed professionally.
- Do not include information that may quickly become out-of-date (such as costs)
- Give contact numbers and addresses.
- Focus on the main message.
- Do not cram in information.
- Write in a clear, concise style.
- Keep sentences short.
- Use bullet points.
- Check that all details are correct.
- Involve children in the design and process of production.

## Posters in public places such as libraries

Posters can be fun and eye-catching, and can help provide people in the community with information. Make sure that they are displayed widely. If they have times or dates on them, check that they are taken down afterwards, so that they do not look out of date. Children enjoy designing posters and can be encouraged to take part in the project.

## Fund-raising

Through fund-raising many settings can help the wider public find out about playwork. Funds can be raised either for the setting itself or for a cause chosen by the children. Fund-raising is potentially a good story, and might also stimulate an item in the local media.

# Keys to good practice

## Fund-raising

- Make sure that you have a definite focus for your fund-raising.
- Encourage the children to be part of the process.
- Have a timescale for the appeal.
- Have a clear plan of how the money is to be raised, and who will be responsible for its safe keeping.
- To collect money on the street or door-to-door, you need a licence from the local authority.
- Do not send children out collecting money door-to-door or getting sponsors.
- Consider whether door-to-door collections will be seen negatively by the local community.
- Popular fund-raising strategies include: encouraging the children to make items for sale; coffee mornings; raffles; washing cars.

## Advertisements

Advertisements can raise public awareness of a setting, but in general it is more economic to try other methods first, such as free publicity in local papers. It is important when considering adverts to think about where they will be placed, and who will actually read them. It may be just as effective to put up a card in the local corner shop as to take out an advertisement in the local paper.

## Keys to good practice

### Advertising

✎ Check the information carefully.

✎ If using local media, find out whether there are any special deals or offers.

✎ Make sure that you have a clear message.

✎ Do not cram in too much detail.

✎ Think about other methods of promoting your setting alongside advertising.

---

## Consolidation

Think of one way in which you have recently promoted your setting or area of work.

◆ *How you did this?*
◆ *Why was this method chosen?*
◆ *What were you hoping to achieve by doing this?*

---

## Communicating the purpose, values and method of your setting or area of work

If you work with other people, it is a good idea to consider together what you see as the principal aims of your work and of the setting. Once this is agreed, everyone will be giving similar messages. One way that many organisations do this is by devising a 'mission' statement: the aim of a mission statement is to express clearly the purpose and values of the setting or area of work.

### Writing a mission statement

There are many styles of mission statement. The best ones are short and to the point. They express briefly the 'keys' of what you are hoping to achieve.

Most organisations create a mission statement by first getting everyone in the setting together and pooling ideas. This is a good teamwork exercise, and helps people to focus on what it is they are aiming to achieve.

## St Nicholas Community Playscheme

**Mission Statement**

'To provide accessible and affordable community-based, out-of-school care'

## NEWTOWN PLAY CLUB

**Mission Statement**

'To provide play opportunities and a safe environment for children aged 5 – 14 years'

*Promoting play opportunities for children*

*Mission statements*

## Using your mission statement

Most settings use their mission statement in their literature, for example in leaflets, posters and adverts. This is why the language of the mission statement has to be clear, and why the overall statement should be short.

### Active knowledge ✔

Does your setting have a mission statement?

1  *If yes, explain how the mission statement reflects the aims of the organisation.*
2  *If no, try to work out what type of message you would **wish your organisation to portray.***

## Communicating information about other organisations

As well as providing information about your own organisation, it is good to be able to give information about other organisations that do similar or related work. There are many reasons for doing this:

- it helps people in the community find out information easily
- it provides a point of communication with people in the community – they are more likely to find out more about your setting if they see you as a source of help and information
- other organisations are likely to do likewise, and to pass on information about your and your setting

- by working in a spirit of partnership with others, you are more likely to further the cause of playwork and out-of-school care.

## Making known the benefits of playwork and out-of-school care

In order to be able to inform the community of the wider benefits of our work, it is essential that we understand these ourselves. The exact benefits will vary from setting to setting, but some benefits apply to most settings – see diagram below.

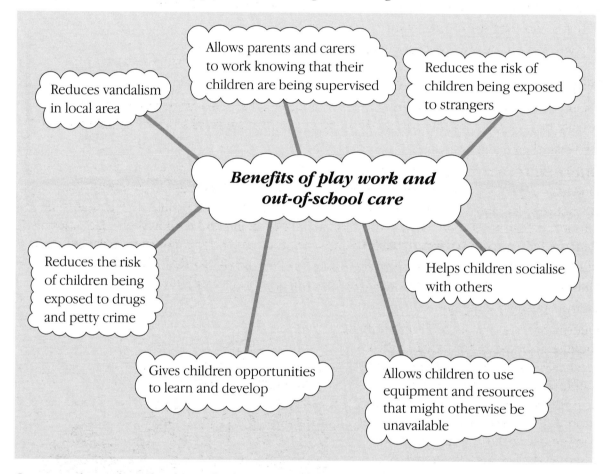

Once you have thought about the key benefits provided by your setting or area of work, you need to consider how best to pass on this information. Make sure that they are printed in your literature and included in any presentations or articles that appear. 'Sell' the benefits of your work to the wider community – you may need their support either in continuing to attract existing funding or in expanding further.

## Active knowledge ✔

Think about your area of work, and the community in which you work.

*What are the key benefits of your work to the wider community?*

# Obtaining feedback about any initiatives

As well as promoting your area of work, you need feedback on your work and on the success of your 'marketing'. This is particularly important following an initiative such as an open day or the placing of an advert.

Feedback serves several purposes. It:

- allows you to find out whether you have managed to get your message across
- allows you to find out who actually *received* the 'message'
- allows you to find out whether your 'message' has been acted upon
- helps you plan for future 'marketing' initiatives
- gives you an idea of the cost-effectiveness of your chosen method.

## Ways of gaining feedback

There are several ways of gaining information and feedback about our initiatives. It is usually best to use more than one form of feedback, and several sources, in order to gain a balanced view.

### Informal face-to-face interviews

One way of gaining information is to ask people face-to-face about the initiative. This should be done in a non-threatening way, and should sound very much like a chat. It is important that people know why you wish to talk to them, and it should be made clear that any information provided will be treated in strict confidence. To gain a balanced view of people's reactions, try to choose a *range* of people to talk to. This should include children, parents and carers, as well as people from other organisations.

### Using questionnaires

Questionnaires can be helpful in judging the effectiveness of the initiative. They can be given out as people leave at the end of a presentation or open day. 'Exit' questionnaires should be kept short and should invite people to pass comments on the event. Ask them whether they would like any further information about your work, and how they had heard about this event.

*Questionnaires can help in judging the effectiveness of an initiative*

## PLAYSCHEME

We are keen to gain any feedback about our open day. Please could you spend a minute or so filling in this form?

*Thank you!*

1. How did you hear about our open day?

......................................................................................................................

2. Why did you decide to come?

......................................................................................................................

3. What have you most enjoyed about your visit?

......................................................................................................................

4. Has your visit met your needs?

......................................................................................................................

5. Were there any ways in which we could have improved our open day?

......................................................................................................................

If you would like any further information about our after-school club, please write your name and address below.

..........................................................................

..........................................................................

..........................................................................

*Thank you for taking the time to fill this form in.*

*An exit evaluation*

## Collating information internally

Another way in which you can evaluate your success is by noting the number of enquiries received after an initiative, for example the number of phone calls or the number of new visitors. It is always a good idea to ask each new visitor or caller how they knew about the play setting, and then recording this. This analysis might show that an advert or presentation had proved very effective, or that one person had proved very influential.

## Presenting information

There are many ways of presenting information and promoting your work. In order to be successful, it is essential that you match your style of language and presentation to your audience – for example, a leaflet produced for children might be very different from one aimed at parents and carers.

# Keys to good practice

## Presenting information

- Ask colleagues for their advice and draw on their experience.
- Look at past materials used by the setting.
- Look at similar organisations' materials and presentations.
- Ask someone from the intended 'audience' for suggestions.
- Test your materials or presentation on a member of the intended 'audience'.
- Make sure that there are no spelling errors or grammatical errors in printed materials.
- Check that the overall message is coming across.
- Use visual images wherever possible, as these tend to be more effective – for example, use photographs and drawings in printed materials, and overhead transparencies at presentations.
- Think short! Do not write too much text: keep presentations concise.

# Promoting in line with organisational policies and practices

It is important that your promotional work is consistent with your play setting's policies and practices. If this does not happen there is a danger of giving mixed messages and confusing people. When mixed messages are given the organisation looks inefficient and embarrassing situations can be created. This reflects badly upon your professionalism.

The best way of avoiding such situations is to make sure that colleagues and others are involved, and are aware of any initiatives that are taking place. Any issues such as costs, and any claims made, can be scrutinised to make sure that everyone is happy with them. You also need to be aware when advertising that you do not breach any trading standards – for example, you must not make any false claims!

## Case study

Mark is a playworker who has just joined the setting. He is keen to help, and has designed and distributed a leaflet about the holiday club.

He asked one or two people for some information, but did not show the leaflet to the manager or deputy of the setting. The leaflet has attracted some interest and several enquiries, but unfortunately the prices quoted in the leaflet are last year's, and it has been decided to increase the fees.

1 *Why might this reflect badly on the setting?*
2 *How might the manager and the deputy be feeling?*
3 *How could this situation have been avoided?*

# Element B212.2 Establish and maintain effective working relationships with other organisations and individuals

One of the ways in which you can help playwork and out-of-school care to become established is by working alongside other organisations and individuals. Making contacts and establishing working relationships is often referred to as 'networking'. This section looks at the ways in which you might make contact with others, and how you can maintain these relationships.

## WHAT YOU NEED TO LEARN

- Identifying other organisations with whom you can work productively
- Establishing contact and exploring mutual benefits of links
- Receiving approaches from other organisations
- Maintaining contact and sharing information with organisations and individuals

## Why is networking so important?

Networking is extremely important for many reasons. In particular, recent funding initiatives have been based on organisations' abilities to work together to provide comprehensive services and information. The diagram below shows other benefits of networking:

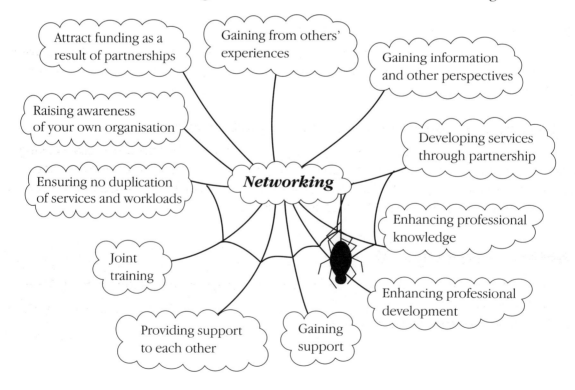

# Identifying other organisations with whom a working partnership might be useful

The type of organisations with which a play setting needs to be in contact will vary from area to area. There are however some specific organisations that you should be aware of, and with which you should try to build up a working relationship. Below is a list of some of these. You should also look at other, smaller organisations and individuals in your area, for example schools, community organisations, and the police. You can find out about organisations by consulting the telephone directory and the local Citizens' Advice Bureau, and also by keeping an eye on your local newspaper.

## Training providers

Training providers such as local colleges and private training organisations are often useful partners because they can often offer staff government-funded training. Usually they are aware of new courses and can advise on career development.

## Employment service

The Employment Service is a useful contact as it can help advertise for staff, and also give information about government initiatives (such as the New Deal). It can also advise on employment issues.

## Training and Enterprise Councils (Learning and Skills Councils)

These regional councils are able to advise on funding arrangements for training, and also give business advice. In the past they have held budgets in order to develop out-of-school care.

## The local council and the local authority

The local council and the local authority can advise about a wide range of services in your area and might also be willing to distribute your literature. Some authorities have funds from Europe for specific projects or because of regeneration grants.

## Early-years and childcare development partnerships

These recently formed partnerships are great places to meet other professionals working in your own or a related field. Most members of partnerships are keen to network and benefit from working together. Partnerships also hold budgets for training and are keen to work with organisations to meet local childcare needs.

## Active knowledge ✔

1 *Make a list of organisations and individuals with which your organisation or setting currently has a working relationship.*
2 *In what ways are these relationships helpful?*

# Establishing contact with organisations and individuals

Once you have identified some key organisations and individuals with which you could make links, you need to make contact. How you do this will depend on how quickly you need to make contact, and also on how confident you feel.

## Networking at meetings

Many contacts can be made at meetings – early-years and childcare development partnership meetings are ideal places to meet others. Look at the attendance list to find out the names of the people to whom you would like to speak. Identify one of these people, then introduce yourself and explain that you have been hoping to meet her or him. Explain your own role. If it seems appropriate, suggest that you exchange work telephone numbers, (not usually home numbers, for reasons of personal security) and business cards.

## Network at training or briefing sessions

You can also make contact with other organisations and individuals at training or briefing sessions: these often attract people in the same or similar fields to your own. As with networking at meetings, you need to be confident enough to approach people and explain your work role.

## Sending out invitations

By sending out an invitation to an open day or a presentation, you can make contact with an organisation or an individual. If you do not know the name of the specific person to whom you could send the invitation, you might need to telephone beforehand. Explain your role, and ask for the name of the person who would be most interested in your work.

## Making contact by telephone

It is possible to make contact by telephone, although this is usually more effective if you already have some proposal or purpose to the call. For example, you might ring the local fire prevention officer to ask whether he or she would be interested in visiting the setting to talk to the children.

# Dealing positively with approaches from other organisations and individuals

Just as your organisation might value partnerships and networking, so other organisations might approach you. You might receive invitations or telephone calls from others. Try always to receive approaches in a friendly and enthusiastic way, as this can lead to an exchange of ideas and an exploration of the shared benefits of working together.

The list suggests how you might deal with approaches from others:

- return the call as soon as possible
- outline the objectives of your organisation
- outline your current role and any ongoing projects

- find out what type of work the other organisation or person is involved in
- consider whether there is any mutual benefit in meeting at this time; if not, keep a note of the person who has contacted you and her or his role
- be enthusiastic, yet professional and courteous in your approach.

## Explore with other organisations the possible benefits of future links

At some time, you need to identify possible mutual benefits to each organisation in co-operating. Although it is pleasant to meet other people, it is also important that your time is used wisely. At some point you need to find out more about the other organisation's aims, objectives and future projects. You will also wish to explain what your own organisation is hoping to do, though without disclosing any confidential information. Be aware of what your organisation can offer to others – for example, your organisation might have particular expertise, such as recent experience of preparing bids.

## Active knowledge ✔

*Make a list that shows what you or your organisation can offer organisations or individuals.*

# Developing and maintaining relationships

For a working relationship to be developed and maintained, everyone must be able to work co-operatively together.

## Keys to good practice

### Effective working relationships

- Be friendly and professional.
- Make sure that you are seen as reliable.
- Deliver any information or work that you have promised.
- Be on time and prepared for meetings. Read through documents in advance, and take them with you.
- Listen carefully to others' points of view.
- Put forward relevant suggestions.
- Keep others within your organisation informed of any developments.

If you are working on a project with others, make sure that you take a fair load of the work that needs to be done, but without taking it all on. If a project needs finance, a written agreement must be prepared to ensure that everyone involved understands their commitments and responsibilities.

## Exchanging information with others

Many working relationships do not lead to projects or initiatives but provide a way of sharing information. Such information might include funding opportunities, legislation, news of future training programmes, and government policies that will affect the sector. There are now many ways of passing information to others, including telephone, email, letter, fax, and face-to-face conversation.

## Passing on information

Before passing on any information that you receive, check its accuracy and whether it is confidential. If you breach confidentiality, your organisation may be excluded from receiving news about sensitive developments, and your own professionalism is called into question. Wherever possible, tell other organisations of the source of your information so that they in turn can get further information directly. It is also important to check that your information is up to date – if you are not sure, make this clear when you pass it on. It is good practice to date and sign written communications, so that the receiver knows who sent it, and when.

## Receiving information

If you have made good working relationships, you should find that you are also receiving information. As with passing on information, you should check its accuracy, relevance and currency.

Here are some questions to consider when receiving information:

- Is the information confidential?
- Is the information up to date?
- Where has the information originated from?
- Is the information accurate?
- Who within your organisation needs this information?
- Where can further information be obtained from?

---

### Consolidation

Think about how you have recently passed information to another organisation.

**Write about this experience, explaining the circumstances. How did you ensure that the information was relevant and accurate?**

---

## Element B212.3 Undertake joint initiatives with other organisations and individuals

In the last few years, there has been much more co-operation between agencies and organisations. This has meant that many projects are carried out in partnership. This has been brought about partly by the way funding has been made available, for example

European social funding *requires* joint working. Partnership working offers many advantages to the general public: instead of providing *competing* services and information, agencies and organisations are providing *complementary* services.

This section looks at the skills that are needed to undertake joint initiatives.

## WHAT YOU NEED TO LEARN

- Agreeing roles and responsibilities in shared work
- Accepting appropriate responsibilities only
- Maintaining contact and reviewing progress
- Keeping colleagues informed
- Resolving any problems, with or without help

## Understanding joint initiatives

The type of initiative in which you might become involved will probably depend on the needs of your local area. In an area where there are no leisure facilities or after-school care, for example, you might work in association with other interested parties to apply for funding to build or convert some suitable premises. This might mean working with the local council, schools, a private leisure provider and social services in order to put in a joint bid for funding.

Alongside working with others to attract funds and develop services, you might also work with other organisations to make campaigns more effective. For example, as part of a joint initiative you might work with the health promotion team and drug awareness workers to produce a local campaign to help children to understand the dangers of using drugs.

*Joint initiatives with other organisations can make campaigns more effective*

## Understanding the bidding process

It is useful to understand a little about the funding process, as you might be asked to support an application to gain funds for a joint project. There is a trend today to awarding funds to projects using a bidding process. This means that your application for a grant will be compared with and scored against competing bids. Bids that show good partnership working, and a project that will help local communities by providing additional services, are generally favoured.

The majority of bids have to be prepared within a relatively short timescale, which means that you have to be able to work well with the other partners.

## Agreeing roles and responsibilities

In order to work well in preparing an application or in working on a particular project, representatives from the different organisations must be able to work effectively together. First everyone must agree on the aim of the project and its design. There is no point in spending time working on a project if one partner later pulls out because they do not agree with the proposal.

Secondly, everyone must understand their roles and responsibilities. Who will take minutes? Who will type the bid? Who will be responsible for collating the information? Agreeing roles and responsibilities is an important part of partnership working, as the diagram shows.

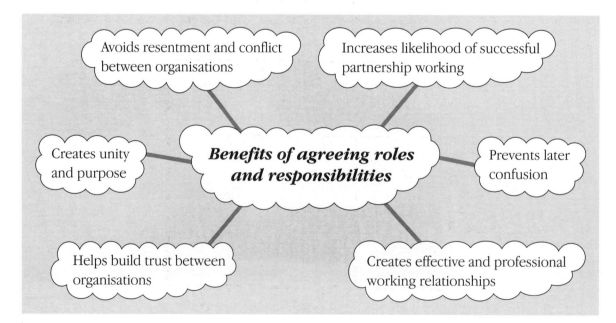

Avoids resentment and conflict between organisations

Increases likelihood of successful partnership working

Creates unity and purpose

**Benefits of agreeing roles and responsibilities**

Prevents later confusion

Helps build trust between organisations

Creates effective and professional working relationships

# Taking on responsibilities

As a project or proposal begins to take shape, it is important that everyone takes some responsibility for the inevitable workload. The work needs to be divided fairly to avoid conflict and resentment. It is usual for the division of work to be in proportion to the gain for the organisation – if one organisation is likely to gain more from a project, then that organisation should take more of the workload.

If you are representing your organisation, discuss beforehand with your colleagues or your line manager how much you can contribute in time and resources. This will prevent you putting your organisation's reputation in jeopardy by promising to carry out something that you cannot achieve, such that your organisation is seen as not pulling its weight. Resentment can quickly build up between partners in a project if one member keeps promising to do something and does not do it in the agreed time.

## Considerations when taking on responsibilities as part of a joint initiative

- How much will your organisation benefit from the joint initiative?
- How much time and what resources can your organisation give?
- Is there anyone else within your organisation who should be involved with the initiative because they have particular strengths or skills?
- What work commitments are you yourself currently carrying?
- What are your personal strengths and skills?

It is a good idea if a written schedule of work is drawn up between members of a joint initiative: everyone is then aware of what needs to be done and who has agreed to do it. It is very important for everyone to keep to the schedule– most projects have to follow a tight time schedule.

## Skills for working with other partners on a joint initiative

Several skills are needed in order to work successfully with others on a joint initiative. They include:

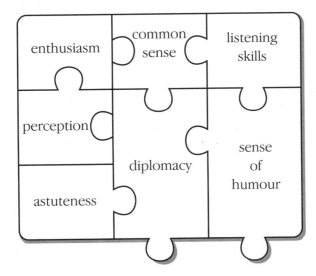

These skills will all be needed. At times, negotiation and compromises will have to be found, and there may be times during the project when people will feel quite under pressure. Diplomacy and common-sense are particularly useful skills as there may be members who do not always agree, and a third party may sometimes be needed to encourage a compromise.

## Maintaining contacts

Once an agreed schedule of work has been drawn up or a proposal has been agreed upon, it is important to keep up the momentum. Without regular contacts, the project is likely to fall apart as partners lose interest or fail to keep to the agreed schedule: this might jeopardise the project. It is also important that contacts are maintained in order to let everyone know of any changes to the proposal or information that might affect their work. It is usual that one or two people become responsible for keeping others informed.

Maintaining contacts usually requires that regular meetings be held at which progress can be discussed. It is often a good idea to agree dates for several meetings at once, so that those involved can keep these times and dates free in their diaries. Notes and minutes of meetings can also help people remain in contact, alongside telephone calls and informal meetings. Timescales for meetings and contacts need to be realistic in order that everyone can achieve them.

## Informing others of difficulties

There might be times when you are unable to meet your responsibilities as a working member, for example due to sickness or because information you have requested will arrive later than expected. If this happens, let others know of the difficulty as soon as possible. The schedule of work can then be adjusted, or someone else might be able to take on your task. In some cases, you might be able to find someone within your own organisation who can help instead, but it is still a good idea to let the others in the partnership know that you are doing this. Failure to let others know when difficulties arise can lead to tension and frustration in the group, and may jeopardise the project if a tight timescale is being worked to. It also reflects badly on your organisation's and your own professional reputation, and might mean that in future you are not seen as effective and reliable.

## Case study

Florence was keen to be her organisation's representative on a steering group that was trying to attract funds to build an outdoor play area for her village. She promised at one meeting that she would be responsible for sending out the minutes of that meeting, and for arranging a venue for the next meeting. After a month, other partners began to be concerned that they had not received any details of a meeting or any minutes from the previous one. One of the members phoned Florence, who said that she had been too busy to do anything and that her organisation was no longer interested in supporting the proposal.

1  *How might Florence's actions affect her organisation's reputation?*
2  *In what ways might Florence's actions cause difficulties for the steering group?*

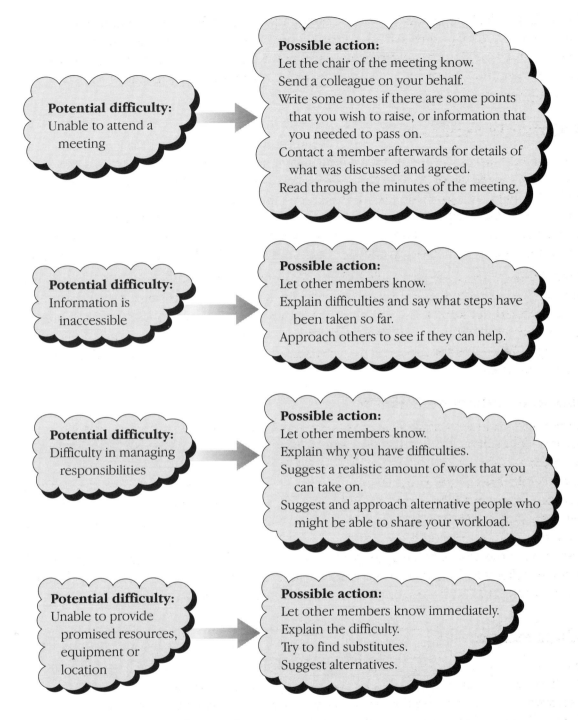

**Potential difficulty:**
Unable to attend a meeting

**Possible action:**
Let the chair of the meeting know.
Send a colleague on your behalf.
Write some notes if there are some points that you wish to raise, or information that you needed to pass on.
Contact a member afterwards for details of what was discussed and agreed.
Read through the minutes of the meeting.

**Potential difficulty:**
Information is inaccessible

**Possible action:**
Let other members know.
Explain difficulties and say what steps have been taken so far.
Approach others to see if they can help.

**Potential difficulty:**
Difficulty in managing responsibilities

**Possible action:**
Let other members know.
Explain why you have difficulties.
Suggest a realistic amount of work that you can take on.
Suggest and approach alternative people who might be able to share your workload.

**Potential difficulty:**
Unable to provide promised resources, equipment or location

**Possible action:**
Let other members know immediately.
Explain the difficulty.
Try to find substitutes.
Suggest alternatives.

## Keeping colleagues informed

It is essential that you keep your colleagues informed of what is happening: remember that you are representing an organisation rather than yourself. Colleagues are often able to provide different perspectives and ideas about a project, and their support and co-operation is vital for a project to be truly successful. It is also a good idea for others to be aware of your role and the agreed responsibilities that you have taken, so that if necessary they can take these over in the case of sickness or unforseeable events.

Sharing information and encouraging feedback also means that others in your organisation can feel part of the process – many projects will eventually have an impact on their current work. Failure to involve others can lead to isolation, conflict and even resentment. Always look for ways of involving people, for example by asking for their ideas, and by finding out if they would like to become involved too.

### Ways of keeping your colleagues informed

There are many ways of keeping your colleagues informed. You might ask for a slot in a staff meeting, or approach colleagues informally for suggestions and comments. Keep records of your meetings with other organisations so that if they need to attend a meeting on your behalf, your line manager or others can find out more about what is happening. Here are some ways of keeping your colleagues informed of the joint initiative:

- memos
- slot in staff meeting
- talking to individual colleagues
- newsletter
- putting information up on staff board
- asking for comments.

## Maintain effective working relationships throughout the initiative

In order for a partnership to work well, it is important that everyone is able to work together effectively over a period of time. This is not always easy. People who come together in this way will have different strengths, weaknesses and personalities. To deal with possible difficulties, everyone needs some basic skills and a good sense of professionalism. The table below outlines the skills and qualities that are needed to maintain good working relationships.

| Skills and qualities | Why they are needed |
| --- | --- |
| Trust and honesty | Everyone has to feel that there are no hidden agendas or power struggles going on. |
| Co-operativeness | Everyone needs to be able to support each other and work towards the agreed aim. This might mean that at times you will need to make some concessions or compromises. |
| Assertiveness | Everyone has to be ready to put forward their own suggestions and comments in a constructive and not a hostile way. |
| Listening skills | As well as making comments, it is also important to be able to listen to others' suggestions and points of view. |
| Reliability | Everyone must be ready to fulfil their responsibilities. |
| Timekeeping | It is helpful if meetings are run to time with a set agenda and if everyone is punctual. |

## Potential difficulties for joint initiatives

It is useful to be aware of the potential difficulties that can face joint initiatives. This means that you might be able to take some action or make some suggestions to avoid them. The table below outlines the major potential difficulties.

| Possible type of difficulty | Possible methods for avoiding them |
|---|---|
| **Clash of personalities** | Make clear divisions about roles and responsibilities.<br>Encourage a climate of acknowledgement and acceptance, saying for example 'That's a useful comment'. Insecure people can feel threatened and may then use opportunities to create 'power' bases. |
| **Breakdown in communication** | Try to make sure that there is good administrative support or that it is clear who should be taking minutes of meetings.<br>Make sure that records are kept of contacts.<br>Circulate minutes of meetings.<br>Make sure that absent members know what is happening.<br>Create a climate in which people can speak openly and honestly. |
| **Work is not being carried out** | Make sure that everyone knows what they are responsible for.<br>Make sure that timescales are realistic.<br>Consider whether the proposal is too ambitious.<br>Check that the workload is distributed fairly. |
| **Lack of trust** | Make sure that everyone acknowledges their intentions and their role in the proposal.<br>Allow time for people to get to know each other. |
| **Time-wasting** | Give meetings a structure. Make sure that a chair is elected who is good at keeping people to the point.<br>Encourage people to speak through the chair.<br>Start and end meetings on time.<br>Make sure that any points you raise are relevant. |

## Consolidation

Think about a joint initiative that you could undertake with another organisation. Consult with your manager and/or other colleagues, and make appropriate contacts with the identified organisations or individuals.

◆ *Write about the reasons why you think that this initiative would be helpful to your organisation.*
◆ *Explain how you made contact with someone from another organisation.*
◆ *Write about the success of this initiative, or what you learnt from trying to forge a relationship with another organisation.*
◆ *Why is it important for organisations to try to work collaboratively?*

## B212 unit test

1  Describe three ways in which a play setting might be able to promote itself in the local community.
2  Describe three benefits of out-of-school care to the local community.
3  Why is it important for people in the setting to be aware of any new initiatives?
4  How can working in partnership with other organisations prove useful?
5  Describe four ways in which you can help to maintain a positive relationship with other organisations and individuals.
6  Why is it important when working on a joint initiative for partners to agree roles and responsibilities?
7  What factors should you consider before offering to work on a joint initiative?
8  Why is it important that your colleagues are kept informed of developments when working on a joint initiative?
9  Why is it important for partners working on joint initiatives to make regular contact?
10  Outline three major difficulties that can face joint initiatives.

# Work with colleagues in a team

Being able to work as part of a team is an important part of being a playworker. A good team is able to provide a harmonious and often a dynamic atmosphere, and this in turn leads to children feeling secure and interested in attending the setting.

The elements for this unit are:

PA54.1  Contribute to the work of a team
PA54.2  Provide support to colleagues
PA54.3  Respond to conflict in the team

## Element PA54.1  Contribute to the work of a team

Good teamwork is important not only to playworkers but to everyone who comes into the setting. A good team creates a pleasant atmosphere: this affects the children, the parents, and others who come into the setting. This section looks at the skills you need in order to be able to contribute to the work of the team.

### WHAT YOU NEED TO LEARN

- Maintaining effective relationships with colleagues
- Carrying out agreed duties and responsibilities
- Seeking support when necessary
- Reporting progress and offering suggestions

### Understanding why teamwork is important

Good teamwork can actually influence the success of a setting or organisation. Its benefits are considerable, as shown in the diagram opposite.

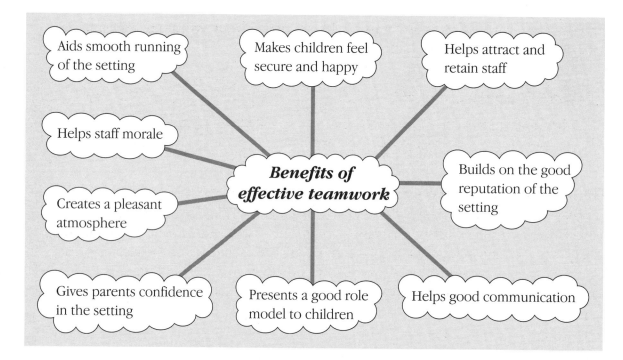

## Maintaining relationships with colleagues

Teamwork requires that people have varied skills and attitudes. It is useful to be able to identify the keys to building and maintaining relationships with those with whom you work. The skills can be represented as a jigsaw puzzle.

*Qualities that help people to work in teams*

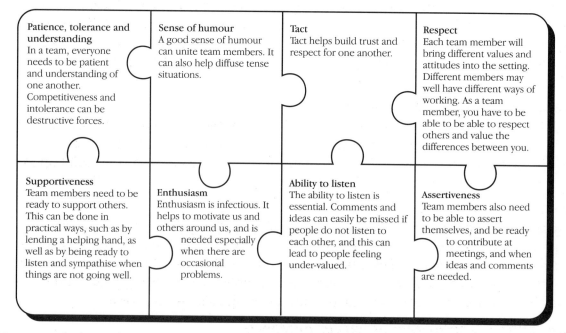

Most people have these skills and attitudes, but to varying degrees – for example, some people might find that they are good at listening whilst being unsure about putting forward their own ideas. It is useful to be able to identify your own strengths, as well as the skills that still need to be developed.

## Active knowledge ✔

1 *What do you think are your personal strengths?*
2 *Are there any areas that you feel still need developing?*

## The importance of carrying out your responsibilities

In order to be a good team member you also need to carry out your workload or responsibilities effectively. No one enjoys working with someone who does not pull their weight, or who does not do their work competently. Mutual trust, or the lack of it, can affect the quality of teamwork and have other consequences in the setting.

When everyone in the workplace carries out their allotted tasks competently, everyone benefits:

- the setting runs smoothly
- conflicts and resentment are minimised
- errors and accidents are avoided
- job security and career prospects are enhanced
- job satisfaction and motivation increase.

### The smooth running of the setting

Teamwork is not just about the quality of relationships in a work setting: it is also about everyone working together and fulfilling their job responsibilities. A good team can be compared to a machine, with every part vital if the machine is to work well. If one part is not working properly, the machine's effectiveness is reduced. In the same way, if one member of the team is not working well the smooth running of the setting might be affected.

### Minimising conflict and resentment

If all the adults in a setting carry out their work responsibilities competently, there is less likely to be conflict between team members. Once one member of a team is not completing their work tasks, or is doing them badly, resentment can quickly build up as other team members have to work harder.

### Avoiding errors and accidents

In some areas of work, the consequences of staff not fulfilling their work responsibilities properly or completely are potentially dangerous – examples include not supervising children carefully, or not following hygiene procedures. Errors might also be made when someone is not doing their work properly – an example is a child being given food to which he is allergic because someone did not record the allergy on a form.

### Enhancing job security and career prospects

If you are able to carry out your responsibilities well and are seen as being reliable, you will significantly improve your job and career prospects. Staff who do not fulfil their job responsibilities, on the other hand, may even find that *disciplinary action* is taken against them: employers have a legal right to expect that their employees will carry out the work they have been employed to do.

### Increasing job satisfaction and motivation

Most people find that they are happier when they feel that they are working well and effectively. Staff who are not working hard at their jobs tend to have lower satisfaction levels, and are therefore less motivated. Motivated staff are likely to produce a better atmosphere and to work more effectively with children.

## Understanding your responsibilities

In order to be able to fulfil your work responsibilities, you need to be clear about exactly what you have to do and the standard to which you must carry out this work. One way in which you can find out about your work responsibilities is to ask for and read your *job description*. This should give you some guidance; if this is not enough, you might ask for more details from your line manager.

### Active knowledge ✔

1  *Make a list of your main duties and responsibilities.*
2  *Explain why these responsibilities are important to the smooth running of your setting.*

### If you are unsure about your job role

Although job descriptions can be helpful in giving you an overview of your role in a setting, there may be times when you need more specific information. For example, you may know that you are responsible for picking up some children from their schools and accompanying them to the club, but you also need to know for which particular children and for which schools you are responsible. This type of specific information is important if you are to be able to carry out your responsibilities competently. Knowing exactly what is expected of you can also help you and the setting in other ways, as you will not waste time getting something wrong, or 'treading on someone else's toes'.

By understanding your duties in advance, you may also feel that you can be more prepared and better organised. For example, if you know that on certain days you are responsible for preparing drinks and snacks, you might start the session by checking that there are enough clean beakers. Good communication and understanding of who is responsible for what are also important in maintaining children's safety. Missing children or accidents due to poor supervision are sometimes the result of inadequate communication, with one person thinking that someone else is responsible.

Clarifying your responsibilities and work duties is therefore important. Although your line manager is responsible for making sure you understand what you need to do, you must also take the initiative and check that you understand. If you are new to this setting but have worked in another establishment, do not assume that the same policies and procedures will be used – each setting has its own way of working.

## Case study

Josie has worked on several playschemes, but is new to this one. She has been told that she should prepare mid-morning snacks. She asks some of the children whether they would like to help her cut up the fruit and make the drinks.

Later on in the morning, the line manager takes her aside and tells her that normally they have a policy of not letting children into the kitchen area, and that if she takes children off for an activity she should always let the other members of staff know as this morning they were looking for the children.

1   *How could this situation been avoided?*
2   *Why is it important not to make assumptions about how you should carry out your responsibilities?*

## Varying from your agreed duties and responsibilities

There may be times when you may find it necessary to change either your work duties or the way in which you carry out a work task. When this happens, it is important that others in the setting, and especially your line manager, know about these changes and agree to them. This gives them the opportunity to consider whether these changes should be made, and allows them to alter their own work plans. You might have good reasons for wishing to change your duties, but your line manager or other colleagues might have information which would show you that this is not a good idea. For example, you might think that it would be a good idea to pop out and get some extra biscuits, whereas your line manager might know that because some extra children are due in at that time you will be needed to maintain the child–staff ratios.

Checking and asking colleagues also helps to avoid potential accidents and misunderstandings. For example, if you are responsible for checking the outdoor area and it is raining hard, you might consider leaving your check until later on. If you inform your colleagues of this, they will know not to send children outside straightaway as the area might be unsafe. In this way, confusion is avoided, and so is the risk of accidents – or of colleagues feeling let down and angry.

In summary, you should always ask relevant colleagues before changing either your duties or the way that you carry them out:

* to prevent confusion
* to avoid conflict and resentment
* to maintain good communication
* to maintain children's health and safety
* to ensure the smooth running of the team
* to maintain child–staff ratios.

## Finding the balance: taking the initiative or creating problems?

Good playworkers are able to take the initiative – for example, they will see that a colleague needs support, and help even if this is not their 'direct' responsibility. Teamwork can sometimes mean doing more than just your standard duties.

There is, however, a fine line between taking the initiative and creating problems in the setting. Although you should look for opportunities to help in the smooth running of the setting, you should also make sure that are not thereby creating difficulties, for example by upsetting another member of staff or by neglecting part of your normal duties. To prevent this from happening, check with colleagues before taking over someone else's duties. Consider also whether in taking on additional duties you will still be able to carry out your own effectively.

*Taking the initiative can sometimes create problems*

## Active knowledge ✔

Carla, a playworker, has gone to collect Ozzie from his school. When she arrives, the school says that he has already been collected by someone else. She phones the after-school club where she works and asks whether he is there. She is told that Jennifer, a new playworker, was on her way to work and was passing the school. Jennifer thought that she would help everyone out by picking Ozzie up and taking him in with her.

1  *Should Jennifer have picked up Ozzie? Explain your answer.*
2  *How might Carla feel towards Jennifer?*
3  *Why is it important to consider carefully your actions when working as part of a team?*

## Asking for additional support

Most playworkers find that from time to time they need extra help or guidance from colleagues. For example, they may be running out of time in which to complete a task, or they may be unsure about the best way to achieve it. Asking for help is not an admission of failure: it is a sign of professionalism. It is better to get help than say nothing and leave the task not done properly. If you feel embarrassed about asking for help, remember that *everyone* has times when they need support. Not asking for support is more likely to upset the team, as tasks not done properly can cause further difficulties (see page 51).

## How to ask for support

Ask for support and guidance as soon as possible. Leaving things until the last minute and only then saying that you need help may be irritating for your colleagues. Make clear exactly what you need. For example: 'Please could you spend a minute just showing me how you normally put these away? I don't want to put them in the wrong place.' Remember to thank your helper and acknowledge the help you have been given; this helps towards the smooth running of the team.

---

## Consolidation

Think of a time recently when you have asked for support or guidance from a colleague.

*Explain why it was important to ask for this additional support.*

---

## Making suggestions to improve teamwork

In order to keep motivated and effective, all teams and organisations need regularly to think about the way that they are working. Teams that never question or look at ways of developing soon become stagnant. When set in their ways they may not be able to respond to the needs of children and parents. Cries of 'But, we've *always* done it this way!' usually indicate that teams have become inflexible.

There are many reasons why it is a good idea for teams to think about what they are doing:

- to meet the changing needs of children and their parents
- to check that the team is complying with the latest legislation and good practice
- to iron out minor niggles before they develop into conflict
- to share problems
- to consider job responsibilities and ways in which staff might wish to enhance their careers
- to make sure that the setting is running as smoothly as possible.

### How to make positive and realistic suggestions

When you make suggestions about the way in which the team might improve its performance, it's important that you do so by discussing your ideas with your line manager or by raising your ideas at a team meeting. It is essential that you are able to be positive about the work of your colleagues and to put forward suggestions in a positive, uncritical way. Remember that many people do not like changes – especially if they were originally responsible or present when the relevant paperwork, procedure or system was introduced.

## Reporting progress and difficulties to colleagues

It is good practice to keep colleagues up to date about aspects of your work – for example, if you have had any difficulties in managing a task, or if you have had some success with a child with particular needs. This helps everyone in the setting to stay informed, which is essential, especially between team meetings. When everyone in the setting shares information about their work and progress, staff are able to support each other and managers are able to identify recurring difficulties which might indicate that staff training is needed. Awareness of others' work also helps when a staff member is absent, as others then know what needs to be done. It could be, for example, that before going off sick a playworker had promised to carry out a particular activity with a group of children.

In some cases, a setting might be adopting a new policy or strategy. Regular feedback among colleagues could allow them to consider its advantages and weaknesses.

### The importance of regular team meetings

Team meetings are essential if staff are to pull together and share information. Snatching odd words here and there is rarely enough to be able to discuss issues or to make proper plans. Team meetings allow everyone in the setting to listen to the same information and to comment about it at the same time.

Many settings have to hold team meetings after hours or before sessions start. It can then be tempting to hold very short and very irregular meetings. Although this approach may seem to save time, in the long run it tends not to be effective as people's ideas and feelings do not get aired. It can also mean that staff become very ineffective and disorganised. Motivated and effective organisations and teams tend to be those have regular team meetings.

### Participating effectively in team meetings

For team meetings to be useful, everyone must attend and do so with some enthusiasm. Be ready to contribute as well as to listen to others' ideas.

# Keys to good practice

## Team meetings

**Do:**

- read anything that has been given to you beforehand
- listen carefully to what is being said
- keep your comments to the point
- keep your ideas positive
- put forward your suggestions concisely
- acknowledge other people's suggestions
- respect others' points of view
- be ready to compromise and go along with the majority view.

**Don't:**

- be late
- switch off
- talk whilst someone else is speaking
- say nothing at the time and then gossip and complain to others afterwards
- nit-pick and comment just for the sake of it
- be critical of others or make personal remarks
- fidget and watch the clock.

---

## Consolidation

Think of a recent occasion when you participated at a team meeting.

- *Explain how you contributed to this meeting.*
- *Why is it important that all team members are willing to put their views forward?*

---

# Element PA54.2 Provide support to colleagues

As well as being a good team member, you also need to have the skills and knowledge to be able to support colleagues. These are essential when you are responsible for managing the setting of a certain area of work, such as oversight of one age group of children, because as part of this responsibility you might need to 'direct' others such as colleagues, helpers and part-time staff.

This section looks at some of the skills and knowledge that are needed in order to monitor others' work and provide guidance and feedback.

- Monitoring the work of colleagues for whom you are responsible
- Offering helpful comments, constructive criticism, and support
- Valuing diversity and challenging discrimination

## Monitoring the work of team members and volunteers

If you are responsible for any area of work within the setting, this may mean that you also have to take on the accompanying responsibility of monitoring others' work. This does not mean 'checking up' on others, but should be about checking in a supportive way that things are running smoothly. Monitoring the work of team members and volunteers is vital for the following reasons.

### Taking on ultimate responsibility

A key reason why you should monitor others' work is that you should be taking *active* responsibility for their areas of work. It is no excuse to say to your line manager or a parent, 'It's not my fault. Jane was supposed to check that all the children were on the bus.' If *you* are responsible for an area of work, all that happens within it is *your* responsibility.

### Identifying difficulties

By monitoring others' work you can identify difficulties and act before these cause more serious problems, perhaps putting children's health and safety at risk. You may need to adjust a routine or the way a task is being done. In some cases, you might identify that an individual is finding it hard to manage an allotted task.

### Supporting team members

By taking an interest in others' work, you can help them to feel supported. If you notice that they are having difficulties, find ways to assist them, such as offering more guidance, or giving them more time.

### Maintaining communication

In monitoring others' work you are also providing opportunities for them to pass on comments to you, thereby maintaining communication. You might find out that a team member is not enjoying her work task; if so, in the longer term she may not carry out this task effectively. Receiving comments will help you in making any further decisions or plans about work allocation.

### Identifying training needs

Whilst monitoring others work you may also identify training needs. Individuals may talk to you about their training needs, or through observation you may realise that training would support them.

*Taking an interest in fellow team members' work helps them to feel supported*

## Assisting with staff appraisals, placement reports, references

You may also be responsible for staff appraisals or required to give students reports. You will find it hard to comment accurately and to assess people's strengths and areas for further development unless you have seen them working and have talked to them about their work. In monitoring people's work you might also be able to recognise in them potential for future career development. If they are very confident in a certain area, for example, they may be ready to take on further responsibility.

## Giving clear direction to other team members

For monitoring to be effective, everyone needs a clear understanding of their job tasks and roles. In many cases, these roles and tasks will be already established. In others, though, such as if you are responsible for an outing, you may need to allocate tasks. It is very important for everyone to understand what they need to do: this can prevent confusion, resentment and potential risks to health and safety.

Allocating tasks or checking that everyone understands their specific roles can be done in several ways, depending on your circumstances.

### Using task sheets

Task sheets break down work loads into specific tasks and ask people to consider what they would like to take on. This is quite a good strategy if everyone has similar knowledge and skills. It also means that everyone in the team understands the roles that others will be taking on. You can circulate the sheet at a team meeting or post it up in the staff area. A disadvantage of this method, however, is that people who come later to sign up may feel that they have less choice. This method does not work well if peoples' skills, knowledge and experience are very different – people may sign up for tasks which appeal to them but to which they are not suited.

### Discussing tasks during a team meeting

Team discussion can work well as everyone is able to share views and understand what others are going to be doing. You will need to explain what needs to be done and record what each person has agreed to take on. If there is an area of work that no one wishes to undertake, you may also need to forge compromises.

## Discussing tasks with individual members of the team

Individual conversation is quite a good method to use, especially if work tasks and responsibilities are already established or if you need to make some small changes to individual team members' tasks. It is also useful if there are many part-time members of staff who have not been able to attend team meetings.

Whatever method you use to check that everyone understands their job tasks, make sure that colleagues feel part of the process. If jobs are allocated rather than chosen, make sure these allocations are seen as fair. Colleagues should also feel that they can make comments and discuss the work that has to be accomplished.

# Ways of monitoring others' work

There are several ways in which you can monitor others' work. The technique you will choose will depend both on the situation and on the person who you need to monitor. To a certain extent, the ability to monitor others' work is also based on trust. Individuals will only feel comfortable in telling you of any difficulties if they trust you and feel secure. Choose your method of monitoring carefully, and make sure that everyone understands that you are not there to criticise but rather to note problems and help solve them.

## Direct observation

This involves watching others whilst they are working. If you use this technique, it is good practice to let them know that you will be doing so. Make sure that they understand your reasons for doing so. Good communication means that they will not feel spied upon; they can even ask you to look out for certain things, such as how certain children are behaving. Most people find direct observation uncomfortable, you will have to work hard beforehand at putting them at ease. You can ask people you are going to observe if they have any preference about where you sit, or whether they would like you to be actively involved as you watch them.

## Indirect observation

In some circumstances *indirect* observation is more appropriate – you might just wish to observe at a distance, for instance to get a feel for whether someone is comfortable with a given job role. This can be done by working alongside the person or just by keeping a general eye on things, checking that everything is going well. Most supervisors use indirect observation as one of their main methods for monitoring work.

## Informal discussion and chats

You can also monitor others' work by listening and talking to them. They may come into the staff area and say how they are feeling. If a member of staff says 'I'm absolutely exhausted', this might indicate a difficulty with the workload or the way it is being managed: perhaps you need to provide extra support. You can also find out how someone is managing by asking them directly, in a friendly way – 'How's it going with that group?' – and then listening carefully to the reply.

## Asking for feedback

Another method is to ask for feedback from individuals. This can be done formally, for example at a team meeting (so that everyone is aware of the progress being made), or less formally, during a one-to-one talk. Be sure to listen carefully to what is said, and notice the accompanying body language. Some people find it hard to admit that they are having difficulties or may feel very defensive of their work. When asking for feedback, always try to make people feel that you are genuinely there to help them, and can do this only if you know of any problems.

## Appraisals

In appraisals, it is usual for staff to talk through their job roles, strengths and weaknesses at the start of the process. What they say will provide excellent opportunities to explore any difficulties that they are having, as well as ways in which they feel they need support.

## Mentoring

If you are mentoring an inexperienced member of staff, volunteer or student, you can use this as an opportunity to monitor her or his work. As a mentor you should try to build up a relationship in which your mentee feels able to talk to you openly and freely. Good mentors listen more than they speak, knowing that their role is not to criticise or judge, but to look for ways for a mentee to move forwards.

### Active knowledge ✔

Rob is a student from a local college. You have been asked to act as his placement supervisor. He is not very comfortable with the idea that someone will be watching him work.

1  *How would you explain to him why it is important for his work to be monitored, and might help his overall practice?*

2  *Explain which method you would use first to monitor his work.*

## Commenting on work and providing feedback to others

An important part of monitoring others' work is to provide them with feedback and comments. If given sensitively, feedback can give people reassurance and recognition for their work, as well as help them to feel that they can ask for help and guidance. Positive feedback should always be sincere. It is a good idea to comment first on what has *impressed* you about the person's work or development.

Positive feedback can benefit everyone in the setting. It helps:

- to motivate individual members of staff
- to give people further confidence
- to encourage people to take on more responsibilities

- to make people feel valued
- to create a friendly atmosphere
- to maintain communication
- to boost overall morale in the setting
- to improve staff retention.

## The importance of constructive criticism

Alongside positive feedback, you will also need sometimes to pass on concerns or to query aspects of practice. This is not always an easy thing to do, especially if you have a close working relationship with someone, or if the person is 'senior' to you or older than you. This part of your role, however, is just as essential as providing positive feedback; if you do not address issues as they arise, more serious problems might result and your abilities to supervise would be questioned. The diagram below outlines why constructive criticism is so important.

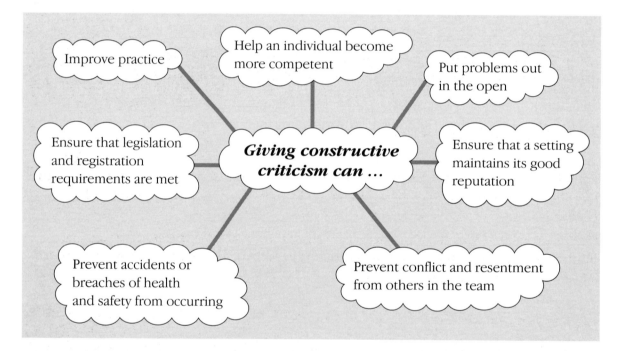

Improve practice

Help an individual become more competent

Put problems out in the open

Ensure that legislation and registration requirements are met

*Giving constructive criticism can ...*

Ensure that a setting maintains its good reputation

Prevent accidents or breaches of health and safety from occurring

Prevent conflict and resentment from others in the team

## Giving constructive criticism

Feedback and constructive criticism must be passed on effectively and sensitively: if mishandled it will leave people feeling negative and demotivated. If you have some criticisms to make, try to ensure that these are discussed in private and at an appropriate time. Begin by making the person feel at ease, and comment on areas of their work that are good or improving. Then talk about the difficulties or concerns that you have. Most people find that an open approach is usually effective: this way the team member or volunteer does not feel that anything underhand is going on.

When bringing up concerns or difficulties, start by exploring whether the person concerned is aware of any problems, or has suggestions to resolve the difficulty. This allows you to get additional information: these may be factors of which you are not aware. (For example, an item of equipment may be broken, or time may be being taken up by something else.)

Once you have explored the difficulty, explain or agree on how the matter is to be moved forwards. This can often be done verbally, but in some situations you may judge it necessary to record what has been agreed, such as further staff training. It is usually a good idea to agree also on a time when the matter discussed can be reviewed. Try to end the discussion on a positive note, as the person may otherwise concentrate only on the negative aspects of what has been said.

## Case study

Sylvia has been working for three months. She has settled in well and has become a good team member. Her practice is generally good, although you have noticed that she is not particularly confident with parents. This means that she tends to keep her distance from them, which in turn has actually upset one particular parent. You have monitored her work in several ways, and you are now about to sit down with her and give her some feedback.

1 *Explain what you would talk to her about first.*
2 *How would you approach Sylvia's difficulty in working with parents?*
3 *What type of action plan would you hope would come from this meeting?*

## Offering support to colleagues

There are times when as part of our role we need to offer support to colleagues. For example, a colleague might be feeling under the weather or might be new to a task or to the setting. Support can be provided in many different forms; if given quickly and sensitively it will maintain the smooth running of the setting.

It is usually a good idea to ask someone whether they would like support, rather than simply to impose it on them. This allows them to feel 'in control' of their support and to indicate the type of support that they need.

## Active knowledge ✔

Look at these two conversations.

SUPERVISOR:  'I'm coming in now, so that you can have a break for a bit. Off you go!'
PLAYWORKER:  'No, that's kind but I really want to finish this activity first.'
SUPERVISOR:  'Look, it can wait – go and have a break.'

SUPERVISOR:  'Look, why don't I come in for a bit while you go and have a break?'
PLAYWORKER:  'No, that's kind but I really want to finish this activity first.'
SUPERVISOR:  'All right, but how about a bit later on, then?'
PLAYWORKER:  'Yes, that would be lovely.'

1 *Which supervisor is able to offer the playworker the support that the playworker wants?*
2 *Explain why you think that this approach was the better one to take.*

## Types of support

### Practical

Practical support is often particularly welcome. It might involve offering to work alongside a colleague in order to make their workload more manageable, or offering to alter someone's hours of work. Practical support might also include providing extra equipment or resources for the setting.

### Emotional

Sometimes people need emotional support. They may need someone to listen to them, or to just take an interest in what is happening to them, especially if they are experiencing some form of stress outside the setting.

## Advice and guidance

In some cases, people will need advice and guidance to help them manage their job role. Check before offering advice and guidance, or they may not follow it but resent its having been given. For example, 'I think that there's a quicker way of doing that. Would you like me to show you?'

## Training

You might realise that a person would benefit from some training in order to work more effectively. As with providing advice and guidance, discuss this with the person before organising the training. When people feel that they have been 'sent', they are less likely to benefit from training.

# Recognising others' contributions

As well as giving feedback to colleagues, we should also look at other ways of valuing their contributions. There are many ways of doing this, including using a staff noticeboard to say 'thank you' for their help, writing a note of thanks, or even buying a small token. Recognising others' contributions can take place at staff meetings, or more privately.

The benefits of taking time to recognise others' work are enormous and wide-ranging: people enjoy their work more and operate more effectively if they feel valued and respected. It is also good practice to give credit where it is due, and this helps to avoid conflict and resentment – people may otherwise feel that their hard work is not valued.

# Sharing information with colleagues

There will be times when you will need to share information with colleagues so that they can do their work more effectively. For example, you might need to pass on some background information about a child which will help a playworker to understand the child's behaviour. There are many types of information that might be helpful, and it is your role to identify it and pass it on promptly.

Whenever you share information with someone, make it clear to them whether or not the information is confidential, so that it is not repeated to others by accident.

Types of information that you might need to share include:

- information about a child's circumstances or state of health (this is likely to be confidential)
- circulars or updates about current practice
- information about where to access further resources or equipment
- information about training courses on offer.

## Consolidation

Think about some information that you have recently shared with a team member.

◆ *Why was it important that this information was passed on to them?*
◆ *Explain why holding back information can sometimes damage relationships in teams.*

## Valuing diversity

Diversity is essential in the workplace. In the same way that you should be valuing and encouraging social and cultural diversity, you should also understand that people will work in different ways and will bring to a setting their own ideas and values. You need to accept that other playworkers will work and relate to children in their own way, and that this in itself is a huge bonus in a play setting. It allows children to see that teamwork means working alongside people who have different styles. It also means that the team is more likely to be able to meet the varying needs of those with whom they work, as different children and parents will be able to identify with the different styles of different team members.

## Challenging discrimination and prejudice

As well as valuing diversity, you should also be aware of the need actively to challenge discrimination and prejudice. Make sure that colleagues are aware of your setting's equal opportunities policies, and make sure that these are being followed. If colleagues confide any difficulties they are having, help them to know that you are supportive of them. Be ready to challenge or question practice if you feel that it encourages discrimination or prejudice. Never turn a blind eye, even if challenging behaviour leads to disciplinary action against a member of staff or talking to parents about their attitudes.

## Active knowledge ✔

1 *What is your work setting's policy on equal opportunities?*
2 *Do you have a complaints procedure?*
3 *How is everyone in the setting made aware of the procedures and policies?*

# Element PA 54.3 Respond to conflict in the team

In an ideal world, there would be no conflict amongst team members. Unfortunately, most teams find that from time to time issues arise which cause conflict. This section looks at the types of issues that might arise, and at the skills that are needed to respond to such conflicts.

## WHAT YOU NEED TO LEARN

- Dealing productively with conflict
- Seeking support if necessary
- Offering support as necessary
- Reporting conflicts

## Managing conflicts sensitively

When a conflict occurs it is essential that it is handled sensitively, to avoid making the conflict larger. The aim is to manage conflicts so that they do not interfere with the main work of the team, as this must come first. Failure to manage conflicts can have serious consequences although these might show themselves only over a period of time. The flowchart opposite shows how a setting can quickly run into difficulties because of a conflict.

## Keys to good practice

### Managing conflicts

- Never turn a blind eye to potential conflicts.
- Consider why the conflict has arisen.
- Encourage people to be open about their feelings.
- Remain impartial and supportive of everyone.
- Find solutions alongside those who are in conflict.
- Monitor the situation for a period of time to check that solutions are working.
- Create a culture of mutual respect and positive feedback.

## Understanding types of conflict

Conflicts arise within a work setting for many reasons. While some conflicts might seem trivial on the surface, they may be hiding deeper problems. Below are examples of causes of conflicts, and ways in which they can be managed without disrupting the work of the team.

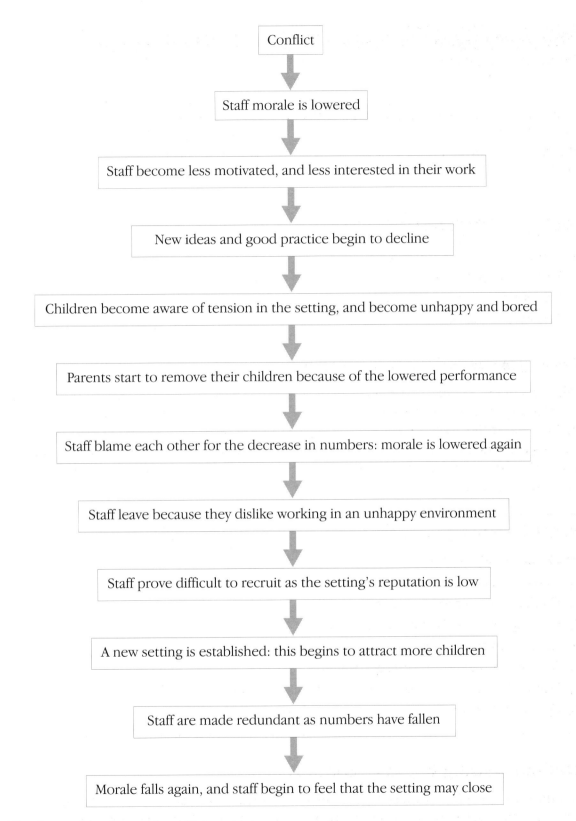

*The damaging effects of conflict*

## Workloads

A major cause of conflict between team members is unequal workloads. Resentment quickly builds up if one member is perceived as not pulling their weight or having less work to do than the others. If one member of the team is avoiding their share of work, address this quickly. Check that rotas for tasks such as washing-up, cleaning and tidying away are worked out fairly – it is just such day-to-day activities that can cause resentments.

*Unequal workloads can course problems among workers*

## Approaches to work

Conflict can also be caused because team members have different attitudes and approaches to their work. Individual members of staff may sometimes believe that their way of working is the *only* way! Elements of competition and resentment may then develop.

To manage this type of conflict, you will need to emphasise the value of each person's work and encourage other members to see that through their different ways of working they are complementing each other. Intolerance can be a starting point for later prejudice and discrimination: monitor the situation very carefully.

## Case study

Sonja has come to see you because Harriet, who works with her, is always coming in ten minutes after the shift starts, by which time Sonja has done much of the setting out and moving of equipment. She wants to know why Harriet has not been reprimanded as she feels that at present Harriet is 'coasting'. Sonja says that other members in the team also have noticed Harriet's laziness.

1  *Why is it important that this conflict is resolved quickly?*
2  *What might happen if the conflict is not resolved satisfactorily?*
3  *Why will it be important to listen to Harriet's point of view?*

# Change

Change is a major cause of conflict within teams. Examples of change include revised rotas, varying opening hours, changing the use of equipment, using spaces differently, or changing procedures. Some people enjoy and look forward to trying out new ideas and practices, whereas others need time to settle into a new way of working. From time to time they have to change some aspects of the way they work in order to meet parents' and children's needs, as well as to conform to registration and legislation requirements.

## *Avoiding conflict when managing changes*

Try to avoid conflict when managing changes. People feel resentment of changes when they feel that they have not been consulted or their views taken on board. Whenever possible, therefore, you should make everyone aware of the need for changes and encourage them to discuss how these changes can be managed. When the changes are required, this should be made clear so that people do not spend time debating how to avoid making them.

Once a plan of action has been decided upon, make sure that anyone who was not present at the meeting is aware of the agreed plan. You may also need to have the plan checked by your line manager or some other professional before going ahead – for example, a change in the registration requirements might mean that the plan needs to be shown to the registering authority. If you need to have the plan approved before going ahead with it, make this clear at the team meeting, so that team members do not feel that their time has been wasted.

Once the plan is introduced, monitor to see whether it is working. Set time aside for team members to comment about any difficulties they are having with the plan. If necessary, amend the plan.

---

# Keys to good practice

## Managing change

- Make sure that everyone is aware of why the changes are needed.
- Make sure that the benefits of the changes are highlighted.
- Explain ways in which the changes can be made.
- Encourage everyone to contribute their comments and suggestions.
- Listen to concerns and look for ways of solving them.
- Agree a plan and a date of review.
- Amend the plan if necessary.
- Give positive feedback to staff, and recognise the contributions that they are making to the plan.

---

## Consolidation

Think of a change that was required in your setting.

- ◆ *Explain how this change was handled. Was it managed smoothly? If so, how?*
- ◆ *Why is it important to involve others when making changes?*

# Managing conflict

## What to do if you cannot resolve conflict

As noted already, conflict can be potentially fatal for a setting. If you are unsure about how to resolve a conflict in the team, or if you have tried and not made much progress, refer to your line manager.

Do not delay with this: remember that your manager has ultimate responsibility for the setting. Conflicts have the potential to escalate quickly, so it is essential that you seek help quickly. It may be tempting to hope that the matter will simply resolve itself but in general this does not happen. By involving your manager rapidly, you might avoid making errors and adding to the conflict.

# Keys to good practice

## Managing conflict

**Do:**

✎ Seek help, guidance and advice quickly.

✎ Explain exactly what has happened so far.

✎ Be honest. Explain the actions that you have taken, even if in retrospect they were not useful.

✎ Learn from the way your line manager handles the situation.

**Don't:**

✎ Wait until the conflict has reached large proportions.

✎ Be defensive or hide information, even if you feel that you have not handled the situation well.

## Being ready to compromise

Occasionally you may find that *you* are the unwitting cause of a conflict. Perhaps you suggested changes that are not working, or perhaps you misread a situation. Be willing to acknowledge your own part in the conflict, and look for compromise.

In other situations you may need to help others find a compromise. Being able to listen to others and work with them is therefore an important skill. The ability to foster and accept compromises in situations of conflict has many benefits. It can:

- raise team morale
- help resolve the conflict
- promote mutual respect between team members
- improve open communication in the future
- avoid further conflict.

### Situations where compromise is unacceptable

There are some situations where you will be unable to compromise. For example, you will not be able to reach a compromise if the compromise results in a breach of any of the following:

- health and safety practices and procedures
- confidentiality

- legal or registration requirements
- equal opportunities practices and procedures.

If a compromise is put forward which would breach one of the above, explain why you are not in a position to accept it. Remember too that any compromise must also be in the best interests of the children, who are after all the people you are aiming to serve. It is often easy to lose sight of this when there is conflict.

## Supporting colleagues involved in conflict

In some situations you might feel that you are caught between two sides of a conflict. This may feel uncomfortable, but you should try to support each colleague and help them find agreement. Do not take sides, and avoid making judgements; instead, listen and try to find out the true areas of disagreement. Where possible, focus on the areas of *agreement* between the colleagues, and the skills that they have between them.

If you meet with them, make sure that you establish clear ground rules about what can and cannot be said – for example, that personal attacks are unacceptable, and that confidentiality must be preserved. Make sure that each person understands the setting's procedures for dealing with conflict. Try to keep any meetings confidential, and discourage those involved from discussing the matter and gossiping with others. Gossip and discussion might cause colleagues to take sides, and the conflict would be fuelled by speculation.

## Reporting conflicts

When there are conflicts, these must be reported. How and when this happens depend on your setting and on the actual circumstances. Occasional moans will probably not be reported, but if one member of staff makes a complaint against another it will be necessary to note this down. Reporting conflicts to your line manager is important: your manager needs to be aware of any difficulties at an early stage. When recording any details about conflicts, be careful that they are accurate and that you follow your setting's procedures. Records may be used later in disciplinary actions.

## Case study

It has been raining for several days and the staff are having to work particularly hard to keep the children amused. The staff are feeling under pressure, and one of the team has suggested that they should have longer lunch breaks. This would mean leaving the children with reduced supervision over the lunch period. The staff member argued that the children could be encouraged to watch television during this time. The team are keen on this suggestion as they feel that they are being overworked at the moment.

1 *Why could you not go along with this suggestion?*
2 *How would you explain this to the staff?*
3 *Can you think of any alternative solutions to help the staff?*

## PA54 unit test

1 Outline some of the skills needed in order to be a good team member.
2 Why is it important to seek guidance if you are unsure how to carry out a task?
3 Why is it important to check before changing your job tasks or role?
4 Outline three reasons why it might be important to monitor others' work.
5 Describe three ways of monitoring others' work.
6 Why is it important to provide positive feedback to team members?
7 Why is it essential that conflicts should be resolved quickly?
8 What should you do if you feel that you cannot resolve a conflict?
9 Describe some of the ways in which you could introduce change.
10 Why is it important to find out about your setting's complaints policy?

# Unit PA 55

# Administer provision

Alongside actively providing play opportunities for children, there is also a lot of 'backroom' work that is essential for the smooth running of the setting. This includes collecting and processing information, keeping accurate records of financial transactions, and maintaining a variety of information.

The elements for this unit are:

PA55.1  Process financial transactions
PA55.2  Implement access procedures
PA55.3  Maintain records of information

## Element PA55.1 Process financial transactions

Most settings do not see themselves as small businesses, yet in terms of keeping financial records of transactions this is what they are. It is essential that anyone involved in handling money is able to do so efficiently and to keep accurate records, as every setting will need to keep a set of accounts. The term 'financial transaction' is used in this section to mean the taking in or spending of money. The section looks at why recording financial transactions is important, and at the ways in which they may be recorded.

### WHAT YOU NEED TO LEARN

- Recording financial transactions
- Checking calculations
- Issuing and collecting receipts
- Storing money and financial documents securely
- Following legal and organisational procedures

### Understanding types of financial transaction

It is surprising how many financial transactions are processed in most settings. The individual sums of money are not necessarily large ones, but over a period the total will be considerable.

The table below shows the common reasons why settings might be carrying out financial transactions.

| Type of transaction | Reason |
|---|---|
| **Petty cash** | Most settings have a petty-cash box. Petty cash is used to buy small items that will help the smooth running of the setting, such as biscuits or drinks. |
| **Trip money** | Many settings will take children out on outings. Parents and carers are often asked to contribute towards the trip, and so money will be brought into the setting. |
| **Pocket money** | Some settings keep children's pocket money for them, so that this can be spent during outings. |
| **Fees** | Most settings need to collect fees from parents and carers. |
| **Fund-raising** | Many settings organise fund-raising events, either for their own setting or for good causes. |
| **Tuck shop** | Some settings sell drinks and snacks in order to help raise funds. |
| **Money for meals** | Some settings provide meals which are not included as part of the overall fees. |
| **Photograph money** | Many settings take photographs of children during sessions. Sometimes these are offered for sale to parents and carers. |
| **Money for stock and equipment** | In some settings a separate budget is kept for stock and equipment. |
| **Wages** | In some settings the manager is responsible for organising the wages. |

## Active knowledge ✓

Using the list above as a guide, find out the circumstances in which your own setting takes in or spends money.

## Recording the details of transactions

Being well organised is one of the keys to coping with financial transactions. Note down all transactions according to your organisation's requirements. In some organisations, staff may record transactions in specific ledgers; in others they might note them down on a general pad, for a bursar or treasurer who keeps the overall ledgers. Whatever the system in your setting, make a note of the transaction whenever you spend or are given money. Record each transaction immediately, or as soon as possible. This is not always easy – children or parents may hand over money while you are doing something else and are not in the office. Nevertheless, you must keep records.

## Safeguarding your reputation

By recording every transaction for which you are responsible, you are protecting yourself if money goes missing, or if later there is a dispute about whether money has been paid or not.

### Ensuring the smooth running of the setting

In order for a setting to run smoothly, it is important that there is enough money. Key people such as treasurers or managers need to know exactly how much there is at a given time, to prevent overspending or having a cashflow problem. Where staff are not keeping accurate records, the key people will have to 'guess' what money is available, and this can lead to many difficulties.

### Meeting auditing requirements

All settings have to keep accounts, and these are often audited once a year. In an audit, the books are checked to see whether the money coming into and leaving the setting can be accounted for. By keeping accurate, up-to-date records, this process is made easier.

### Avoiding disputes and disagreements

Where record-keeping is poor, there are more likely to be disputes and disagreements. Classic problems include parents being asked for money that they feel they have already paid. Parents and carers may claim that they have paid: if staff have not kept a record, this can lead to unnecessary irritation or bitterness, especially if the sums of money are large.

*Security is important – if money is left lying around it can be a temptation*

## Preventing theft

The presence of money may be a temptation to some, so there is always a danger of money being taken. Poor record-keeping can lead to money being stolen and it will be hard to trace what has been taken. Theft of small sums of money might go unnoticed, but the loss of larger sums of money may lead a setting into financial difficulties.

| Date | Details of Expenditure | Cheque Number | Amount | Authorised by |
|------|------------------------|---------------|--------|---------------|
| 13/7/00 | Stationery order – Hammonds Sales Ltd | 048878921 | £24.09 | JPW |
| 13/7/00 | Refund to parents of fees – Mrs F Kingdon | 048878922 | £34.00 | JPW |
| 19/7/00 | Group Insurance – Swindles Insurance Ltd | 048878923 | £48.09 | JPW |
| 19/7/00 | Phone Bill – British Telecom | 048878924 | £33.23 | JPW |
| 19/7/00 | Petty cash float – Pay Cash | 048878925 | £25.00 | JPW |
| 19/7/00 | Overtime payment for cleaner – P. Perkins | 048878926 | £18.00 | JPW |
| 19/7/00 | Training for Ann – Edlearning College | 048878927 | £67.00 | JPW |

*A financial record*

## Making sure that calculations are accurate

There are often occasions when calculations are needed. For example, children may bring in money and need change; or money for a trip may be paid in instalments.

It is therefore essential to be able to calculate accurately. Most people find that they make simple mistakes when they are busy or pushed for time, so it is always a good idea to double-check your calculation. This can be done using a calculator or by asking a colleague. Checking through your sums at the time avoids having to refund money, or ask for more money, later.

| Date | Expenditure/Income | Debits | Credits | Balance |
|------|-------------------|--------|---------|---------|
| 13/7/00 | Balance brought forward | | | £25.00 |
| 13/7/00 | Biscuits for break time | – £4.25 | | £20.76 |
| 14/7/00 | Fruit and Juice | – £7.83 | | £12.17 |
| 14/7/00 | Stamps | – £2.26 | | £9.89 |
| 14/7/00 | Donation towards party food | | + £5.00 | £14.89 |
| 15/7/00 | Party poppers/hats and crisps | – £5.32 | | £8.56 |

*Can you find the mistake in this petty cash record?*

## The value of receipts

Receipts act as proof of a transaction. They show the amount of money that has changed hands and the date; often they show also the service or goods that have been provided.

Receipts are important for many reasons. They act as a record of money changing hands, and so can be used to validate financial records. They can also be helpful if goods or services bought are not to the required standard – for example, a receipt can prove that a broken slide is only six months old, and is still within the warranty period.

## Issuing receipts

Most settings give receipts when they receive money – for example, parents may be given a receipt when they pay an instalment towards a trip. Issuing receipts shows that the setting has made a note of the money given and allows parents and others to keep their records up to date. In some cases, parents will need receipts in order to claim benefits or grants.

The number of receipts issued varies from setting to setting, with some settings issuing receipts only if sums are large or if money is being paid in instalments. It is generally a good idea to use receipts wherever possible, however, as this can minimise disputes later.

Some settings also use a receipt book if they are looking after items belonging to the child, such as a watch or purse.

### Filling in a receipt

Most receipt books are very easy to fill in: if there is no receipt book in your setting, you can draw up your own. As a minimum, a completed receipt should include:

- the date
- the amount of money received
- the name of the person from whom the money came
- the signature of the person issuing the receipt.

It is always a good idea to add onto the receipt what the money was for: this can avoid potential confusion later. Most receipt books also produce a duplicate or include a section that allows you to keep a record of the receipts as you issue them. You should always fill this in as well.

## Obtaining receipts

Receipts are also needed by the setting to record where money has been *spent* – for example, receipts are needed when snacks are bought using petty cash, to prove that this is where this money has gone. When you spend the money belonging to the setting, you should always ask for a receipt. These receipts can be used as proof that the money in the setting has been legitimately spent.

When you are given a receipt, always check that all the details on it are correct – for example, the amount spent, the date, and the type of goods purchased. If there are several amounts on the receipt, it is a good idea to write on the receipt what each refers to.

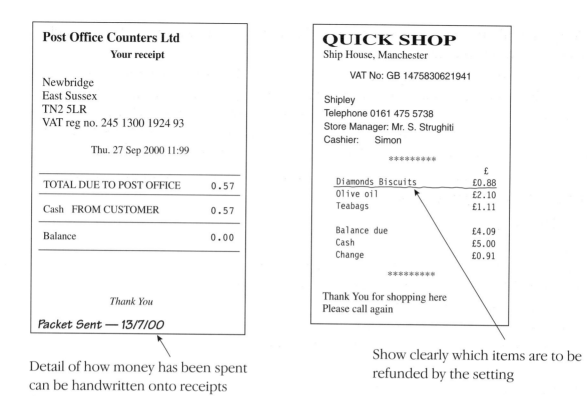

**Post Office Counters Ltd**
**Your receipt**

Newbridge
East Sussex
TN2 5LR
VAT reg no. 245 1300 1924 93

Thu. 27 Sep 2000 11:99

| | |
|---|---|
| TOTAL DUE TO POST OFFICE | 0.57 |
| Cash FROM CUSTOMER | 0.57 |
| Balance | 0.00 |

*Thank You*

*Packet Sent — 13/7/00*

Detail of how money has been spent
can be handwritten onto receipts

**QUICK SHOP**
Ship House, Manchester

VAT No: GB 1475830621941

Shipley
Telephone 0161 475 5738
Store Manager: Mr. S. Strughiti
Cashier:    Simon

\*\*\*\*\*\*\*\*\*

| | £ |
|---|---|
| Diamonds Biscuits | £0.88 |
| Olive oil | £2.10 |
| Teabags | £1.11 |
| Balance due | £4.09 |
| Cash | £5.00 |
| Change | £0.91 |

\*\*\*\*\*\*\*\*\*

Thank You for shopping here
Please call again

Show clearly which items are to be
refunded by the setting

### Receipts

### *Obtaining receipts to claim money back*

In some settings, there may be times when you need to spend your own money and then claim this money back. You will then need to provide a receipt as evidence, to validate the records in the setting. In some settings it will be impossible to make the refund unless you provide this proof.

## Storing money, receipts and records securely

Once money has been taken in and recorded, it needs to be carefully stored. This is to prevent money from being stolen or 'disappearing'. For example, a cheque inside a crumpled envelope might easily be thrown away as rubbish. Most settings try to keep different 'pots' of money separately to avoid confusion – for example, petty cash is generally kept separately to avoid any overspending. In some settings, money is banked in several accounts in order to make record-keeping easier – for example, there might be a separate account for trips.

Records and receipts must be stored carefully, both to prevent them from becoming mislaid and to maintain confidentiality. Confidentiality is important: parents and others have a right to know that details of their financial transactions will not be disclosed to others.

### Following your organisation's system

It is important that you follow your organisation's system for storing money. Provided that you do, if money is stolen or lost you will not be held responsible. Most settings have a lockable office or desk: this provides an area for keeping money, receipts and records secure. It is a good idea to use this area whenever possible to receive money from parents, children and others: they can see the financial transaction taking place, and you can give change or raise any queries in privacy.

When accepting cheques, make sure that they are signed, dated, and written out correctly. This avoids needing to return them later. If you need to give change via a child, put it in a labelled envelope with the child's name on it and a message that states clearly that it is change to be given out later. Avoid mixing your own money with that of the setting – this could be misinterpreted, even if you were simply trying to provide some change.

## Keys to good practice

### Handling money

**Do's:**

- Try and record the transaction in the office or specific areas
- Put money into labelled envelopes or plastic wallets if it is loose
- Label money if there is no specific 'pot' for it to go in
- Put records and receipt books back in their place
- Ask for assistance if you are unsure what you should do with money

**Don'ts:**

- Be tempted to store money in your pockets for safe keeping
- Leave money lying around unattended
- Take receipt or record books out of the office or area
- Leave receipt or record books lying around
- Ask children to look after money for you
- 'Borrow' money, even if it is a very small sum
- Mix up your own money with that of the setting's – for example using some of your own money to act as change

## Passing on money and records to others

In many settings, you will need to pass on the records and money to others – for example, to a colleague who does the book-keeping or to the treasurer. This person may be keyholder to a safe, or be responsible for banking the money.

Keep the person up to date with any financial transactions for which you have been responsible, and check that they know exactly where money is stored and its purpose. Do not give out any information or provide access to money other than to the people in your setting who have this responsibility.

### Active knowledge ✔

1 Make a list of people who have access to money and records in your setting.
2 Who is responsible for the day-to-day book-keeping?
3 Who is responsible for the overall financial decisions and performance of your setting?

# Referring problems

There may be times when you will need some advice or guidance about financial transactions. For example, you might be asked by a parent for information, or you might be unsure how to record a transaction. Seek advice or guidance straight away: 'having a go' and getting it wrong might cause confusion later.

The table below outlines some of the common problems that occur.

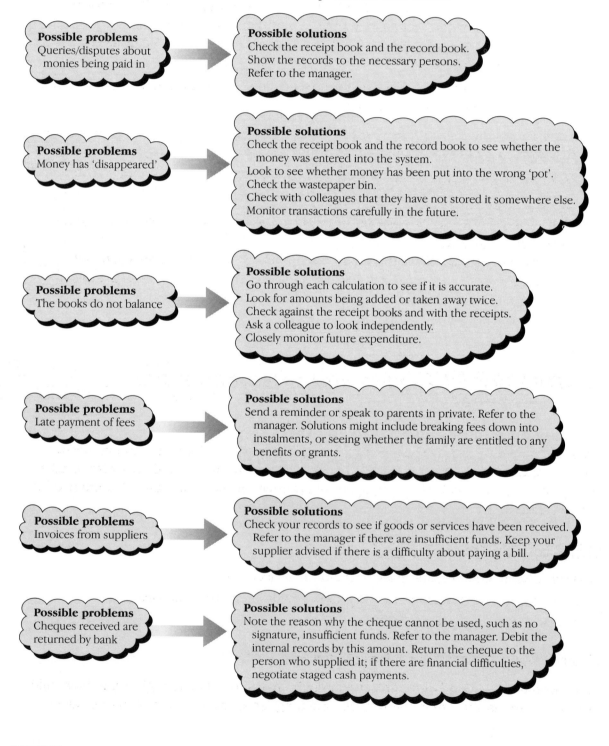

**Possible problems**
Queries/disputes about monies being paid in

**Possible solutions**
Check the receipt book and the record book.
Show the records to the necessary persons.
Refer to the manager.

**Possible problems**
Money has 'disappeared'

**Possible solutions**
Check the receipt book and the record book to see whether the money was entered into the system.
Look to see whether money has been put into the wrong 'pot'.
Check the wastepaper bin.
Check with colleagues that they have not stored it somewhere else.
Monitor transactions carefully in the future.

**Possible problems**
The books do not balance

**Possible solutions**
Go through each calculation to see if it is accurate.
Look for amounts being added or taken away twice.
Check against the receipt books and with the receipts.
Ask a colleague to look independently.
Closely monitor future expenditure.

**Possible problems**
Late payment of fees

**Possible solutions**
Send a reminder or speak to parents in private. Refer to the manager. Solutions might include breaking fees down into instalments, or seeing whether the family are entitled to any benefits or grants.

**Possible problems**
Invoices from suppliers

**Possible solutions**
Check your records to see if goods or services have been received. Refer to the manager if there are insufficient funds. Keep your supplier advised if there is a difficulty about paying a bill.

**Possible problems**
Cheques received are returned by bank

**Possible solutions**
Note the reason why the cheque cannot be used, such as no signature, insufficient funds. Refer to the manager. Debit the internal records by this amount. Return the cheque to the person who supplied it; if there are financial difficulties, negotiate staged cash payments.

## Following legal and organisational requirements

Most settings have established ways of processing financial transactions. You need to follow these so that your organisation can show its accounts. Failure to provide reliable accounts could mean that funding would be taken away from the setting, or (in the case of a charity) it could lose its charitable status. In addition, settings need to be aware that any personal information that is stored either on paper or on a computer falls under the Data Protection Act 1998. This says that personal details cannot be passed on to others without their permission, and that any information stored on the system about a person may be seen by them. Settings need also to be aware that they should not destroy any financial records for 5 years.

If you are setting up a financial system for a setting, it is a good idea to seek advice from a professional accountant or book-keeper.

---

### Consolidation

Think about a time recently when you took money from a parent, a child or someone else.

◆ *What was the money for?*
◆ *Explain how you made sure that the money was stored securely, and that an accurate record was kept of it.*
◆ *Ask whether you can take a photocopy of the record or the receipt that you issued.*

---

## Element PA55.2  Implement access procedures

An important administrative task in any setting is to provide information to prospective parents, carers and children, and to complete registration with them if they wish to take up a place. This section looks at the types of information and procedures that are needed within this task.

### WHAT YOU NEED TO LEARN

- Dealing with enquiries, and passing them on as necessary
- Collecting and recording information about children and their families
- Providing information about access conditions

### Answering enquiries about places

Most parents and carers will want to find out about a setting before registering their child. For many parents and carers the way that a setting responds to their first phone call or visit can be a deciding factor in whether they wish their child to attend the setting. Settings that respond to enquiries promptly and warmly are therefore more likely to fill places.

A good first contact between the setting and parents helps to establish a good working relationship. It also makes the setting look efficient and professional. This is important, especially to a setting that has just started up and needs to attract new children in order to keep going.

In order to be able to respond to parents' questions promptly and accurately, you need already to have absorbed basic information about the way your setting operates. If you are unsure about any area of information, ask a colleague or line manager. If you are responding to a telephone enquiry and cannot answer a question, ask if you can return the call once you have the information. Then ring back promptly with the answer or to explain why the information is not available.

*A good telephone manner is important when answering queries*

If a parent or carer arrives for an impromptu visit, welcome them warmly. If possible, show them around. If it is not possible to spend time answering their enquiries – for example, because you were just about to go out on a trip – explain why and arrange another time that will be convenient to them.

The table below shows some of the common questions that parents and carers ask. Parents will also ask questions specific to the needs of their children – for example, a child who enjoys art and painting may wish to be in a setting where there are plenty of creative activities going on.

| Area of information | Types of questions that are asked |
|---|---|
| Cost | How much does it cost per session to send a child?<br>Is there any reduction for more than one child?<br>What does the price include?<br>Is there a cancellation fee?<br>What happens if a child cannot attend due to sickness? |
| Session times and availability | What are the session times?<br>What sessions are available?<br>Is there any flexibility about sessions? |
| Food, drink and snacks | Are these included in the price?<br>Can the setting cater for children with specific dietary requirements, such as a gluten-free diet or a vegetarian?<br>What does a typical menu look like? |
| Activities | What type of activities are provided?<br>Are all activities free?<br>Is any special equipment or clothing required? |
| Settling in/transport arrangements | Is there a collection service from schools or from the local area?<br>How are children made to feel welcome?<br>Are the children divided into age groups?<br>How many other children are in the child's age group?<br>Are there any other children from the child's school?<br>Who looks after children once they have arrived? |

During the course of a conversation with a parent or carer it may become apparent that you will not be able to offer a place. For example, it may become clear that the setting will not meet the requirements of the parent or child. Be honest about what your setting can and cannot provide. Invite the parent or carer to leave you a contact number in case a place becomes available or in case you think of another setting that might be suitable. This type of gesture helps build a good reputation for your play setting.

## Active knowledge ✔

Look at the table above, of the types of questions that parents and carers commonly ask.

*Write a short answer to each of these questions, based on your own setting's procedures.*

## Collecting information about children and their families

It is important to keep basic information about children and their families on file in the setting. This will be needed in the event of an emergency, for example, or to prove to an auditor the number of children attending the setting. The information is also useful in helping setting to meet children's particular needs, such as dietary or medical requirements.

Most settings collect this information either by sending out a form or by filling in a form with the parents or primary carers. Filling in the form with parents or primary carers can be particularly useful because it allows parents to discuss issues as they are covered on the form – for example, the medication that children may need in a setting. This can help to build a relationship with parents and will provide more detailed information about the child's habits and needs. Filling in the form with or for parents can also help those parents who find form-filling difficult because their vision is impaired, for instance, or because they have difficulty in reading. It is helpful if parents are told why the information is needed, and that it will remain confidential. Under the Data Protection Act 1999, they have the right to check any stored information.

You can also use this opportunity to explain to parents how the setting is run, and give them any additional information that they might need. Some settings produce handbooks or starter packs.

*Filling in forms with parents gives them the opportunity to discuss issues as they are covered on the form*

The table below outlines the type of information that is generally collected when children take up a place at a setting.

| Information | Reason for its collection |
| --- | --- |
| **Address of parents/carers** | To send letters, or to contact parents in an emergency. |
| **Full name of child** | To make sure that it is correctly spelt. It will be needed in case of an emergency. |
| **Date of birth** | To help find a child's medical records in an emergency. The age of the child is also important in meeting registration requirements. |
| **Emergency contact numbers and addresses** | To contact parents/carers quickly in the event of an emergency. |
| **Doctor's name and address** | To access children's medical records in the event of an emergency. |
| **Health** | In case of an emergency, and also to make sure that any particular needs can be met – for example an allergy to bee stings will mean that staff would be extra-vigilant and would seek medical assistance if the child were stung. |
| **Dietary requirements** | To make sure that all foods and drinks are suitable for the health, cultural or religious needs of children. |

# Recording information clearly and fully

If you are responsible for recording information about the child, be sure to do this accurately and legibly. Although many settings have one main form, there might also be other documents to be filled in. Common additional forms include:

- forms giving permission for children to go on outings, to have their photograph taken and shown in the setting
- forms to entitle parents to bursaries or subsidised places.

Once information has been collected, you may have to transfer details onto other day-to-day documents such as the register, the list of children who have snacks, or the list of children who need to have inhalers near them. Information must be transferred carefully and accurately or children might not have their needs met.

## Passing on information to others

The information gathered must be carefully stored and passed onto others as necessary. The manager or senior team in the setting will need to know at all times how many children are in the setting, their ages and their needs.

Every setting has its own way of passing on such information – in smaller settings, the manager will want to meet the prospective parents and the child if possible; in larger settings, it might be the responsibility of the group leader to do this. Whatever the procedure, most settings pass on information quickly to avoid potential problems.

Efficient access and registration procedures:

- ensure accurate information
- help meet children's and parent's needs
- help build positive relationships with parents
- prevent confusion in the setting
- aid the smooth running of the setting
- are needed to meet legislation and registration requirements (see page 87).

## Handling enquiries about future places

You may receive enquiries about future places: this will happen if no places are currently available, or at the end of one playscheme where parents wish to find out whether another will be running.

Give honest and accurate information to parents, so that they can make their childcare arrangements based on what has been said to them. Sometimes you may not be able to give a complete answer, for example if the committee that organises the playscheme has not yet been appointed. In such cases you should refer to a colleague or write down the names and contact details of the interested parents, and pass these on to your line manager so the parents can be informed of future developments.

# ADMISSION FORM

Please use capitals

1. Full name of child: ..............................................................................................

2. Date of birth: .................................................... Age: ............................................

3. Proposed date of admission: ...........................................
   For each session required please state the approximate arrival and departure times:

   Monday ...............................................

   Tuesday ...............................................

   Wednesday ...............................................

   Thursday ...............................................

   Friday ...............................................

4. Name of parent/guardian: ...............................................................................

5. Home address/telephone number:        Work address/telephone number:

   ...................................................        ...................................................

   ...................................................        ...................................................

   ...................................................        ...................................................

   ...................................................        ...................................................

6. Position of child in family: (e.g. 2nd of 3 etc.) ...............................................

7. Name/address of Health Visitor ...............................................

   ...............................................................................

   ...............................................................................

8. Has your child had all the usual inoculations including whooping cough?

   Yes ☐        No ☐

*A registration form*

# Element PA55.3 Maintain records of information

In order that settings are able to run smoothly, it is important that good records are kept and maintained. This section looks at the types of records that most settings need to keep and ways of maintaining them.

## WHAT YOU NEED TO LEARN

- Ensuring that records are up to date and usable
- Storing records appropriately
- Maintaining confidentiality as required
- Passing on appropriate information to authorised colleagues

## Types of records

Records are vital in all settings. There is a legal obligation to maintain some records, such as an accident book, while others allow the setting to make plans and monitor their success. The table overleaf lists the types of records that are usually kept in most settings.

### Active knowledge ✔

1 *What type of records does your setting keep?*
2 *Who has overall responsibility for making sure that these records are kept up to date?*

### The Children Act 1989

The Children Act 1989 was introduced to ensure that childcare settings were regulated and safe. This has meant that settings have had to apply to be registered. As part of the registration requirements, settings that fall under the Act are required to keep certain records. It is interesting to note that even settings that do not *have* to comply with the Act still keep similar records as these are seen to be good practice. The list below shows some of the records settings need to keep:

- daily attendance register
- current information on children
- accident/incident book
- records on staff/volunteers
- insurance.

| Type of record | Reason |
|---|---|
| **Accident books** | It is a requirement of the Health and Safety at Work Act 1974 that employers keep a record of all accidents to their employees that take place in their setting. Play settings often keep separate books – one for the children and one for employees. The accident books must be accessible and available for inspection. |
| **Attendance registers** | These are needed for several reasons. In case of an emergency they give the number of children in the setting at that time. Some settings are funded according to the numbers of children 'on roll': attendance registers provide evidence of the numbers on particular days. |
| **Emergency contact details** | These are needed in the event of an emergency. Many settings ask for several contacts in case one is not available. |
| **Outing consent forms** | Consent forms are needed when children are taken out on trips and outings. Some settings ask parents to sign one for every outing. |
| **Health and dietary needs** | Records are kept of children's particular needs in relation to their health or diet. This enables staff to make sure that any activities, food and drinks that they are planning are appropriate. It also allows them to take the correct course of action if they see that a child is looking unwell. |
| **Records of medicine administered** | Where settings are willing to administer medicines to children, it is important that records are kept of the type of medicine that is brought into the setting, whose it is, and how it is to be administered. Parents have to sign the records to show that they have given their consent for medicine to be given to the child, and staff must keep a record of what has been given and at what time. |
| **Information about children and their families** | Most settings fill in a general form when a child first enters a setting. This form includes details about the child and the family, such as their address and full name. This form must be kept up to date, as some details may change – for example, a child's name might be changed or the family might move. |
| **Inventory of equipment** | Many settings keep a list of the equipment and the resources that they have. This allows them to check from time to time that equipment is still in good order and has not gone missing. Inventories must be kept up to date in case there is an insurance claim, when they can be used as evidence. |
| **Insurances** | Up-to-date records of insurance details are important; and some, such as public liability, must be displayed in a setting. Common insurance policies include public liability and employers' liability, buildings insurance and contents insurance. |
| **Staff/volunteers records** | Employers need to keep records about the staff. This should include a copy of their job descriptions, application forms or curricula vitae, and details about their pay, including National Insurance contributions and income tax. Staff also need to be approved from the registration department; and staff and volunteers in settings need to have police clearance. |
| **Work rotas and logs** | Most settings find it useful to keep a work rota or log so that they can pay staff accurately and check that rotas are fair. |

# Maintaining records

Many records are essential to a setting not just because they help the setting to run smoothly, but also because there is a legal requirement to keep them. This means that they need to be kept up to date, legible and accurate. This means being very disciplined and organised. You will be wise to note down information in the correct place soon after it has been given, or write a note to yourself as a reminder to do so later.

Some records need updating rather than adding to, such as the list of emergency contact numbers – is it still correct? At least once a year, parents are asked to check the information on file. In the same way, staff files might need to be checked periodically so that the information stored is still accurate.

To keep the records straight, some people build in a regular daily time slot when they know that they will be able to concentrate on the administration and are less likely to be disturbed. It is not uncommon to find playworkers doing this after the end of sessions.

# Storing and organising information

It is helpful to have a systematic filing system. If information is put away in order it can be retrieved quickly.

There are many ways of storing information. Some people use large files, while others store the majority of information in filing cabinets. Whatever system you use, make sure that you label everything clearly and logically so that others can find information if you are not available. This will be essential in an emergency situation, when a child's or a staff member's folder will be required immediately.

As part of the filing system, distinguish between information that needs to be secure and information that needs to be easily accessible to others in the setting. Staff files, for example, will need to be locked away, whereas the week's work rota will need to be displayed. Some information, such as children's records, might be kept unlocked during the sessions, but locked when the setting is closed.

To help others find information easily, it can be helpful to put a 'contents' list on the front of the filing cabinet drawer or at the front of a file. This helps people to check quickly whether the information they are looking for is available.

The diagram shows the reasons why information needs to be stored and maintained effectively.

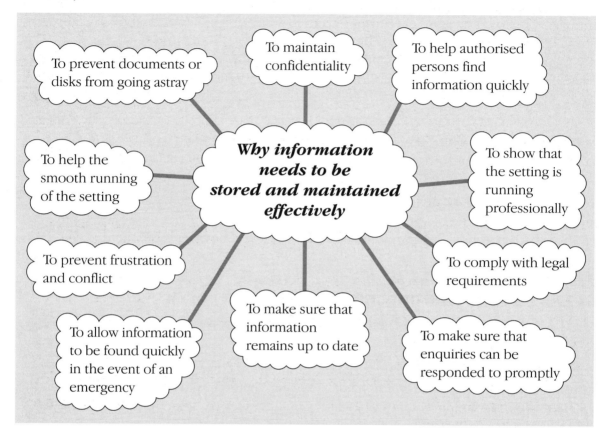

## Restricting access to information

Restrictions on access means that information is more likely to be kept confidential, and if there is a breach of confidentiality it is easier to discover the source. If you are responsible for maintaining some records, it is important that you understand who can have access to them. This will often vary according to the type of information that is being stored.

All playworkers within a setting will probably need access to attendance registers and information about children, but this is likely to be restricted for helpers or students working within the setting. In the same way, only the manager and the person responsible for personnel may have access to staff files, although most settings have a policy whereby they allow staff to have access to their own files.

If you are asked to provide information and you are unsure whether the person asking for it should have access to it, refer to your line manager or another senior colleague. To prevent unauthorised people having access to information, always lock away information and make sure that the key is kept in a secure place. If several types of records are being stored together, it may be best to take out the records that the person is authorised to look at, rather than allow her or him to retrieve the information and perhaps stumble across information that is sensitive and confidential.

Look at the following list of records that might be kept in a setting:

- attendance register
- emergency contact numbers
- staff employment details
- accident book
- telephone numbers of staff.

For each type of record, write a list of people within your setting who have free access to this information.

## Access to information

The Data Information Act 1984 was brought in to protect people. Personal information that was being held on computer must not be passed on without their knowledge. This Act applied only to information that is held on computers, not on paper; but the Access to Personal Files Act 1987 extended it to paper-based records kept by local authorities. The Access to Health Records Act 1990 further extended the law, this time to health providers. A new Data Protection Act passed in 1998 updated the law and provided for *all* records about clients, whether on paper or held electronically.

Under the law, anyone who is storing personal information about others on computer must register with the Data Protection Register; and everyone must abide by the following code:

- Individuals have the right to know what data is being held about them, and the right to correct it if it is inaccurate.
- Individuals may refuse to provide information.
- Data must be lawfully collected and processed fairly.
- Data cannot be passed on or used for other purposes without permission.
- Data must be accurate and kept up to date.
- Data can only be collected and stored for the purpose that has been registered.
- Data should not be kept longer than necessary.
- Data must be kept secure, so that confidentiality is protected.

## Case study

Mary is convinced that she is being underpaid in comparison with other playworkers at the setting. She does not want to ask the others how much they are getting paid, but is very keen to find out. She decides to look at the staff files to see what everyone else is being paid.

She wanders into the office where you are working, and asks you if you have a key to a filing cabinet to check something out. When you ask her what she needs, she says that she wants to look at her own employee file.

*Explain how you would handle this situation without breaching any confidentiality.*

# Providing information promptly to authorised people

If you are responsible for storing some types of information, you might on occasion be asked to provide it for your line manager or others such as auditors, registration officers and the emergency services. Being able to provide the information quickly is important, not least because it shows that the setting is being run professionally and efficiently. In extreme cases, such as where a child has a medical condition, it might even be life-saving. The diagram below shows some of the reasons why information might be requested from authorised people.

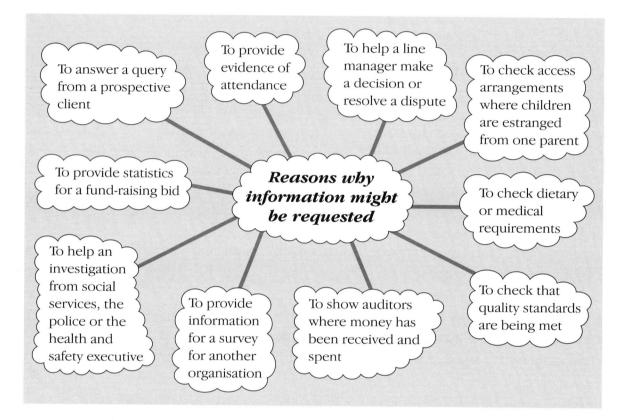

To answer a query from a prospective client

To provide evidence of attendance

To help a line manager make a decision or resolve a dispute

To check access arrangements where children are estranged from one parent

To provide statistics for a fund-raising bid

**Reasons why information might be requested**

To check dietary or medical requirements

To help an investigation from social services, the police or the health and safety executive

To provide information for a survey for another organisation

To show auditors where money has been received and spent

To check that quality standards are being met

## Consolidation

Choose an example of one type of record that you are responsible for maintaining and storing.

◆ *Why is this information needed?*
◆ *How do you make sure that it is kept up to date?*
◆ *Who has access to this information?*
◆ *How do you ensure that this information is easily retrievable?*

# PA55 unit test

1 Why is it important to keep accurate records of all transactions?
2 What might happen if money, records and receipts were not stored safely?
3 Outline three problems for which you might need to seek help from others.
4 Why is it important to answer all enquiries about places courteously?
5 Outline three areas of information about which prospective parents may wish to find out.
6 Why is it important that information is gathered about children?
7 Why is it important to refer to your line manager or colleague if you are unable to answer a particular enquiry?
8 Outline three types of records that have to be maintained.
9 Give three reasons why records must be stored and maintained effectively.
10 What is the Data Protection Act, and how might it affect your setting?

# Unit PB 23

# Promote children's development through play

All children need to play and to have access to good-quality play opportunities. Helping children by providing play opportunities is a major yet enjoyable part of being a playworker. Every setting will have its own way of providing for play, which will be affected by the environment, the resources, and most importantly by the children themselves. This chapter looks at how playworkers can promote children's all-round development through play.

The elements for this unit are:

PB23.1  Plan play opportunities
PB23.2  Provide opportunities for children to develop individually through play
PB23.3  Provide opportunities for children to develop socially through play
PB23.4  Take part in play with children
PB23.5  Bring play to an end

## Element PB23.1  Plan play opportunities

### WHAT YOU NEED TO LEARN

- Involving children, parents and colleagues in planning
- Matching play to children's needs and interests
- Offering children choice, balance, variety and equal opportunities
- Negotiating ground rules
- Being flexible, and planning for contingencies

### Understanding the role of play in children's development

A good starting point when looking at play is to understand how a range of enjoyable play experiences can help children's overall development. To look at how different types of play can help development, we can split children's development into different areas.

There are many ways of doing this, but one common way is by using the SPICE model, named from the first letters of each of the five areas. This is shown in the table.

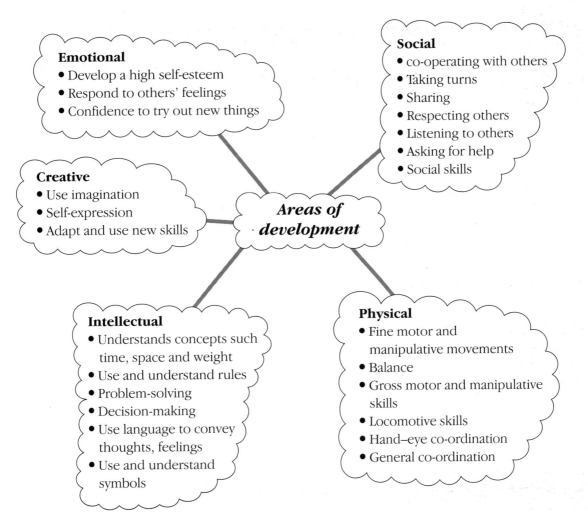

**Emotional**
- Develop a high self-esteem
- Respond to others' feelings
- Confidence to try out new things

**Social**
- co-operating with others
- Taking turns
- Sharing
- Respecting others
- Listening to others
- Asking for help
- Social skills

**Creative**
- Use imagination
- Self-expression
- Adapt and use new skills

*Areas of development*

**Intellectual**
- Understands concepts such time, space and weight
- Use and understand rules
- Problem-solving
- Decision-making
- Use language to convey thoughts, feelings
- Use and understand symbols

**Physical**
- Fine motor and manipulative movements
- Balance
- Gross motor and manipulative skills
- Locomotive skills
- Hand–eye co-ordination
- General co-ordination

*The SPICE model of areas of development*

Some play opportunities will develop specific individual areas of development, but many will develop several areas.

Consider the many areas of development that would be promoted by a play opportunity such as working with others to build an obstacle course:

- **Social development:**
  – co-operating with other children.
- **Physical development:**
  – moving and handling equipment.
- **Intellectual development:**
  – considering space and size
  – problem-solving.
- **Creative development:**
  – designing a 3D area.
- **Emotional development:**
  – self-reliance and satisfaction.

## Planning play opportunities

Although there are games that children can play which require no equipment or resources, most play does require some support, equipment or resources. Planning for play is therefore essential: it allows children to enjoy play opportunities fully, as they use and adapt equipment and props in their play.

Most settings that spend time planning for play find that children are then more likely to play spontaneously. This is because they can see a range of opportunities that interest them. Such settings are also able to provide more interesting opportunities for the children because they have thought ahead, such as going on trips or making full-size papier-mâché dinosaurs! This in turn means that both staff and children are motivated, and so helps the setting to run smoothly.

*Planning for play is essential – most play requires support, equipment and resources*

The diagram below shows some of the reasons why planning is important.

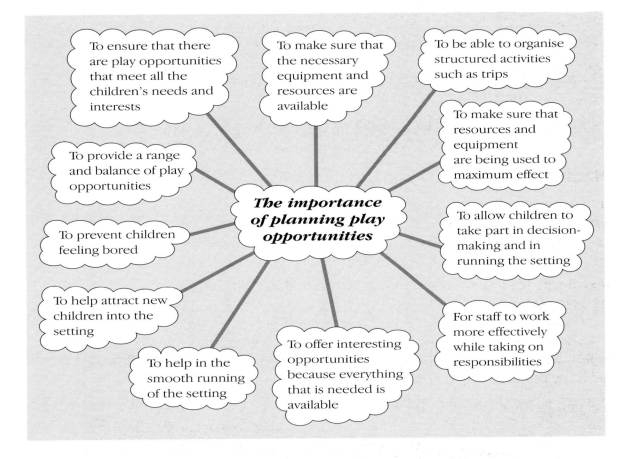

To ensure that there are play opportunities that meet all the children's needs and interests

To make sure that the necessary equipment and resources are available

To be able to organise structured activities such as trips

To provide a range and balance of play opportunities

To make sure that resources and equipment are being used to maximum effect

**The importance of planning play opportunities**

To prevent children feeling bored

To allow children to take part in decision-making and in running the setting

To help attract new children into the setting

For staff to work more effectively while taking on responsibilities

To help in the smooth running of the setting

To offer interesting opportunities because everything that is needed is available

## Involving children, colleagues and parents in the planning

It is good practice to involve others, especially children, in the planning of play opportunities. Children should be involved because they are the 'consumers'; in the same way that supermarkets try and find out what we like to buy and eat, we should be doing the same with children. If children are *not* consulted, staff may work very hard and be disappointed that children are not interested in the play opportunities or activities they have prepared; or children may not enjoy attending the setting, which they may not find stimulating.

Involving others in the planning also tends to be an enriching experience – other people, such as parents and carers, may have resources, equipment or ideas that will be fun to play with. You will also feel more motivated if instead of just 'minding' children, you can be actively involved in working with them to prepare play opportunities.

## Types of planning

Planning will often operate on at least two levels: long-term and short-term. Many settings also carry out some medium-term planning. The type of planning, and the way in which it is recorded, varies enormously between settings.

## SPORTS WORLD PLAYSCHEME

| DATE | MORNING ACTIVITY | AFTERNOON ACTIVITY |
|---|---|---|
| **Monday 26th July**<br>Fire & Evacuation Procedures<br><br>Welcome games | Name your Sports Team<br>– design your team's crest or logo & make into a giant banner<br><br>Knex Construction – New Equipment! | Sports Team Races & Games Outdoors<br>"Sports Star Gallery"<br>– draw your sports hero & write a caption about them<br><br>Video Session |
| **Tuesday 27th July**<br>Fire & Evacuation Procedures<br><br>Circle and group games | "Olympics"!<br>– make Olympic Rings torches to display in the playroom<br><br>Parachute Games & Outdoor Play | "Medal Mania"<br>– design & make medals and ribbons<br><br>Video Session<br><br>Badminton |
| **Wednesday 28th July**<br>Fire & Evacuation Procedures<br><br>Circle and group games | "Wembley Towers"<br>– make & build the Wembley Towers or –<br>"SPORTY STUFF"<br>– make your own sports equipment or model | Football & Outdoor Games<br><br>Video Session<br><br>Sport Pictionary & Charades |
| **Thursday 29th July**<br>Fire & Evacuation Procedures<br><br>Circle and group games | Bouncy Castle!<br><br>"Formula 1"<br>– make a racing car or a "Winners Flower Garland" | Bouncy Castle!<br><br>Video Sessions<br>Outdoor Games<br><br>"Question of Sport Quiz" |
| **Friday 30th July**<br>Fire & Evacuation Procedures<br><br>Circle and group games | "Rattles"<br>– make rattles, pom poms & other 'noises' to cheer with<br><br>Cheer Leader<br>– make up cheers and dances | Rounders Match<br>& final team games<br><br>Presentations & Team Winners<br><br>Video Session |

Children's free choice of play activities, such as board games, construction toys, reading, basic art and team games, will be available throughout the day. There will also be quiet activities during group time, usually at the beginning and end of the day, and during mid-morning and mid-afternoon snack times, when juice and a snack will be provided. Please provide your children with suitable clothing for outdoor activities which take place each day.

### A plan for a theme-based approach

Most settings carry out some long-term planning in order to be able to order stock and equipment, and to organise outings and visitors. Some settings also use a theme-based approach, such that sessions have slightly different focuses. Short-term planning tends to happen on a day-to-day basis which allows for adjustments according to the weather, the number of children, and the immediate interests of the children.

## Ways of involving others in planning

There are many ways of involving others in planning play opportunities, both on a day-to-day basis and on a long-term basis. Most settings use a combination of methods to help them get ideas and a feel for what children are interested in doing.

### Informal discussions

Many day-to-day planning ideas might grow out of informal chats with children, parents, carers and colleagues. A group of children might mention something that they have seen on television that they would like to do, or a parent might say to a playworker that she has some large pieces of fabric that could be used to make dens.

The key to encouraging others to put forward their ideas in this way is to *listen* and if possible *act* on them. If it is not possible to follow up on an idea, explain why or make a note of it so that it can be used at another time. Responding to ideas and suggestions creates a climate in which more ideas will flow.

### Planning meetings

One way in which other people and children can be involved is by holding planning meetings. In some settings brief meetings are held at the start of each session: at these, children are asked what they would like to do in addition to activities that have already been arranged. In other settings children and parents are encouraged to contribute to the longer-term plans. The input of colleagues at planning meetings is also important – they may have ideas, resources or comments that they would like to put forward.

### Questionnaires and comment slips

Some settings regularly distribute questionnaires which include questions about which activities the children have enjoyed, or what type of play opportunities children would like to have organised. Other settings provide a comments and suggestions box, which allows anyone in the setting to put forward their ideas.

### Children's meetings

Some settings have meetings in which children can give their input as to what they would like the setting to provide. In settings where there are older children, they often take the responsibility for reporting back to the playworkers; or the playworkers can sit in with the children and work with them on what they would like to be arranged.

# Types of play opportunities

In order to cater for different children's interests and needs, it is important to offer a wide *range* of play opportunities. Play opportunities can be grouped into different types, although some are hard to categorise neatly. Play types often go under a variety of titles: find out how your own setting refers to different play types, to avoid any misunderstanding in your planning.

The table below shows the common play types, and the ways in which these can help children's all-round development.

| Play type and definition | Examples of play opportunities | Aspects of children's skills and overall development which may be promoted |
|---|---|---|
| **Creative play** – play that is inventive and/or productive | Junk modelling<br>Painting and drawing<br>Writing<br>Dancing<br>Making music<br>Origami<br>Clay modelling | Fine motor skills<br>Hand–eye co-ordination<br>Decision-making<br>Learning about properties of materials<br>Self-expression<br>Self-esteem and confidence<br>Working together with others |
| **Cultural play** – play that celebrates and/or raises awareness of different cultures and their values and practices | Cooking<br>Celebrating festivals such as the Chinese kite festival | Widening awareness<br>Self-esteem and confidence<br>Working together with others |
| **Environmental play** – play that involves and/or raises awareness of natural elements and/or wildlife and their survival | Projects such as making bird boxes, counting ladybirds<br>Water and sand play<br>Nature walks<br>Science kits using magnets, electricity and the like | Awareness of their world<br>Confidence<br>Self-expression<br>Working together with others<br>Self-reliance |
| **Imaginative play** – play that involves 'pretend' roles or acting out fantasy situations | Making dens or hideouts<br>Dressing up<br>Producing plays and sketches | Language skills<br>Confidence and self-esteem<br>Co-operation with others |
| **Physical play** – play that is physically active | Rounders<br>Football<br>Dodge ball<br>Obstacle courses | Locomotive skills<br>Gross motor and manipulative skills<br>Fine motor and manipulative skills<br>Stamina<br>Balance<br>Strength<br>Co-operation with others<br>Self-esteem and confidence |
| **Special events** – planned specific occasions | Parties<br>Discos<br>Fund-raising events<br>Performances<br>Visitors | Awareness of others and the world around them<br>Self-expression<br>Co-operation with others<br>Self-esteem and confidence<br>Social skills |
| **Off-site activities** – trips and visits, locally or further afield | Camping weekends<br>Trips to a local park<br>Visits to museums or the cinema | Social skills<br>Awareness of the world around them<br>Self-reliance |

## Free play and structured play

*Free play* is spontaneous play, which happens when children choose and use the materials and resources in their own way. Their play may then fall into one of the play types listed – for example, a pair of children might create their own den out of fabric and some chairs, and then begin to act out roles: this would be imaginative play. Free play allows children to play following their own moods and interests, although they still need good resources and supervision.

*Structured play* is play that has been pre-arranged in some way, as with team games or cooking. Structured play is usually carefully planned to be sure that materials and equipment are available.

When planning opportunities for children, most settings create a mix of free play and structured play opportunities. This approach is more likely to meet the needs of all the children, some of whom will need more support and guidance than others.

# Providing play opportunities

For play opportunities to work well and for the setting to run smoothly, it is important not only to consider individual play activities that can be offered but also the *range* that will be available to the children. You will need to consider the following factors when planning:

- time
- space
- age and interests of the children
- supervision requirements
- equipment and resources available
- numbers of children
- particular needs of children
- cost.

## Time

The amount of time available for play opportunities can be a serious restriction and may influence planning. This is a particular factor for clubs with very short session times, or for crèche and drop-in centres. Children and staff will find it very frustrating if they cannot finish an activity because there is not enough time. When planning for play, therefore, you must consider how much time might be required – for example, a very complicated cooking activity might take a whole morning.

## Space

Space can be a factor, and especially floor space. Where space is limited, you may not be able to have certain activities running alongside each other – for example, it might not be possible to have indoor parachute games at the same time as having the racing car track out.

## Ages and interests of the children

When planning play opportunities, think about all of the children in the setting and their needs. It can be easy to overlook the needs of younger children if there are significantly more older children who are good at voicing their needs. You might need to talk to particular children about the type of play activity that they enjoy, and then make sure that you can provide it.

## Supervision requirements

Different activities require different levels of supervision and support – cooking often requires close supervision, for example, whereas playing football may require more general supervision. Planning must therefore take into account the supervision requirements for each activity. Are there enough staff to meet these requirements?

## Equipment and resources available

Individual play activities may require certain resources or equipment. Before scheduling an activity, check that these resources will be available and in sufficient quantity. Planning avoids situations in which children begin play and then find that there is not enough paint, or that the glue has run out. Consider also whether any activities happening side by side will require the same resources, such as scissors.

## Numbers of children

The number of children who might wish to take part in any play activity is a further factor. If there is not enough equipment or supervision for all the children to join in, should they wish to do so, how will the activity be managed? In some settings there are extreme differences in ages and needs of children: here play activities could be targeted first at younger groups of children, then repeated in a slightly different way for older children.

## Meeting particular needs

When planning activities and programmes, be aware of children who will need special equipment or support in order to join in. Consider this separately for each activity: a child who needs support or equipment for one activity may not need any in order to join in another. If children have medical conditions such as eczema, you will need to consider whether the activity is suitable, or how it can be adapted so that they can join in.

## Cost

Some play opportunities may have a cost factor. Check this before an activity is planned into a programme.

# Providing choice, balance and variety

Most adults enjoy some variety in their lives, and children too need variety and choice in their play opportunities. When planning sessions or programmes, make available a good *range* of play opportunities and activities. Some children may choose always to play quite repetitively, but they should still be offered the option for trying new play opportunities. Most children, however, enjoy trying out new things, especially if they have been involved in some way in setting them up.

When planning activities, make sure that all children can access them. Bear in mind any special needs, such as making sure that a painting easel can be adjusted for a child who has a leg frame. Be aware that one group of children may dominate the others, for example by saying that an activity is babyish. Be ready to intervene so that children who might otherwise feel intimidated do feel that they can take part.

## Making sure that plans are flexible

Allow for some flexibility in your planning, so that you can respond to changes in circumstances, such as rain, or larger numbers than expected. When working out types of play opportunities, identify those activities which are liable to be postponed or altered, including outdoor play activities and visits.

## Encouraging children to take control of play opportunities

Whilst providing play activities, wherever possible provide scope for the children to take ownership of them. Some of the best types of play activities are flexible and have several possibilities. Children can then adapt them to suit their own needs. Activities that are very structured and that can only be done in one way tend to be more limiting and less appealing.

There are enormous benefits for children if they are able to take ownership of their play activities, as shown in the diagram.

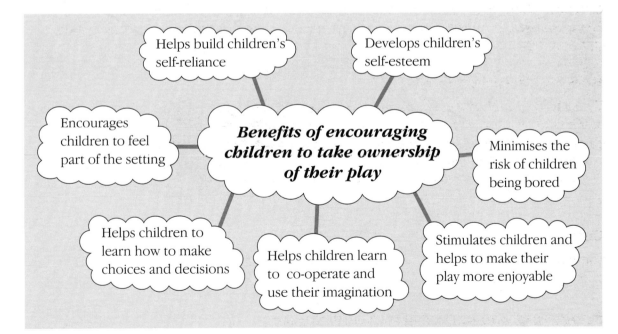

## Having realistic plans for contingencies

Sometimes plans have to be changed at short notice, so your setting needs to make sure that there are plenty of other activities that can be quickly brought out. The list below shows some reasons why plans may need to be changed:

- *Staffing difficulties* – absences due to sickness can mean that the playworker responsible for an activity is not present, or that there are not enough staff to supervise adequately several activities.
- *Weather* – outings, visits or outdoor play are activities that can easily be affected by sudden changes in the weather.
- *Cost* – an activity might have to be postponed because not enough contributions have been received, or a grant has not been received.
- *Equipment or resources are not available* – this may happen because of a lack of communication or because they have 'disappeared'.
- *Children are not interested in the play opportunity* – there may be times when children have changed their minds, or are uninterested in play activities: other opportunities will need to be provided.

In order to be able to think of ideas quickly and easily, you need to know what equipment and resources are available in your setting. It is surprising how often resources lurk unused in settings!

### Active knowledge ✔

Think about the equipment and resources that are available in your setting, including:

- board games
- art and craft materials
- equipment for physical play
- musical instruments
- videos
- computer games and programmes
- miscellaneous.

*Make lists of the equipment and resources, perhaps using these headings.*

Playworkers gradually acquire a store of ideas that can be drawn on at short notice. The table below shows some examples.

| Types of activities | Comments |
| --- | --- |
| **Treasure hunts** | It is quite easy to have an impromptu treasure hunt, either indoors or out-of-doors. Children can be asked to look for a single object, such as a walnut, or several items, such as raffle tickets. Treasure hunts can be organised by older children, and clues can be written. |
| **Card games** | Card games such as 'beat my neighbour' or whist can provide hours of entertainment for children. Consider buying a simple card game book and a pack of cards! |
| **Origami** | Origami needs only thin pieces of square paper. Children can very easily make animals, boxes, windmills and waterbombs. |
| **Party games** | Most children enjoy the traditional type of party games such as musical statues and hunt the thimble. Most party games do not need many props, only music. |
| **Create dens** | Dens and hideaways can be created indoors using fabric, cushions and furniture. |
| **Paper chase** | Confetti or other scraps of paper can be thrown down by one child. The others try to follow him or her and collect as much paper as they can. |
| **Team games** | Team games are a good way of organising groups of children who may enjoy some physical activity. Games such as 'port and starboard' and obstacle courses are always popular. |
| **Board games** | There are many good board games available that are simple to play, but enjoyable. |

## Obtaining parents' or carers' consent for play opportunities

As part of the planning process, you may need to consider whether parents' or carers' consent is needed. This is usually needed for play activities that require children to leave the setting or that involves some level of risk. If you are unsure about the suitability of an activity for particular children, such as for a child with asthma, check with the child's parents or carers. Here are examples of the types of activities that might require the consent of parents or carers:

- swimming
- ice skating
- rafting
- rock-climbing
- canoeing
- pony-riding
- assault courses
- abseiling.

## Active knowledge ✔

Find out how your setting asks parents and carers for their consent.

1  *Is there a standard letter or format?*
2  *What types of activities would require the consent of parents or carers in your setting?*

## Setting ground rules of play opportunities

Ground rules are the basic boundaries that help children understand what they can and cannot do during the course of their play. Ground rules are usually based on keeping children safe and encouraging them to respect each other. It is good practice to encourage children to think about the ground rules for an activity for themselves. By giving them this responsibility (although usually with some guidance), they are more likely to respect the ground rules and to remember what they are. For more information about ground rules, see also page 138.

---

### Consolidation

Think of a play activity that you have recently planned.

◆ **Write about how you planned this activity.**
◆ **How did you make sure that the planned activity would interest the children?**
◆ **How were the children able to take 'ownership' of the activity?**

---

## Element PB23.2 Provide opportunities for children to develop individually through play

As well as working with *groups* of children, playworkers must also be able to meet the needs and interests of *individual* children. This section looks at the importance of working with individual children, and ways in which we can give them support.

### WHAT YOU NEED TO LEARN

■ Encouraging spontaneous play
■ Providing support as necessary, while fostering independence
■ Showing children that they are valued

## The needs of individual children

Each child will have slightly different needs and interests, so each child will respond in different ways to play opportunities. Some children might wish to repeat certain types of play for long periods of time; others might be more restless and enjoy changing activities frequently. The play opportunities that you plan and provide must therefore be flexible enough for children to develop their own interests. For example, a child who loves dinosaurs might happily play with them in the sand pit, whereas a football enthusiast might enjoy creating a league table to record matches.

Children gain many benefits from being able to play spontaneously, as shown in the diagram. Look for opportunities to encourage them.

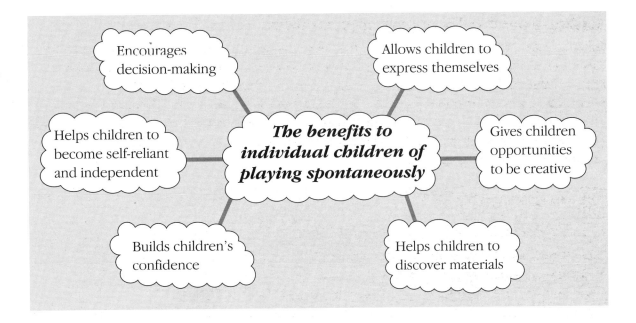

## Monitoring children's involvement and stimulation

It is important to monitor children individually during play, especially during group activities. Check that each child is gaining from and enjoying their play. This kind of monitoring will help you avoid possible problems such as clashes between children.

There are two main ways in which we can monitor children; most playworkers will use a combination of them, depending on the play situation and the child.

### Informal questions and chats

Informal chats are effective if children are playing by themselves. Questions such as 'Are you enjoying this?' or 'Do you have one of these at home?' can often help us to see whether the child is really enjoying the play activity. It is important that the questions do not make the child feel interrogated, however, and that they do not intrude into their play. You can gauge whether a child is responding to the play opportunity by spending a moment chatting to them, 'This is going to be quite a large puzzle, isn't it?'

Look out for:

- Children who seem more interested in talking to you than in carrying on their play activity – this can be a sign that the play activity is not really working, and that they need some company.
- Children who sigh, shrug their shoulders or sound flat and bored – this can be a sign that they are merely doing this activity because they have found nothing else.

### Observing body language and facial expression

Non-verbal signals are a key way in which we can see whether children are enjoying their play. Watching these is non-intrusive, and is especially useful when children are playing in groups. It is often useful to stand back and watch a particular child for a moment: facial expressions can quickly change, and a child whose face looks sullen one moment may be smiling the next.

*Children who are not joining in may need extra attention*

Remember also that facial expressions can be misleading – for example, some children (and adults) can look solemn and sad when merely concentrating!

Look out for:

- Children who seem 'on the edge' of a game or activity – this might indicate that they are lacking confidence to join in, or that they are not really interested in participating. In some cases, it may be an indication that there are friendship difficulties.
- Children whose body language seems tense or awkward – this can be a sign of unhappiness or tension.
- Children who are boisterous and aggressive, and who may be using equipment inappropriately – this can mean that the activity is not stimulating enough.

In addition, we might also find that some children are clingy, 'fussy' and attention seeking. This can be a sign that they are not involved and stimulated by the activity.

## When children seem not to be enjoying play

Although in some cases, you might decide to monitor the child for a little longer before taking action, in most cases it will be important to respond to a child that is not showing signs of enjoying the play activity.

Ways of responding include:

- Playing alongside the child
- Giving the child some more assistance
- Finding other equipment or resources
- Encouraging the child to try a different play activity
- Talking to other children who are playing to encourage them to play with the individual child.

## Encouraging children to extend themselves through play

Play is a marvellous medium as it allows children to try out new things and to go that one step further without fear of ridicule or failure. This is the idea behind play being used to 'extend' children. Play workers have an important role in helping children to extend themselves, as children can lack confidence in certain areas of their development – for example, a child might want to climb a little higher or try cycling without stabilisers, but is slightly afraid or unsure.

### Active knowledge ✔

The list below shows a few of the things that children might wish to do in which they would need support.

- rollerblading or ice skating without holding on
- aspects of cooking, such as cracking an egg or using an electric whisk
- performing or talking in front of others
- using a telephone to get information.

*Can you add five more items to this list?*

### Helping children to extend themselves

The key to helping children to overcome their own barriers is to allow them the space and time to edge further towards their goals at their own speed. It is essential not to 'push' children, as this can curb their confidence – and in any case, we want children to learn to do things from choice rather than to please adults. Pushing children into situations where they fear failure can also lower their self-esteem: they may become disappointed with themselves that they cannot do as much as they want.

You can help children by praising what they can already do, and be ready to help them when they want to 'have a go'. In practical terms, this might mean standing underneath a climbing frame, ready to catch them, or standing behind them as they make their first phone call. Take your lead from the children, asking them what type of support they would like: that way they are more likely to meet their own goals.

### Giving prompt support when it is needed

There may times when children will need particular help, for example during a treasure hunt a younger child might need help in reading the clues. Supporting children needs to be done sensitively, so as not to undermine a child's confidence or 'credibility' in front of other children. This is particularly important when helping *older* children.

The table below shows how the support needs of children might change according to their age.

| Age group | Support needs | Ways in which support might be offered |
|---|---|---|
| **5–8 years** | Younger children might need help with skills such as reading, writing, cutting, and using tools.<br>It is important to encourage this age group to 'have a go' as they may be inclined to ask adults to do things for them.<br>Children in this age range will need continual monitoring: some children find it hard to come and ask for assistance.<br>Children will grow in confidence if given plenty of praise, both for their efforts and their achievements. | Directly approach children to see if you can help in any way.<br>Provide different tools and resources to 'get around' problems.<br>Do not rush children.<br>Encourage them to take their time and have a go. |
| **9–12 years** | This age group are becoming increasingly independent and very aware of their own and others' achievements.<br>This can mean that some children are reluctant to say that they need some help.<br>Praise is still important, but might need to be given discreetly! | Offer children 'a hand' and ask them what they would like you to do.<br>Give suggestions and let the children decide what to do. |
| **13–15 years** | This age group are usually very capable and will not need much adult support. They may come to adults to 'check' things out. Older children sometimes feel that they are 'beyond' praise, yet still need some acknowledgement. | Let this age range know that you are around if they want to check anything out, or if they need any equipment or assistance.<br>Make sure that you do not come across as either patronising or bossy.<br>Acknowledge rather than praise this age range – for example, 'That's a good idea, I haven't come across it before.' |

## Making sure that support is fair

When giving support to an individual child, be sure that other children do not feel neglected and that they too are given the adult support they need. Children can easily feel resentful, and parents and carers might think that playworkers have 'favourites'. Treat every child as an individual, and make sure that you listen to and interact with them on a one-to-one basis at some time during each session – even if this is simply a greeting, and find out whether they are enjoying the session.

In order to balance the needs of individual children with those of the group, you may have to 'juggle' between children. One way in which children can gain high levels of individual support is by maintaining good staff ratios. Bear this in mind when planning, considering the supervision requirements of the range of activities you propose.

## Active knowledge ✔

Look at the list of play activities below, for children aged 5–12 years.

- making kites
- playing computer games
- making papier-mâché masks
- playing football
- designing a puppet theatre
- board games.

*Work out which activities are likely to require a lot of close supervision or individual support for children.*

## Encouraging children to be independent and self reliant

Self-reliance and independence are important skills for children to develop. Children who are *confident* enough to have a go at activities are more likely to enjoy them and persevere with them. Self-reliance and independence also allow children to be more creative in their play, because they are not afraid of doing things 'wrong'.

The diagram below shows the benefits to children of acquiring these qualities.

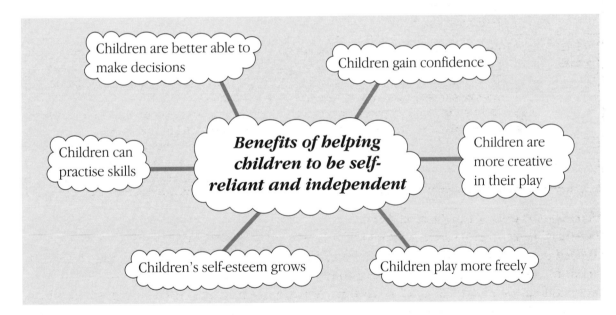

Whenever possible, encourage children to be independent and self-reliant. This does not mean refusing to give them assistance, but making sure that you do not 'take over' an activity, and looking for ways to encourage them to take on responsibility. An example of this would be if a young child wanted some help cutting some fabric: the playworker might look for a sharper pair of scissors so that the child could do the cutting himself, or ask the child to hold the fabric in place whilst it was being cut. You can also help children to be independent by making sure that they can have access to equipment and resources.

# Responding to children's ideas and suggestions

One of the lovely things about working with children is their creativity and their enthusiasm. Responding to children's ideas and suggestions positively will develop this further, so knowing how to do this is an important skill for the playworker. As children get older, they may sometimes lose the confidence to make suggestions, fearing that their ideas will not be accepted. Whenever children are putting forward ideas and suggestions, therefore, always show them that you are interested, and keen to listen to them.

In group situations, make sure that all children have the opportunity to contribute. Younger or less confident children can sometimes feel intimidated by those who are more vocal. You might need to develop some ground rules about listening to and respecting each others' ideas. Do not let other children 'shout down' ideas, as this could lead to those who spoke losing their self-esteem. If age ranges are very wide, it might be an idea to break into smaller groups, so that everyone's ideas and suggestions can be explored.

Another way of encouraging children to pass on ideas and suggestions is by developing a 'suggestion box', in which children can post their ideas. This can be very popular, but it is important that children who need support with literacy skills are not discriminated against. Suggestions may not always be feasible, but it is still important to handle the ideas sensitively. One approach is to take an idea to its logical conclusion by asking some further questions. This allows children to think through their ideas, and they may then realise for themselves that these might not be practical.

The following case study shows a playworker working with a child.

## Case study

Wesley is very inventive and enjoys making things out of junk. Today he is keen to make a kite to fly, as it has recently been very windy. He asks the playworker if he will come and help him. Wesley suggests that the main body of the kite could be made from large pieces of wood. Mike, the playworker, knows that this will make the kite too heavy.

| | |
|---|---|
| MIKE: | Have you flown a kite before? |
| WESLEY: | Yes, I have got one at home. |
| MIKE: | What is it made of? |
| WESLEY: | It's blue and has things like bamboo canes in the back. |
| MIKE: | Why do you think that they used thin sticks? |
| WESLEY: | To keep the kite light. |
| MIKE: | We have got some garden sticks that you can use, if you want to. |
| WESLEY: | Instead of these pieces of wood? |
| MIKE: | Well, it's up to you. You can see if the wood will work, or you can try with the garden sticks. I'll get them out of the cupboard so that you can see them. |
| WESLEY: | Yes, these might be better than the wood. I think I'll use these. |

1  *Why was it important that Wesley kept control of his project?*
2  *How did Mike manage to help Wesley without undermining his confidence?*

## Showing children that they are valued as individuals

All children need to feel that they are special, and valued as individuals. This is particularly important in large group settings, where children might feel more anonymous. There are several ways of organising a setting to help children feel that they belong, and this is particularly important in settings that have many younger children:

- allocate particular staff to groups of children
- separate children into smaller groups according to their ages or interests
- allocate a higher staffing ratio to younger children
- make sure that staffing remains stable.

Another way to help children feel that they are valued as individuals is to spend time with them regularly. You might ask them about the things that interest them, or listen to their concerns. Building individual relationships with children will help them to come forward when they need assistance or if they have ideas that they wish to share.

---

### Consolidation

Think about a time recently when you gave assistance or support to a child.

◆ *Explain the circumstances.*
◆ *How did you make sure that the child was still in control of the play activity?*
◆ *Why is it important for adults to offer support promptly to children?*

---

## Element PB23.3 Provide opportunities for children to develop socially through play

Play settings allow children to mix together in a non-competitive environment whilst enjoying themselves. This helps children's social development as they learn to understand how to relate to children of different ages and from different home backgrounds. This section looks at ways in which playworkers can help children to socialise whilst playing.

### WHAT YOU NEED TO LEARN

- Encouraging co-operative play
- Fostering respect and mutual understanding between children
- Helping children to resolve conflicts

## Social development

The ability to co-operate and mix with others is an important life skill. Children who are comfortable in the company of others, and who know how to interpret others' signals and gestures, will gain in confidence and find it easier to form adult relationships. There are many skills that children need to develop:

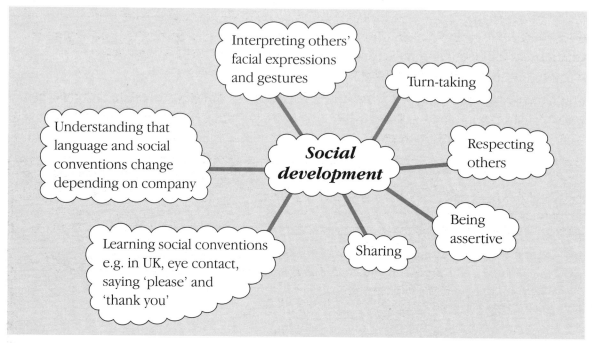

## Providing opportunities for co-operative play

There are many play opportunities and structured activities that will help children to develop the skills of co-operation. Team and party games are particular favourites and can help children new to a setting to settle in quickly. Similarly, many children enjoy working in pairs or in small groups on creative projects such as putting together puppet shows, and making kites or water bombs.

The types of play opportunities that children will enjoy will often depend on their interests and their ages. Many children also enjoy doing things with an adult, such as cooking, painting or canoeing. Opportunities to play and to be alongside playworkers can also benefit children, as they then learn to relate with adults who have different roles from their parents or teachers.

### Helping children to co-operate

As well as planning particular activities for children, there are other strategies that we can use to help children co-operate with each other. These include:

- agreeing ground rules at the start of activities
- encouraging children to keep to the ground rules they have agreed
- being a positive role model so that children learn from our behaviour
- praising children when they are co-operating well
- encouraging children to take responsibility for helping one another.

# Stages of development and ability to co-operate

Children's stages of development tend to affect their social skills and their ability to co-operate with others. Bear this in mind, when planning play opportunities, and also when judging how much supervision or support a group of children might need.

Although there is a strong link between age and stage of development, you need to get to know children as individuals, as their experiences can affect their development. In some areas of development children may have some developed some skills but not others. For example, a child might be good at using social conventions, such as showing table manners, yet find it hard to share with others during a play activity.

The table below shows some of the areas of development that are important if children are to be able to co-operate with others, and ways in which playworkers can help children who need support in these areas.

| Areas of development | Effect on children's ability to socialise with others | Ways in which the playworker can encourage children |
|---|---|---|
| **Language and communication** | Being able to communicate is extremely important when socialising. By 5, most children are beginning to use language fluently, but it is not until around 8 years that children have mastered a language. Children who have a language or communication impairment or who do not speak the language of the setting fluently may find it hard to get others to understand them. This can lead to isolation and frustration. | Play or work alongside the child. Praise the child when he/she tries to communicate. Provide play opportunities that do not rely heavily on language and communication. |
| **Cognitive/ intellectual** | Children's intellectual/cognitive stage of development affects the way in which they play. Younger children tend to enjoy more hands-on activities and role-play. Older children tend to enjoy games and activities that rely on their abilities to follow rules, use their memory or think in the abstract – for example, noughts and crosses, crosswords, board games. Children's intellectual and cognitive development tends to follow a certain pattern which relates to their age and experience, with most children being able to follow and understand rules by the age of 6 or 7. | Younger children and children with learning difficulties may need adult support when playing games which requires following complex rules. Make sure that there are some games and activities provided which do not rely heavily on intellectual skills. |
| **Emotional development** | Children's emotional development and social development are often inter-related. Skills such as being able to take turns and share gradually develop, along with empathy – children learn to be thoughtful and to think about how others might be feeling. Children who lack confidence or have poor self-esteem can find it harder to make relationships with children of their own age. Some children tend to be aggressive, while others might be attention-seeking. | Make sure that children are given praise and feel valued. Consider playing alongside or working with individual children. Plan some play opportunities for pairs and very small groups. |

## Promoting understanding between children of differing backgrounds

Every family operates differently: it has its own rules, values and personalities. This is a good starting point when working with children, as once children understand this they are more likely to be tolerant of cultures, religions and ways of life that are different from their own.

Children also need to take pride in their *own* family and traditions in order that they can grow in confidence and feel positive about themselves. It is interesting to note that some people who show discriminatory behaviour and prejudices are insecure and lacking in confidence; this is why they find it hard to cope with things that are different. Helping children to be confident and secure is therefore one way in which we can foster respect and tolerance. In addition, children need to learn that lifestyles different from their own are to be valued. This can be encouraged by helping them to find out about a range of cultures, traditions and religions other than their own.

We can help children learn about the ways in which families are all different by planning appropriate play opportunities. Examples include activities such as organising a 'favourite recipe', or games such as 'Guess our family's favourite TV show'.

*Children from different backgrounds can enjoy shared experiences*

Make sure that there are clear ground rules about respecting others. Children must learn not to make comments or gestures that are offensive. Any behaviour that is offensive has to be challenged and worked on – turning a blind eye cannot be an option. In addition, playworkers need to develop a warm, tolerant atmosphere within the setting. They can do this in several ways, as follows.

### Acting as a good role model

This is a key way in which children learn how to co-operate and respect each other. Playworkers need to show that *they* are interested in finding out more about other's traditions and ways of life. Comments such as 'I don't know if I would like that much' should be avoided, as should words such as 'strange' and 'funny'. Playworkers can also demonstrate to children by example that although they may have different views and beliefs, they can still work together.

It is helpful if playworkers have some knowledge about different cultures, religions and languages. They can then make links when they are talking to children – for example, 'If you like kite-flying, you should go to China – there are festivals there and races and competitions'.

## Trying out new play experiences

Games, music and videos are all examples of things that can vary from culture to culture or from family to family. Provide a wide range, so that children can experience each other's favourites. Encourage children to try out play experiences to which they might otherwise not have access, such as toys and games that are seen as being 'for boys' or 'for girls'.

Children may also need to be encouraged to play alongside children with whom they normally do not mix, for example because they do not go to the same school, or because they are of different ages. Team games and parachute games which encourage co-operation can break down this type of barrier.

## Celebrating festivals and events

You can help children to become aware of other cultures and traditions by finding out about festivals and events. It is important that this is not done in a stereotypical way, however: take time to make sure that food or artefacts are realistic or authentic.

## Using technology

The increasing availability of the Internet should allow children to be able to 'talk' to children across the world. This may be a good way of helping children to find out about other children's interests and ways of life.

# Encouraging children to resolve conflict themselves

All children have minor squabbles and conflicts as they are playing. Whenever possible, let them learn to resolve these and find compromises themselves. By all means monitor situations closely if you hear raised voices or can see a minor dispute going on, but give the children time to try to deal with the situation themselves. Where children *have* managed to resolve a dispute for themselves, they are more likely to respect the solution; and they will also have learnt something about working with and listening to others.

## Ways of encouraging children to resolve disputes

Do offer children encouragement.

- Make sure that children are praised (or even rewarded, in some cases) if they have managed a dispute well.
- Make sure that solutions such as rotas and lists are used in the setting so that children learn to use these as strategies.

- Play games that encourage problem-solving in teams. One example is putting out a range of materials and challenging the team to construct a hat within four minutes.
- Make sure that children can see the adults in the setting working and finding solutions to everyday problems in a mature way.

## Supporting children in resolving conflicts

In some situations, it may become clear that children are not managing to find a solution. You may still try to encourage them to find a solution by acting as a facilitator. In this role you would see if you could get the children to think about the conflict and ways in which it could be resolved. The aim would be to see whether the children could come up with the solutions themselves, and then implement them. Most children have a good sense of fairness and justice: by working with these, most conflicts can be resolved.

## Case study

Three children are crowding around the computer game. One child keeps saying that he wants a turn, whilst the other two keep pushing him away and saying that he can have a go later. Eventually the child who wants to go puts his hand in front of the computer to stop the others from seeing the screen. This action results in raised, angry voices and some pushing and shoving.

With no sight of a settlement ahead, it is clear that adult intervention is needed. Raj, the playworker, asks the children what the problem is. He then asks them whether they could see a way that this problem might have been avoided. One of the children suggests that a rota system would be a good idea. Raj asks if devising a rota system now would work. Two of the children agree, but the one who was waiting says that he still hasn't had a go, and that a rota system would mean that he might have to wait even longer. Raj asks the other two if this is true and whether this child should have his turn first. The other children agree and one suggests that they should also find out whether others in the setting want a turn too.

Finally, it is agreed that while the one child has his long-awaited turn, the other children will go and make a list of everyone who wants a turn, and then together they will draw up a rota.

Raj tells the children that he is extremely impressed by their maturity, and the way in which they have been able to organise themselves.

1  *How did Raj help the children to find a solution?*
2  *Why is it important for adults to avoid imposing a solution?*
3  *Why is it important for Raj to praise the children?*

## Intervening in children's disputes

There are some occasions when adults should always intervene in children's disputes. This is to prevent children from being harmed either physically or emotionally.

Adults should always intervene:

- if there is name calling
- if offensive remarks are being made (for example, racist or sexist remarks)

- if one child is dominating or intimidating others
- if aggressive or physical behaviour is being used

In situations where this is happening, make it clear that this behaviour is not acceptable and will not be tolerated. Use honest and open discussions to help the children involved see the damage that their behaviour might cause. As intimidating behaviour and offensive behaviour are often the result of insecurity and low self-esteem, be sure to praise children when they are acting appropriately.

## Element PB23.4  Take part in play with children

There are specific times when playworkers need to play alongside or with children, in order that the children will be able to benefit further from the play opportunity. This section looks at the reasons why playworkers might join in the play, and ways in which this can be done appropriately.

### WHAT YOU NEED TO LEARN

- Participating in play only if this helps the children
- Playing in a way appropriate to the children's ages and needs
- Allowing the children to play alone

## When to take part in play

Whenever possible, children should be allowed to play together and create their own play world. This gives them freedom, opportunities to be with their peers, and chances for them to learn to socialise. In some circumstances, however, it is desirable for playworkers to join in children's play. The main reasons why play workers might join in children's play are as follows.

### Supporting particular children

Sometimes playworkers will play with particular children or alongside them, for example, if a child is unfamiliar to the setting and needs to settle in, or if a child is having difficulties in understanding the rules of a game.

### Preventing or resolving a conflict

A playworker might join in a game to avoid, or to help resolve, a conflict. The presence of an adult can help children to calm down, whilst allowing the play opportunity to continue.

### Extending a play opportunity

Sometimes, children run out of ideas but want to carry on with the play opportunity. For example, they may be enjoying using large outdoor equipment, but be finding it hard to think of any games. In these situations, an adult might join in to inject some new ideas, of which the children can then take ownership.

## Ensuring health and safety

Some play activities might need very close supervision in order that they are safe. The adult might then decide to join in and be part of the activity so as to ensure safety, for example at a swimming pool or when canoeing. Being part of an activity means that the adult is in a position to intervene quickly should it be necessary.

Playworkers might also join in an activity if the children are particularly keen for them to do so. This is often the case with younger children, who may enjoy having some adult attention and input whilst they are playing.

---

## Consolidation

Think about a time when you joined in with children's play.

◆ **What were the circumstances?**
◆ **Explain why you decided to join in.**

---

# When not to take part in play

As well as understanding that at times it will be important to join in children's play, it is important to recognise that these are times when adults should *not* join in.

Once adults join in play, the play tends to take on a different feel. Adults bring an adult perspective. Try where possible to allow children to play spontaneously alone. In particular, it is not a good idea to join in children's play in the following situations.

| When children are playing happily |

When children are happily playing and enjoying their play, it is not a good idea to join in. Children gain more from being able to play freely with each other.

In some cases, children will ask a passing adult whether she or he wants to join them. In such a situation you need to make a judgement: will they still continue their game without you? Unless they seem *really* keen for you to join in, decline their offer pleasantly.

| When children have made it clear that they wish to play alone |

In some situations you will see from children's body language and play that they wish to be away from adults. They may huddle and create a den, or their play may stop as adults come near. Once you have satisfied yourself that their play is safe, take the hint! If play seems particularly secretive, however, you should maintain a close but discreet eye, in case the children are doing something dangerous.

## When children's safety might be compromised

If equipment is not designed to take adults or if you might put the children in danger, you should not join in. Even if children wish you to join in, you should not be tempted onto equipment that is not designed for adults, such as swings and climbing frames.

Remember too that your body weight and size might create a dangerous situation, for example if during play you toppled onto a child.

### When an adult's presence will inhibit children

Sometimes children may invite you to join in, but you might see that your presence would stop them from gaining the most out of their play. For example, they might wish you to join in a performance they were putting on. By not taking part, however, you will be able to give the children greater ownership of, and so more satisfaction from, the activity, which they will then have done by themselves.

*Sometimes children may invite you to join in, but do not take control unless absolute necessary*

### Playing appropriately and positively with children

As a playworker, do not take control of the play activity unless there is a real need to do so, such as because children have asked for ideas, or because otherwise a conflict may result.

You need to be able to adjust your play to suit the needs and level of the children. This does not mean that you become childish, but that you try to play at a pace that children can relate to. For example, during a board game with younger children, you might have to count out the number of squares that your piece has to move, so that they can understand your go.

Whilst playing with children, take the opportunity to boost their self-esteem. Listen to their ideas, compliment them, and show that you are enjoying their company. Be a good role model when playing with children, so that they can learn co-operative behaviour from your. Take turns, encourage others to choose first, and – of course – be prepared to lose gracefully!

## Keys to good practice
### Playing appropriately and positively with children
- Let them steer the game.
- Be a good role model.
- Find out from them what they would like you to do.
- Do not be competitive in play.
- Make sure that you do not appear to have any 'favourites' when you play.
- Look for opportunities for children to take control of their play.
- Consider whether your presence is inhibiting their play.
- During play look for ways to boost children's self-confidence.

## Case study

Robin has just joined the playscheme staff. He is keen but inexperienced, and spends most of his time playing with the children. The other staff are starting to feel a little irritated by his approach, as he rarely does other important tasks such as washing up the beakers after snack time, or tidying away the equipment.

You have recently noticed that whilst playing with children, Robin tends to be quite competitive and wants to win any board game. You overhear some older children having a moan about him and the way he always seems to dominate their games.

1 *How would you handle this situation?*
2 *What points would you need to explain to Robin about joining in children's play?*

## Leaving children to play on their own

As well as being able to *join in* children's play, playworkers also need to learn how to *leave* it!

Children gain a lot of skills from being able to play independently of adults, so once children seem settled into their play, consider looking for ways of leaving them to it. Do this without disrupting the play or making the children feel that the play is not interesting enough. In some situations, especially with younger children or where you have been involved in the play activity, spend time gradually becoming less involved. You might ask another child if she would like to play on your side during a board game, or in a role-play situation, and then begin to say less and less. (This tends to work better than abruptly leaving the play activity.) In other situations, if you can see that children are no longer needing you and have become very involved themselves, you might acknowledge how well they are doing and ask if they still need you.

If you originally joined in the play because of a conflict or tension, it is a good idea once you have left the play to remain nearby in case the difficulty reappears. Where you have helped younger children in their play, you might need to keep popping back discreetly in case they need further support.

---

**Consolidation**

Recall a time when you joined in and then left children to play on their own.

◆ *Explain how you left their play without disrupting it.*
◆ *How can children benefit from being able to play without the involvement of adults?*

---

## Element PB23.5　Bring play to an end

Unfortunately, however successful the play opportunity, there will be times when play must be brought to an end. You need to be able to help children to finish their play activity in such a way that they do not become frustrated and disappointed. This section looks at ways of doing this.

### WHAT YOU NEED TO LEARN

- Allowing children to complete play, when possible
- Bringing play to an end appropriately
- Encouraging feedback from children
- Recording any issues or incidents during play

### Why play may need to come to an end

There are many situations in which play might need to be ended. The reason why play is being brought to an end may determine how you handle the situation. Common reasons why play opportunities need to be ended include these:

- the session is ending
- it is time for the children to leave the setting
- other children are waiting to have a turn
- weather conditions mean that children can no longer play outside
- it is time for lunch
- staff can no longer supervise the activity because of other commitments
- children are beginning to show signs of boredom or conflict.

# Allowing children to finish play spontaneously

Whenever possible, let children finish play spontaneously. They then feel in control, and will leave the play activity feeling satisfied.

If there is a time pressure, let children know well in advance at what time play must come to an end. This helps them to pace their play accordingly, and they are more likely to bring it to an end within the time limit. (They may, for example, decide at the start of a game how many turns each person is going to have.) With younger children who cannot tell the time, you might ask them if they would like a ten-minute reminder, so that they know how much time they have left.

Children may also bring their play to an end if they can see that something else more tempting is going on.

# Bringing play to an end

It is not always possible to let children finish their play spontaneously. They may be too involved, there may be time pressures, or other children may be waiting for the resources or equipment. The playworker must then help the children to bring the play to an end.

Children who have enjoyed their play opportunity may feel a range of emotions, including frustration, resentment, anger and disappointment. Understanding and acknowledging the way children feel is important.

Below are some strategies that can help you bring the play to an end.

### Providing 'advance notice'

This should be done whenever possible. Tell children ahead of time that they will need to end their play: this allows them to finish off what they are doing. The more involved the children are, and the more complex the activity, the more time children will need. You will need to judge how much time they will need. Creative play, in particular activities, such as making objects, tends to need plenty of finishing time.

### Negotiating the end of play

It can be helpful to *negotiate* with children the end of their play. This works quite well with older children, who can then feel that they have some control. You could ask the children how quickly they think that they could end the play, or they might ask for two more turns. Agreeing a solution with children as to how to end the play can mean that they feel happier about ending their play.

### Suggesting a 'play pause'

In some situations, you might be able to suggest that the play can be put 'on hold' rather than brought to a complete end. The offer of a 'pause' may not always be taken up, but it will be appreciated by most children.

In order to 'pause' some types of play, notes will be needed as to whose turn it is or what the exact score or layout is. Help children with this recording, especially if there will be a period of time before play can be resumed.

## Inviting children to show their parents or carers what they are doing

If play needs to end because parents and carers are waiting, it is sometimes a good idea to ask children if they would like to show parents and carers what they are doing. This allows parents and carers to feel involved, and lets children talk to them about what they have been doing.

## Keys to good practice

### Good practice in bringing play to an end

- Always try to give children plenty of warning that play needs to come to an end.
- Explain to children why play needs to come to an end.
- Look with the children for ways of putting the play 'on hold'.
- Make sure that children know when they can repeat or resume the play activity.

---

### Consolidation

Think about an occasion when you helped children to bring play to an end.

- ◆ *Explain the reasons why the activity needed to end.*
- ◆ *How did you encourage the children to leave the activity?*
- ◆ *Did this approach work well? If it did, why was this? If not, why not?*

---

## Encouraging children to give feedback about play

If children give feedback about their play, you can find out what they have enjoyed doing and why, and bring this into your planning. Try always to get the feedback quickly, while children's thoughts are fresh when they are more likely to be able to comment effectively.

Feedback also rounds off an activity, and can be a way of making children feel part of a group. Children can show each other what they have done, and staff can use this as an opportunity to praise helpful or co-operative behaviour. Some settings organise feedback sessions at the end of each play activity, in which children not only talk about what they have done, but also about what they would *like* to do, in the next session or in future sessions.

The diagram below shows some of the benefits of encouraging children to provide feedback.

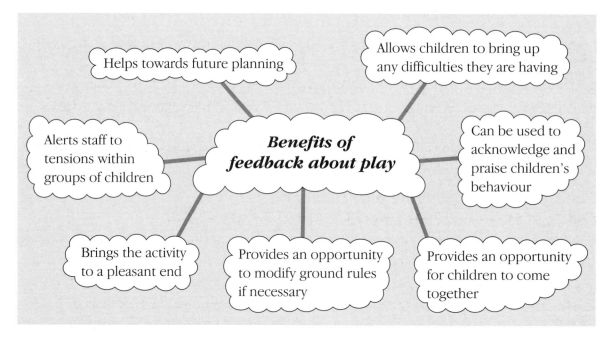

Helps towards future planning

Allows children to bring up any difficulties they are having

Alerts staff to tensions within groups of children

*Benefits of feedback about play*

Can be used to acknowledge and praise children's behaviour

Brings the activity to a pleasant end

Provides an opportunity to modify ground rules if necessary

Provides an opportunity for children to come together

## Finding out about issues during play

Feedback times also allows children and staff to reflect upon any difficulties, and to consider ways of resolving them. For example, a couple of children might say that they did not get a turn, or others might say that there was not enough equipment. Listening to feedback provides an opportunity to establish new ground rules or to change the activity slightly.

## Telling children about other play opportunities

Often when one play opportunity comes to an end, there are other possibilities for children. Explain to the children what is on offer. This is particularly important in situations when children were reluctant to leave the previous play. In some ways playworkers need to be a little like salespeople: some children will need to be 'sold' a play opportunity. You will need to sound enthusiastic and positive while explaining the possibilities of the new play opportunity. Being able to do this is especially necessary when working with some older children, who tend to adopt an 'It's boring' attitude because they do not want to be seen as 'children' who play.

When telling children about play opportunities, it is generally a good idea if you can give them ideas of how they might like to adapt them – this sometimes triggers off an interest that the children can then develop. A group of football-mad children who cannot play football outside because it is raining might be enticed to a craft table with the idea of making something for their team, such as rosettes or medals. When giving suggestions, be sure that they do not sound like instructions – 'What about making something for your team? You could make rosettes or a wall chart is better than 'At this table you can make rosettes'.

It is always easier to make play opportunities sound attractive if the *children* can see that there are many possibilities within the activity. Wherever possible, plan play opportunities that are flexible and adaptable.

> ## Case study
>
> Suppose that your setting has just bought a large pack of modelling clay, some glazes and some tools. There is also a book of ideas on how to produce different models, and one of the other playworkers has been a potter.
>
> **Write down how you would 'sell' this activity to a small group of 11-year-olds who have been reluctant to take up other play opportunities.**

## Acting on issues from and incidents during play

During feedback we might find out that problems have arisen during play. Staff might have noticed other difficulties which need to be shared.

It is important that all issues and incidents are acted upon, so that future play can be safe and can run smoothly. In some situations, staff might lead the children to change the ground rules of an activity if it is to be repeated later on. Issues such as shortage of equipment and resources might be noted by staff so that new stock and equipment can be ordered. Where staff have noticed that there are tensions between particular children, or that a child is not settling in well, extra supervision and support might be considered.

Sometimes staff may realise that the layout or the play opportunities they had planned are not working well. This might need a quick team meeting in order to regroup.

## Making sure that records are complete

When play and the session have come to an end, playworkers will need to spend time tidying up and completing administrative tasks. There is always a temptation to cut these activities short, because by then people are often very tired! This is not an option, however: the setting will not function effectively if records are incomplete. Also, tensions and anger may grow within the team if some people are seen not to be carrying out their duties properly.

As well as checking and bringing records up to date, you will also need to make sure that the records are tidied away. If it is the end of the day, the records must be put in a secure place. The table below shows the types of records that will need to be updated at the end of sessions.

| Type of record | Purpose |
|---|---|
| **Accident book and slips** | To make sure that any accidents have been correctly recorded, and to provide information to parents/carers about accidents that have occurred. |
| **Attendance registers** | This is a requirement of registration, and also needed in the event of a fire. Many settings also receive funding according to the numbers of children who attend. |
| **Petty-cash book/other financial records** | Any financial transactions should have been noted at the time, but records should be checked at the end of the day. |
| **Daily log** | Some settings keep a daily log which records any particular events of the day. |
| **Planning** | At the end of each session, plans will need to be drawn up for the next session – children may have requested particular activities. |
| **Notes to other staff** | If you know that you will not be present in the play setting at the start of the next session, you might need to leave some notes for your supervisor or manager. |
| **Staff hours sheet** | Part-time or temporary staff will need their hours recorded, in order that they are paid correctly. |

## Consolidation

Plan and organise a play opportunity for children in your setting.

◆ *Which areas of children's development was this activity intended to promote?*
◆ *How did you involve the children in the planning of this activity?*
◆ *How did you work with the children to set some ground rules for the activity?*
◆ *Explain your role during the activity. Did you support any individual children?*
◆ *How did the play opportunity end?*
◆ *What feedback did the children give about this play opportunity?*
◆ *What did you learn from carrying out this activity?*

## PB23 unit test

1 Why is it important to encourage children, parents and carers and colleagues to contribute to planning?
2 List four types of play opportunities.
3 Choose an example of a play activity, and explain how it might contribute to children's overall development.
4 What are the benefits of individual children playing spontaneously?
5 Describe three ways in which you might recognise that a child is not enjoying a play opportunity.
6 Explain how you might help a child to extend herself or himself when learning how to ride a bicycle.
7 Why is it important when planning activities to think about a child's stage of development?
8 Why is it important for adults who work with children to act as good role models for social development?
9 How could you help children to learn co-operate and respect each other?
10 Why is it important that children learn to manage disputes for themselves?
11 What are the benefits for children of being able to play without the involvement of adults?
12 List three circumstances in which playworkers might join in children's play.
13 Why is it important to leave children's play once they are settled?
14 Explain how children might feel if their play were brought to an end abruptly?
15 Give two strategies that you might use to bring play to an end positively.

# Unit PC 12

# Promote positive relationships in the play environment

The ability to develop positive relationships with children and their parents or carers is an important skill for playworkers to develop. Positive relationships create a good atmosphere, which means that children can feel relaxed and will enjoy coming to the setting. Good relationships are also the key to managing children's behaviour in a way that allows boundaries to be set in partnership with the children.

The elements for this unit are:

PC12.1  Contribute to positive relationships with children
PC12.2  Encourage children's positive behaviour
PC12.3  Respond positively to children's unwanted behaviour
PC12.4  Develop positive relationships with parents and carers

## Element PC12.1  Contribute to positive relationships with children

The playworker's brief is quite a challenging one. It requires working with different ages of children, and in some cases for quite short periods of time. Playworkers need to be skilled at getting to know children quickly, and responding to their needs. This section looks at ways of building positive relationships with children.

### WHAT YOU NEED TO LEARN

- Helping children to feel welcome and secure
- Developing caring and anti-discriminatory relationships
- Communicating effectively with children
- Ensuring children's physical and emotional safety
- Responding to complaints

## Helping children to feel welcome and secure

Most *adults* find it at least a little stressful to go into a new environment where they do not know many people. So do children. You can help by making all children who come into your setting feel comfortable and welcome. Remember that older children may present themselves as being relaxed and confident, yet in reality be unsure of themselves.

The way in which you welcome children will be slightly different according to their age and needs.

## Welcoming younger or less confident children

Younger children often need plenty of adult attention and supervision. It can be a good idea to allocate one member of staff to take a particular interest in each child from the beginning. Talk to children about the opportunities and activities that are going on, and help them join in, guiding them if necessary. Some younger children will find it hard to ask for the toilet or for drinks, so it can be helpful if they are told about these early on. In some settings, older children enjoy taking care of younger ones; this too can be a useful way of welcoming the younger child.

## Welcoming older or more confident children

Older children still need reassurance and adult support, but this might be given in a more discreet way, with adults taking the lead more from the children. For example, you might ask a child, 'Do you want me to introduce you to Sandie, who I think lives near you?' This approach allows children either to take up the offer of help or, if they are confident, to find their own way. Even with outwardly confident children it is still a good idea to keep a discreet eye on them at first, in case they are finding it hard to join in with the others.

If ground rules have been already established, it is a good idea to outline these so that older children can understand the framework they are in.

## Planning activities to help children to get to know each other

In some settings, several children will start at once. It is a good idea to have some activities planned which will allow the children to get to know each other and be able to play with each other. Party-type games are quite good, as are games in which children learn each other's names.

## Activity
### Name game

The children form a circle, and a beanbag or ball is thrown across or around the circle. As children catch it they shout out their own name.

Once children have begun to know each other's names, the game can be varied. This time the beanbag can be thrown high into the middle of the circle, and the child's name is called out. That child then has to catch it. She or he then throws it up again, calling out another child's name.

# Greeting children

Even when children have settled into a new setting, it is still important that they are made to feel welcome. Take time to greet each child, and have a word or two with them. This will allow you to pick up on any signs that a child is not happy – for example, they may have had a bad day at school, or be feeling tired.

Most settings have areas where children can sit and read or play board games, and be quiet if they wish. If they don't feel like joining in with the other children straight away, these can also be places where you can chat to children and they can tell you what they have been doing.

*Children need to be made welcome individually*

## Showing children care, consideration and respect

In order to build positive relationships with children, it is essential that you respect them and show this in the way that you work with them. This means listening to them, taking on board their ideas and feelings, and making sure that you do not patronise them or make them feel uncomfortable by your tone of voice. Adults who do not show children care and consideration are at best tolerated by children, and at worst avoided. If they feel that they are not liked or wanted, some children may even refuse to come to the setting.

### Active knowledge ✔

Look at the table below, which shows some do's and don'ts when working with children.

| Do | Don't |
|---|---|
| Listen to children<br>Explain rules and ideas<br>Treat all children well | Patronise them<br>Make sarcastic comments<br>Make fun of them<br>Pretend to listen to them<br>Shout<br>Have favourites |

1  *Copy and add to this table.*
2  *You might like to find out from the children you work with how they do and don't like to be treated.*

# Communicating with children

The most successful playworkers are those with good communication skills who are also able to develop an affinity with children. Most people working with children find that although their style of communication varies slightly with the age and needs of the children they are working with, the basic principles such as listening remain the same.

## Basic communication skills

Most people find that they *have* basic communication skills, although they may not be able to identify and understand how these work. There are many facets to good communication: below are outlined four elements that are particularly important.

### 1 Listening

Many children feel that adults are not very good at listening to them. Younger children, for example, may need time to think through what they want to say, whereas older children often want to talk in detail.

For children to understand that you are interested in what they are saying, you need to use *active* listening skills. Do not interrupt children or burst in with suggestions, but allow them to talk to you at their own pace. Show in your face and your body language that you are interested.

### 2 Speaking to children

Children recognise and dislike adults who patronise them or order them around. It is therefore essential that you talk to children at an appropriate level, which shows them respect. Many children dislike equally adults who pretend to be one of them, so you need to try to adopt the role of being supportive but friendly.

### 3 Facial expression

Facial expressions are sometimes more important than words. Our faces can show interest, boredom or anger, as well as warmth. Just using the right words is not enough – your face will tend to show what you are feeling, and children will notice whether this matches what you are saying, so they will detect whether or not you are sincere in what you are saying.

### 4 Tone of voice

Tone of voice also sends out messages, and your own tone of voice will tell children whether or not you are being sincere, whether or not you are really interested in what they are saying, and whether or not you really care for them and respect them.

## Communicating with different ages of children

Playworkers have to adapt their communication according to the needs of the children they are working with. For example, a younger child will enjoy an adult saying 'Well done' because they need reassurance, whilst an older child might find this patronising. It is hard to define any particular rules about how to communicate with different ages of children, but in general, communication with older children should recognise their independence and their need to talk at a more grown-up level.

## Involving children

For children to be comfortable with you and the environment you are providing, it will help if you encourage them to ask questions, offer ideas and make suggestions. The aim is to make them feel that they are active participants. Some adults find this difficult at first, especially if in their previous experiences adults have been seen very much as all-powerful and the decision-makers, while children are expected to be passive. As an adult, you need to keep sight of your overall responsibility to keep children safe and protected, but you can still create secure and respectful relationships such that children can *really* talk to you.

Whilst encouraging children to feel that they can be active in their communication with you, you should be aware that some children may use this as an opportunity to test the boundaries of politeness. Try to see this as a learning process for children as they learn about true communication, though you will need to explain to children when their comments are not appropriate.

## Applying anti-discriminatory practice

It is essential that you make positive relationships with *all* children in the setting, regardless of their age, gender, or any other factor (such as their home background or needs). In practice this means that no child should be favoured above others, and that all children should be given the time and help that they need.

Most people find that they have to work quite hard at making sure that all children in the setting feel welcome and developing positive relationships with them. Children are very quick to pick up on prejudices, and may avoid being with any adult with whom they do not feel comfortable. Children who have already felt that adults are in some way 'against' them often develop a 'don't care' attitude, to protect themselves from further hurt. This can make it harder at the beginning for playworkers to win their trust and respect, but with time most children will learn that they are truly welcome.

### Avoiding labels and assumptions

In some settings, children quickly gain *labels*, such as 'shy' or 'wilful'. Labels are potentially limiting for children; in the end, they begin to live up to their labels. Be careful in commenting on children to other members of staff, and avoid comments to the child that suggest a certain type of behaviour.

Similarly, be careful not to make assumptions about children based on their lifestyle, gender, or any other characteristic. Classifying children is another way of labelling them and prevents us from seeing them as individuals.

## Active knowledge ✔

Rosemary has been working as a playworker for a number of years. She knows most of the children in the group, as most of them live near her. Today as she is looking at the list of children who are due to start in the setting, she says, 'I see that little Sophie's starting. She's from a rough home, that one. Her brother was a little terror and I know she's been in trouble, too.'

1 *Why are these comments inappropriate?*
2 *How might they affect the way the staff see Sophie?*
3 *Explain how you would tactfully let Rosemary know that her comments were inappropriate.*

## Treating children as equals

Anti-discriminatory practice requires that children are treated as equals. This does not mean that they are treated *equally*, that they will necessarily get exactly the same amount of attention or help. For example, a younger child might require *more* adult attention than an older child who has been attending the setting for a number of years, although all children have a right to some individual adult attention.

Be sure to speak to and greet all of the children for whom you are responsible; do not spend so much time with one child, or group of children, that others find it unfair.

## Providing a safe atmosphere for children

For children to feel safe and secure, playworkers must ensure their physical and emotional safety. In the context of 'contributing to positive relationships with children', this means being aware of their feelings and insecurities. This might mean considering whether a child is being bullied, or encouraging children within the setting to play and behave co-operatively.

You need to make sure that children see you as a responsible person who would look after them if they had a problem. It is unwise and unprofessional for playworkers to tell their own problems to children. You can help children to feel safe by supervising their play activities and keeping an eye on relationships within the setting. This can be done sensitively, yet in a way that allows children to see that there are people around who would take care of them.

### Responding to children's complaints

On page 125 we looked at the importance of your gaining children's feedback in order to inform your practice. In the same way, you should take children's *complaints* positively: complaints are a sign that children feel that they can talk to us. It is a good idea to develop a policy in your setting to ensure that complaints can be followed up. If you ignore children's comments and complaints, they may feel dissatisfied and hurt.

Sometimes the complaints will be niggles, such as 'He's always having longer goes than anyone else'; these can easily be resolved by talking through the situation. At other times you might need to take the complaints more seriously, especially if children feel that they have been bullied or mistreated in some way. This means investigating sensitively what has happened, and finding strategies to prevent it from recurring.

In rare cases, children may make complaints against a member of staff. If this happens, it is essential that the setting's policy is followed: the complaint must certainly not be ignored.

---

### Consolidation

◆ *What is your setting's policy if a complaint is made against a member of staff?*
◆ *Can you think of a 'niggle' that you dealt with recently?*
◆ *What was the child's complaint?*
◆ *Why was it important that the child felt that she or he was being listened to?*

---

It is always a good strategy when working with children to encourage positive behaviour, and to have a policy that encourages *wanted* behaviour rather than focussing too much on *unwanted* behaviour. This section looks at the ways in which we can help children to show desirable behaviour.

## WHAT YOU NEED TO LEARN

- Negotiating ground rules for play
- Monitoring children's verbal and non-verbal communication
- Encouraging positive behaviour
- Reviewing ground rules

## What is positive behaviour?

Positive behaviour is behaviour that you wish to encourage in children in order that they can socialise effectively. This includes being able to share and co-operate with others, as well as being able to take on responsibility. The diagram below shows the types of behaviour that you should be encouraging children to show.

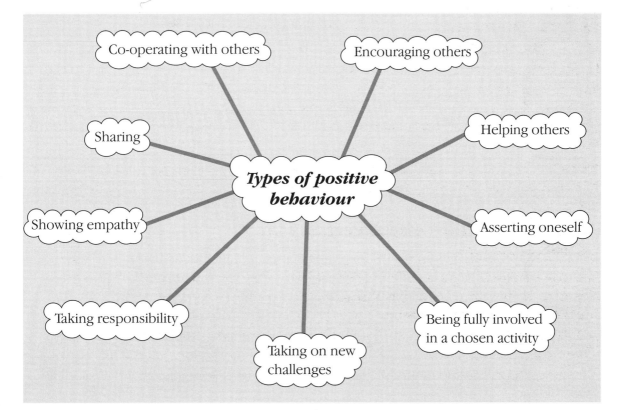

## Providing opportunities for children to show positive behaviour

In order to foster positive behaviour, you need to create an environment in which children have opportunities to learn and to use the relevant skills. This will often mean making sure that children can take on responsibility: true co-operation and sharing come from within rather than being imposed.

*Co-operation is an aspect of positive behaviour which should be encouraged*

## Active knowledge ✔

The table shows a list of activities that settings might provide which include opportunities to show positive behaviour.

| Activity | Positive behaviour |
|---|---|
| Children are involved in decision-making and in the running of the setting, via a children's committee<br>Children organise fund-raising events for charity<br>Children choose play activities<br>Children are involved in deciding with the adults some of the ground rules for the setting<br>Children are responsible for putting up displays and keeping the environment tidy<br>Children are involved in 'marketing' the setting, by designing posters<br>Children are involved in decorating the setting | Co-operating with others<br>Encouraging others<br>Helping others<br>Asserting oneself<br>Full involvement in a chosen activity<br>Taking on new challenges<br><br>Showing empathy<br>Sharing<br>Taking responsibility |

*Look at each activity, and work out what opportunities it offers for demonstrating positive behaviour.*

## Using ground rules effectively

Ground rules provide children with a clear understanding of the boundaries in the setting or during an activity. When they understand clearly what they can and cannot do, they are less likely to show unwanted behaviour. Most rules are very simple, and are designed to make sure that children respect one another, and do not put themselves or others in danger.

In some settings ground rules are decided on by the staff alone, while in others children are given the opportunity to contribute. There are many advantages of involving children in the process of drawing up ground rules, one being that this enables them to take on responsibility.

# How to draw up ground rules

There are several ways of drawing up ground rules with children. In some settings, staff ask all the children to come together for a general discussion about what they think the ground rules should include; in other settings, members of staff work first with smaller groups, and then all the ideas are pooled together. The choice of approach will probably depend on the number of children and the group dynamics within the setting. The advantage of splitting into smaller groups is that the younger or less confident children may feel more able to contribute their ideas – the aim, after all, is to create a situation where *all* children's views are heard.

The next step is to look at the ground rules that have been suggested and consider the reasons behind them. It is interesting to see that most groups of children are very interested in fairness, and are able to establish some very good ground rules. If you feel that there are important issues that have not been covered, you can always ask the children how these should be addressed – for instance, 'What about snack time – do you think that we need some system worked out, because sometimes there is quite a queue?' Check that all the adults in the setting are happy with the ground rules.

Once the ground rules have been drawn up, most settings find some way of recording and displaying them. Sometimes the children themselves take responsibility for this. In other settings, staff members might write the rules and then display them. Settings that encourage children to draw up ground rules find that children tend to enjoy this process, and it is easier later to deal with situations in which a child has not kept within the agreed limits.

# Ground rules for particular activities

You may also need ground rules for particular play activities, especially where there is a safety element – for example, when going out on trips or playing certain games. A good approach is to gather together the children who are involved and ask them to think about the potential difficulties, and then what they think the ground rules need to be. Instead of rules being imposed on children, you are then helping them to think through situations.

In some situations, this may not be possible, and you might need to say to the children, 'Look, just before you start, can I remind you that you will need to think about making sure the ball does not stray into the road. It's probably a good idea if you play away from the fence.'

There might also be times when you need to check with parents that *they* are happy with the ground rules that are being set. For example, when a trip is being organised, there might be an issue over how much, if any, pocket money should be brought. (Thinking about and checking parental wishes is also considered on page 158.)

# Reviewing ground rules

Review your ground rules regularly. Are they still valid? Are they proving effective? Don't slip into a situation where rules never change – 'This is the way it's always been'! This could create a situation where the rules were no longer effective or were preventing children from taking up opportunities.

Handle the review sensitively. Remember that there might be specific reasons why a member of staff or child has suggested a particular rule. When people have contributed to the organisation's running, they may feel defensive if rules appear to be 'challenged', especially if the rules are not changed or reviewed.

## Ensuring that adults agree with ground rules

It is essential that all adults in the setting come to some agreement about ground rules, otherwise tensions can be created. If you are responsible for a setting's policy on behaviour, consider making sure that rules are reviewed regularly, and that everyone knows this will happen from time to time. If you feel that a ground rule set by an adult is not appropriate, talk this through with colleagues first, rather than with children: this prevents staff from feeling undermined.

## Case study

The village playscheme has been run successfully for several years, and has some established rules which by and large work well. Anna, a new member of staff, was puzzled, however, when she was told that she could not take any of the gym mats outside. She asked her line manager if there was a reason why, and was told that this was because they were new and had been expensive to buy. Anna decided to ignore this rule, thinking that it was more important that the children had fun, especially as the mats seemed in quite poor condition.

1 *Why might Anna's actions create tension in the team?*
2 *What might have been a better way for this to have been handled?*

## Listening to and observing children

It is always better to anticipate potential difficulties than wait until unwanted or unsafe behaviour becomes evident. Observe and listen to children during their play. Sometimes tone of voice or body language will indicate that a potential problem is brewing. By supporting children straight away, you are more likely to prevent the unwanted behaviour. Often, just by wandering over and listening further you will be able to work out what the problem is and give the children some solutions. For example, if a group of children are trying to share insufficient equipment, some are likely to become restless and frustrated.

Experienced playworkers also find that by observing and listening to children as they *arrive* in the setting, they can pick up subtle messages about how the child is feeling. Children might be feeling tired, for instance; and when working with older children, you need also to remember that their bodies keep producing sudden surges of hormones which can alter their moods and behaviour.

## Case study

The play setting has a small outdoor area and one group of children are playing dodgeball. Two of the older children have taken responsibility for the game, which has been running well for 20 minutes. Now one of the children who is out has become restless and is trying to take the ball away from the game. Other children are shouting at him because they want the ball back to carry on the game. Suddenly the atmosphere has become tense.

1 *How would you handle this situation?*
2 *Why is it important for staff to keep an eye on children's play activities, even if they are not being directly involved?*

# Praising children's positive behaviour

It is always worth acknowledging children's positive behaviour: this is a great encouragement for them. Commenting on their positive behaviour has been shown to make a difference, especially if praise is given at the time. It is also a good idea to explain to children what effect their behaviour is having. For example, you might say 'It's good that you were ready to move up like that, to allow Alicia to join in – that will have made her feel welcome.' This helps children to learn why positive behaviour is so important.

## Ways of praising children

The way in which we give praise will tend to vary according to the children we are working with – older children sometimes prefer discreet praise, rather than with an audience listening: they reach a stage when they may feel embarrassed. Rather than saying 'Well done', you could say 'You really handled that well.' With younger children, the approach might be different: younger children may prefer a wider recognition, and 'Well done' in front of others will often be welcomed.

## Types of behaviour to praise

Make sure that you praise children regularly. This can have a positive effect on their self-esteem. Watch out for ways in which to praise them, including small incidents such as a child holding open a door for another, or a child waiting patiently to have a turn.

---

## Consolidation

Look at the following examples of positive behaviour.

- Mark (8 years) has waited for other children to move out of the way before kicking the ball.
- Chris (12 years) has realised that a new child is not really joining in, and has asked if he would like to play a game of cards with him.
- Evie (5 years) has been sitting at a table quietly doing a puzzle for 15 minutes, singing happily to herself.
- Ravi (13 years) has collected up the cups and put them on the side before going out to join in a game of football.

- ◆ *Why should each of these children be praised?*
- ◆ *How would you praise them appropriately?*
- ◆ *Think of a time when you have praised children recently. Explain why you did this, and how you made sure that the praise given was appropriate.*

---

# Reinforcing positive behaviour by example

Studies on the way children learn show that learning through watching other people is extremely powerful. This is sometimes called *social learning*, or learning by *modelling*. For adults who work with children, this means that we must act as good examples. Another term used is *role models*.

Children imitate many people around them, including those whom they see on television or in videos, but it has been shown that they especially model adults whom they admire in some way. If you have won the respect of a child, you may be able to influence their behaviour positively.

It is a good idea to explain this concept to the older children, too, so that they can feel that they are contributing to the positive atmosphere and behaviour in the setting.

## Types of behaviour that children might copy

Children will copy many types of behaviour, including anti-social or unwanted behaviour. In your day-to-day work with children, be aware of the effect of your own actions. For example, if an adult whom a child admires smokes, the child is more likely to smoke also. (This is partly why the children of parents who smoke are more likely to try smoking.)

The diagram below shows the types of behaviour that children should be seeing from the adults who work with them.

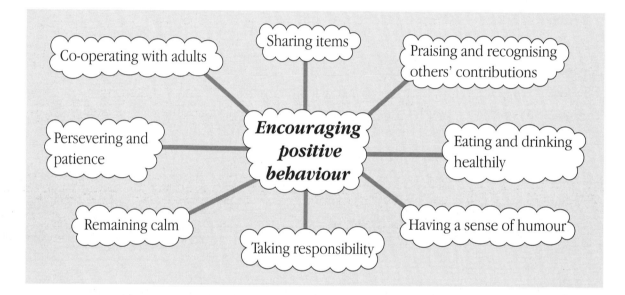

## Fostering positive behaviour

Another way in which you can help children show positive behaviour is by ensuring that the time they spend in settings is enjoyable. Children who are feeling bored or who feel they are in 'babyish' settings are more likely to show unwanted behaviour. Look carefully at the types of opportunities available to the children who attend the setting, and make sure that they are fun, challenging and appropriate.

This is not always an easy task: some settings are working with a very wide age range, and the play needs of younger and older children will often be different. When working with wide age ranges, some settings create spaces where older children can play together, with periods for the whole group to come together; whereas other settings work in a more integrated way.

It is also a good idea to look at activities and consider how they can be made simpler or more challenging as necessary. The example below shows how this can be done with one simple activity, a treasure hunt.

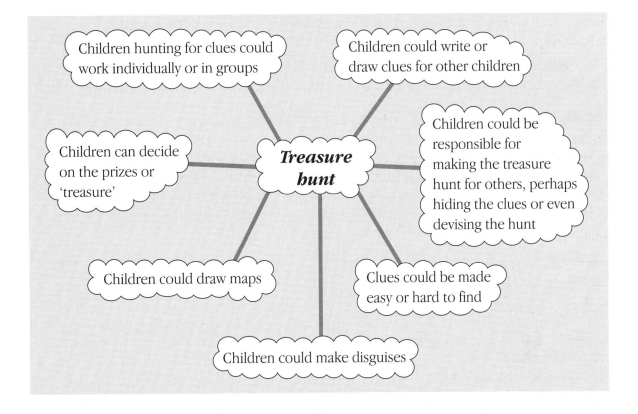

Children hunting for clues could work individually or in groups

Children could write or draw clues for other children

Children can decide on the prizes or 'treasure'

**Treasure hunt**

Children could be responsible for making the treasure hunt for others, perhaps hiding the clues or even devising the hunt

Children could draw maps

Clues could be made easy or hard to find

Children could make disguises

## Element PC12.3 Respond positively to children's unwanted behaviour

On pages 137–142 we looked at the ways in which playworkers can promote positive behaviour. Encouraging positive behaviour is always better than reacting to unwanted behaviour, but there will nevertheless be times when you will have to respond to unwanted behaviour. This section looks at ways of doing this positively.

### WHAT YOU NEED TO LEARN

- Identifying unwanted behaviour
- Noticing changes in children's behaviour, and interpreting these, especially if inappropriate for the age and stage of development
- Reviewing strategies
- Encouraging children to express negative feelings

### What is meant by 'unwanted' behaviour?

Unwanted behaviour can be defined as behaviour that is harmful or hurtful to others, or harmful or hurtful to the child herself or himself. Such behaviour could include one child spoiling others' enjoyment of play activities, or a child doing something that is potentially dangerous, such as smoking or taking drugs. It is vital that staff working together agree on a policy for responding to unwanted behaviour, and that they take an agreed view about what constitutes unwanted behaviour.

## Promptly identifying unwanted behaviour

You need to identify unwanted behaviour quickly. By stepping in quickly and in a positive way, problems can often be solved easily. This means that your setting must provide good supervision of children's play activities, and watch carefully to see whether children's body language indicates a potential problem. In some cases, simply strolling past the children's activity, or a direct look across at a child, might be sufficient to help children remember the ground rules of the setting. In other cases, you might have to move quickly to avoid a child hurting themselves or each other.

## Signs of unwanted behaviour

Most playworkers develop a 'sixth sense' for unwanted behaviour. This comes both from experience and from being able to read signs accurately. As well as looking for obvious signs of disturbance, it is important when working with older children to look out for children who seem to be hiding something, or sneaking off. This may sometimes be a sign that they are experimenting with drugs, alcohol or cigarettes.

Here are some of the signs that might indicate unwanted behaviour, either happening already or about to happen:

- Raised, angry voices
- Children isolating themselves from play activities
- Angry body movements
- Inappropriate and offensive speech
- Over-excited gestures and noises
- Covert glances or hiding
- Tense atmosphere
- Dramatic changes in noise levels.

## Case study

Robin has noticed that one of the children who had been playing a ball game with others is looking rather red and has stormed away from the rest of the group. The other children are carrying on playing, although the noise level has dropped. The child picks up a bat that was on the side, swings it around aggressively and then starts running towards the group.

1 *Does Robin need to react to this situation quickly or more casually?*
2 *What are the potential indicators that unwanted behaviour might be shown?*

## Identifying changes in children's behaviour

Children sometimes show unwanted behaviour as a cry for help or as a reaction to circumstances. For example, a child who is being bullied might show aggressive behaviour towards other children. You need to be aware, therefore, that changes in children's usual pattern of behaviour might be signs of a deeper problem.

If you notice that a child's pattern of behaviour has changed and feel concerned, you might need to bring this to the attention of parents, colleagues or your line manager, depending on the unwanted behaviour being shown. They might be able to provide you with background information that would make it easier to respond to the behaviour.

If you think that a child's behaviour is due to being in an abusive situation, you should follow the child protection procedures of your setting (see also Unit PC23).

### Interpreting children's behaviour.

Children may also show unwanted behaviour as a reaction to changes in their lives. Some changes may be short-term and affect children temporarily, while others may affect children more deeply. Although it is not always easy to predict how children may react to changes in their lives, the table below shows types of changes that might affect some children.

| Long-term factors | Short-term factors |
|---|---|
| Parental separation<br>Loss of a sibling, parent or near relative<br>Health problems | Moving school<br>Moving house<br>Falling out with friends<br>Tiredness<br>Bullying |

Understanding what is happening in children's lives, without prying, can therefore help you to respond more effectively to children's unwanted behaviour. To gain this understanding you will need to be able to work with a range of people, but often parents and carers will be able to give you valuable information.

## Strategies for dealing with unwanted behaviour

There are various strategies for dealing with unwanted behaviour, and many playworkers find that some work better than others with particular children. The choice of strategy may also vary according to the age of child with whom you are working. Getting to know the child is almost as important as the strategy itself.

Whatever strategy you adopt when dealing with unwanted behaviour always remember that children have a right to respect and dignity. Your methods should not humiliate children or be aggressive, either in voice or in action. (Adults who employ methods that humiliate children tend to be less effective in dealing with unwanted behaviour, as children feel alienated.)

## Keys to good practice

### Dealing with unwanted behaviour

**Don't:**

- jump to conclusions
- shout
- be aggressive
- humiliate the child
- ignore what the child is saying
- isolate the child (e.g. 'You have to wait outside')
- use physical restraint or punishment.

**Do:**

- remain calm
- make sure that the child and others are safe
- consider taking the child aside
- listen to the child
- explain to the child why their actions are inappropriate
- involve the child in deciding how to prevent the unwanted behaviour from recurring
- consider whether there is an underlying reason for their behaviour.

## Talk to the child away from other children

Privacy prevents children from feeling embarrassed and from losing confidence. It is effective with all ages of children, but is particularly important with older children. The aim is to have a word with a child quietly, without the other children in the setting necessarily knowing that you are dealing with behaviour.

## Explain why the behaviour is inappropriate

Children do not always know why their behaviour is unwanted, especially when they have simply become over-excited during a play activity. It is always helpful to explain briefly why they need to stop their behaviour. This should be done in a non-confrontational way. For instance, 'Look, I know that you're having a lot of fun, but the bad news is that you might get hurt if that stick gets near your eyes.'

## Offer alternative activities

In some cases, you can distract children by offering them alternative activities. This is particularly useful if the reason for the unwanted behaviour is partly that children feel unchallenged or that the children are not co-operating with each other. Alternative activities should be offered in a way that does not feel like a punishment.

## Help children to consider the consequences of their behaviour

It can be helpful if children are encouraged to think through the consequences of continuing their unwanted behaviour. Again, this should be done in a non-confrontational way, and is useful as a strategy with older children. (Younger children are not always able to empathise with others or to consider the results of their actions in the same way.)

## Case study

Martha has been intimidating the younger children by swearing at them, and telling them to get off the computer as it is her turn, which it isn't. One of the younger children complains to a playworker. The playworker talks to Martha about what is happening.

PLAYWORKER: The younger children seem to be a little unhappy about what is happening. Why do you think that is?

MARTHA: 'Cause I was messing around and said a few swear words.

PLAYWORKER: Why isn't that such a good idea?

MARTHA: 'Cause the younger children weren't getting their go.

PLAYWORKER: That's right, and they might also pick up some of the words that you were using.

1 *Why should playworkers listen to the complaints of younger children rather than let children 'sort it out' themselves?*

2 *How did the playworkers give Martha an opportunity to talk about what was happening?*

3 *How did the playworker help Martha to think about her behaviour?*

## Encourage children to share responsibility in finding solutions

Older children in particular respond very well to taking on some responsibility. Asking children to talk through the situation and come up with their own solutions can therefore be a useful strategy.

## Give children time away from a situation

This strategy is sometimes referred to as 'time out'. The idea behind 'time out' is to separate children from a situation and allow a pause. This may be useful, for example, if a child is becoming over-excited and aggressive, or if she is finding it hard to be with other children. It is important that neither the child nor the playworker sees this as a punishment.

It is often a good idea to spend time with the child during the 'time out' period, so that they do not feel isolated or punished. You may want to use the 'time out' to talk through why the child is finding it hard to act appropriately.

## Case study

Karim (10 years old) has been making inappropriate noises during group circle time, and these are preventing the younger children from enjoying the game. The playworker has already asked Mark if he would like to do something else: he has said he wants to play, but is still making the noises. Another playworker comes over and asks whether he could borrow Mark to help him set out another game.

PLAYWORKER: Actually, I really needed you because your behaviour there wasn't brilliant, was it? You were stopping the younger ones having their fun. Did you realise that?

KARIM: I was only messing around.

PLAYWORKER: I know that, but the younger ones love that game and normally you are very good about joining in with them. Do you want to go back and join in, or would you prefer to help me set up?

KARIM: I want to join in the game, but I'll stop messing around.

PLAYWORKER: That's a good plan. Look, do you want to help me for a minute, so the others won't know that I had a word or two, or would you like to go back straight away?

KARIM: I'll help for a minute and then I'll go back.

1 *How did the playworker help Karim think about his behaviour?*
2 *How has the playworker helped Karim to 'save face'?*

## Consolidation

Think about an incident of unwanted behaviour that you managed effectively.

◆ *Write about what happened, and how you managed the unwanted behaviour.*
◆ *What strategy did you use?*

## Reviewing strategies for individual children

You may find that the child is showing unwanted behaviour in other situations also, with different people. Talking with others may give clues as to *why* the child is showing this behaviour, and its extent. It can therefore be very helpful to meet with others such as parents and carers, colleagues and teachers, in order to find a common and effective strategy to help the child. Adopting a common approach in dealing with unwanted behaviour brings some consistency into a child's life: this can be particularly useful if the child's behaviour stems from changes in her or his life.

Once a strategy has been agreed with others, keep contact so that its effectiveness can be reviewed and monitored. In cases of extreme unwanted behaviour, which may indicate a deep-seated problem, it may be a good idea to get some specialist advice and help for the child. Parents can access this help by visiting their GP or health visitor, who will refer them to a specialist.

## Case study

Robert's father died six months ago. Robert's behaviour now is a cause for concern: at times he is extremely aggressive towards other children, to a point where other parents have complained about his behaviour. The playworkers at the after-school club have decided that it might be a good idea to have a chat with his mother, to try to work out how to help him. She is more than happy to come because she also has found his behaviour worrying. She suggests that his class teacher should also be involved.

A meeting is arranged, and it emerges that Robert is reacting in a variety of ways – at home he tends to be sleepless and very moody, while in school he is very withdrawn. It is decided that whenever possible Robert's positive behaviour should be praised, that he should get as much one-to-one attention as possible, and that a 'time out' strategy should be employed when Robert becomes aggressive.

The playworker suggests that they should make contact again after two weeks, so that they can look at how he is coping. Robert's mother says that she now feels that she is not so alone in dealing with Robert, and everyone agrees that the meeting has been very helpful. The teacher has said that he will find out whether the local education authority has a counselling or support service, as this might be useful. A date is fixed for another meeting.

1   *Can you explain the advantage of the strategies chosen?*
2   *Why was it important for everyone to meet again?*
3   *Why might Robert need some specialist support?*

## Reviewing organisational procedures

Every play setting needs a policy on behaviour management, and everyone within the setting must agree with it and follow it. Where a policy is not followed, or where people within a setting do not agree on how to manage behaviour, children are often given very mixed messages: this makes it hard for them to know what is and is not acceptable. In order that policies work, it is therefore useful if settings regularly review procedures and agreed strategies, especially if there has been a change in staffing. New members of staff should be given copies of policies, and it is useful to spend time talking with them about the strategies that are used and the way in which incidents of unwanted behaviour are reported.

## Reporting and recording unwanted behaviour

As part of the behaviour policy, settings should have a procedure for reporting and recording unwanted behaviour. Most settings will usually only report and record *serious* incidents of unwanted behaviour – almost all children will at some time need to be reminded about showing appropriate behaviour. It is usually a good idea to let parents and carers know about more serious incidents of unwanted behaviour; they may be able to provide background information that will help you adopt appropriate strategies. When telling parents about their child's behaviour, handle the situation sensitively – no parent or carer wants to hear bad news about their child. Talk to them in private and in a positive way.

## Case study

PLAYWORKER: I'm so pleased that you have a minute. Can we just pop into the office?
PARENT: Is there a problem?
PLAYWORKER: Yes and no! We just wanted you to know that Sasha has not seemed himself of late, and we were a little worried by his behaviour. Have you noticed any changes in his behaviour?
PARENT: Well, he has been very irritable at home, but I just put that down to being back at school.
PLAYWORKER: Well, what made us particularly concerned today was that he suddenly lashed out at another child, and when we tried to find out why, he just wouldn't say. We were quite surprised, because normally he seems so easy-going. He did say sorry and we do have a policy here of 'live and forget' so we would prefer you not to say anything to him, but if he says anything to you that might help us understand his change in behaviour, we would very much like to know.
PARENT: Yes, that's unlike Sasha. I'll keep an eye on him and perhaps find out from his teacher how he's settling in.
PLAYWORKER: That would be brilliant. If you think of anything we should be doing, please let us know.

1 *Why is it important to involve parents when dealing with any changes in children's behaviour?*
2 *How did the playworker encourage Sasha's mother to keep in contact?*
3 *Can you think of some reasons why Sasha might be showing a change in behaviour?*

Records of unwanted behaviour are important in case a child or parent complains about how an incident has been handled, as well as providing information about how often a child is showing unwanted behaviour.

When recording incidents of unwanted behaviour, be careful about being judgemental or labelling children. Most settings note down briefly the date, what happened, and how the behaviour was managed.

## Allowing children to express negative feelings

There are many different theories on aggression. Some suggest that aggression is instinctive, while others suggest that it is learnt behaviour linked to frustration.

Most settings find it helpful to provide some outlet for aggression and negative feelings. There are many ways of doing this, of which a common one is providing opportunities for vigorous physical games and activities. The diagram shows some of the activities that can be provided.

*Vigorous games can provide an outlet for aggression and negative feelings*

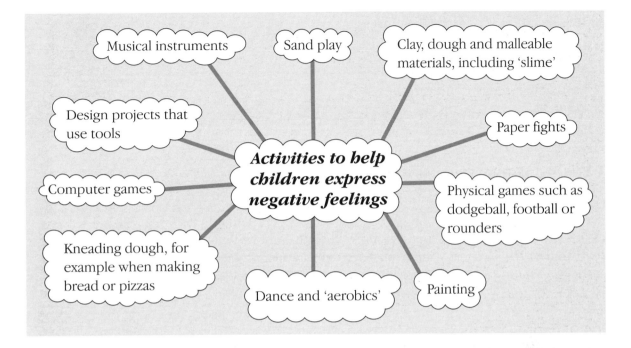

## Consolidation

Think about the types of opportunities that exist within your setting for children to express their feelings.

◆ *Write down a recent example of how you helped to provide an activity to help children express negative feelings. Explain how you did this.*

◆ *Why is it important that children are given opportunities to express themselves?*

# Element PC12.4 Develop positive relationships with parents and carers

Parents and carers play crucial roles in children's lives, and provide – or do not – the love and stability that is so essential to children. Most know their children better than anyone else, and can often pick up on their joys and sadnesses with a single look. By seeing yourself as being in partnership with parents, you should be able to learn more about the children with whom you are working, and how to meet their needs.

There are other benefits, too, for play settings that are able to develop positive relationships with parents and carers. Such settings often find that they receive enormous support in return, and in some cases this helps them to attract new children, resources and funding.

- Being polite and courteous with parents and carers
- Demonstrating anti-discriminatory practice
- Respecting parents' and carers' wishes
- Dealing with disagreements
- Maintaining confidentiality

## Making parents and carers feel welcome

A good starting point when thinking about parents and carers is to consider how you can make them feel welcome. This is important: parents and carers who feel relaxed about coming into the setting are more likely to talk to you and feel confident when leaving their children in your care. There are many aspects to making people feel welcome, but at heart what matters is to make them feel wanted. If you ignore a parent or keep a carer waiting, you give the message that they are not valued or wanted. In contrast, if you greet a parent or ask a carer whether she needs any help, you send out a positive message.

These are some of the practical ways in which you can help parents and carers to feel welcome:

- tell them about what their children have done
- invite them to sit in during sessions
- greet them positively
- ask them for feedback
- acknowledge their ideas and comments
- listen to their concerns and feelings
- take an interest in them as people.

## Case study

Jade is a playworker who enjoys her work with the children. She is a brilliant administrator and organiser, but has the attitude that most parents are basically a nuisance.

She has recently started work as a deputy manager of an out-of-school club, which needs to increase the numbers of children attending. Today some parents and their children are being shown around the club. She talks to each child and explains to them about the structure of the club, but barely says a word to parents, apart from telling them that if they send their child to this club, they should make sure that they pay on time and collect their children punctually. When one parent tries to ask a question about the club, Jade gives a very gruff response.

1 *Why might parents need more information about the club before sending their children?*

2 *How might Jade's attitude affect their decision-making?*

## Valuing and respecting all parents

One of the elements in building good relationships with parents and making them feel welcome is valuing and respecting them. Whatever the situation, always remain polite and courteous to all parents. Find out how they would like to be addressed, for example, rather than assuming that you should call them by their first names.

Respecting parents and carers also means that we must accept that each parent and carer will have personal views and a personal lifestyle, as well as individual ways of relating to their children. This is often easier to say, than to do, although it is essential in showing good anti-discriminatory practice. Valuing and respecting parents and carers will mean not just saying and doing the 'right' things, but thinking positively about them, remembering that your tone of voice and your body language send out messages which might make people feel unwelcome.

## Recognising your own values and prejudices

Everyone has values and prejudices. These are learnt during childhood, and through our life experiences.

Values and prejudices tend to affect us without our realising this. We tend to get on better with people who have similar attitudes and lifestyles to ourselves. To show true respect and to value others, it is important to be aware of your own starting point and then consider whether these are likely to affect the way you might relate to others.

## Communicating with parents and carers

Most good relationships depend not only on respect but also on good communication. Good communication can help prevent potential misunderstandings, as well as help parents and carers to feel that they can talk to you openly about their children and give you feedback about what you are doing.

There are many ways of communicating with and passing information on to parents and carers. Even if they can rarely visit the setting, you may still be able to maintain some contact.

The following list shows some of the methods of communication that are commonly used:

- face-to-face contact
- notes home
- telephone calls
- open sessions
- home book or diary
- newsletter
- noticeboards
- photos and videos.

## Face-to-face contact

Some parents and carers might be able to pop into the setting regularly. You will be able to build a relationship with them, by talking about their children, and listening to them. Face-to-face contact allows each person to respond immediately, and often small issues can be resolved quite quickly. If they have something that they wish to discuss, many parents and carers will find it easier to talk to a playworker rather than to send a letter.

### Skills needed

For this method to work well, you will need to be able to listen attentively, to show that you are interested, and to consider the effect of your words and body language on the other person.

> Dear Mrs. Martin,
>
> Just a quick note to let you know that Mark has settled down really well. This week he has especially enjoyed playing with the mini-golf set we have here.
>
> Hope to see you in the near future.
>
> Please do not hesitate to get in contact.
>
> Best wishes
>
> Sarah Godwin
> Manager, Clowning Around out-of-school club

*A note to a parent*

## Notes and letters home

There might be times when a letter or a note home is needed, for example if a child has had an accident or has lost an item. It is also good to write a note to pass on positive feedback about a child if parents and carers are not able to come in to the setting very often, especially if you are working with a very young child.

### Skills needed

Before sending out any letters or notes, check your presentation and spelling. Some people now prefer to type notes and letters, but you should always sign them personally. It is also worth checking that the tone of the letter or note is suitable.

## Telephone calls

The telephone can be used effectively as a method of communication. It is less formal than a letter or a note, and allows people to respond instantly or to seek clarification.

### Skills needed

As the person to whom you are speaking or listening cannot see your facial expression or body language, it is important to consider your tone of voice. Switchboard operators, for example, are taught to smile as they speak so that their tone of voice becomes warmer.

## Open sessions

Some settings have open sessions during which parents and carers can simply drop in and see what their children are doing. One playscheme, for example, planned an afternoon where parents and carers could join their children in learning some circus skills. Open sessions provide opportunities for parents and carers to see at first hand the benefits of children's play activities whilst also allowing them to talk to staff in an informal way. Open sessions are also a way of encouraging other parents and carers to consider sending their child to the setting and helping the wider community to see the work that is being done.

### Skills needed

For open sessions to work well, parents and carers must be made to feel welcome. Staff need to find time to talk to them and answer any questions that they may have.

**22nd August**

Ling has had a good day today, despite seeming a little drowsy at times. Could this be a side effect of the medication? She enjoyed our treasure hunt in the garden this morning and also the painting activity this afternoon. We have put one of the paintings in her bag. Please could you send in some spare clothes tomorrow, because we are going to have the water out if it is a hot day.

Jenny

**23rd August**

We have not had a very good night! You might find that Ling is very tired today as she had a fit last night. I am going to take her to the doctor tomorrow to check whether this new medication is working.

Ling showed us her painting and we have put it up in the kitchen.

I have put two changes of clothes for Ling in her bag as well as some photographs of our new kittens. She loves the kittens – one is called Max and the other is called Theo.

*A home book*

## Home book or diary

Many settings that work with children with special needs, for example difficulties with communication, find that home books or diaries can provide parents and carers with valuable information. They might often be used with younger children who are settling in to the setting. The home book or diary allows the staff to jot down any messages or information about a child that they need to pass onto parents and carers. The children return the book or diary with any comments in that the parents or carers have made.

### Skills needed

Most settings using home books with children find them very valuable as a tool for communication. If children have limited communication, they must be filled in accurately and regularly.

## Newsletters

Some settings send out newsletters from time to time. These can help parents and carers find out about forthcoming activities, trips, and other information. They can also be useful as a marketing tool, attracting the attention of potential new parents and children.

### Skills needed

Information in newsletters needs to be well presented and accurate. Producing newsletters can be time-consuming, although some settings produce these in co-operation with the children.

## Noticeboards

Many settings rely on noticeboards to pass on information. They are often put near cloakroom areas or where parents and carers meet their children. They can act as reminders, as well as help parents and carers find out what has been happening.

### Skills needed

Noticeboards need to be updated regularly. If information is out of date or never changes, the board will fail to attract attention. It is also important that any writing produced by playworkers be accurate and legible. Some settings involve children in producing information for the noticeboard – for example, children might design a poster asking for some party food!

## Photos and videos

Taking photos or producing a video of what is happening in a setting is a popular way of helping parents and carers to find out about what is happening in settings. Children love to help, either taking the photos or seeing themselves on them. Photos can either be displayed on a noticeboard or sent out to parents.

### Skills needed

It is useful if a few comments are put underneath or on the back of a photo, to put the photo in context.

## Brochures

Many settings produce a simple brochure that explains to potential and new parents and carers the main aims of the setting, and gives information about times of opening, costs and so on. Brochures can then be kept as a reference. In some settings, the children help to produce parts of the brochures.

### Skills needed

It may be a good idea to talk to existing parents and carers about the type of information they would have found helpful at the outset. The presentation of the information needs to be good, and the information itself as up to date and accurate as possible.

# Providing accurate and clear information to parents and carers

There is a range of information that parents and carers might need, once their children attend a play setting. It is an important part of the playworker's role to ensure that when parents and carers request information they are given it accurately and promptly, unless this is likely to break confidentiality. If you are unable to provide information, you might refer the parent or carer to your line manager, or give suggestions as to where they might find it.

## Active knowledge ✔

Look at the following types of information that parents and carers might need.

- Information about the costs of sessions.
- Reassurance that their child has settled in.
- Information about the types of activities and resources on offer to children.
- Details about opening and closing times.
- Information about finding lost property.
- More information about how an accident occurred.
- Information about how a parent or carer can help in the setting.

1 *Why might parents and carers need each of these pieces of information?*
2 *Think of ways in which this type of information could be passed on.*
3 *Why is it important that parents and carers are given accurate information promptly?*

## Respecting the wishes of parents and carers

There will be many times when you must consult with parents and carers and listen to their wishes. For example, you might plan a trip to the swimming pool but find that a parent or carer would prefer their child not to attend, for religious or health reasons.

At such times you might need to remind yourself that it is the parents or carers, not you, who have legal responsibility for the children. If you fail to respect their wishes, you are in effect sending a message that you do not value them.

## Case study

This morning a parent popped into the setting to tell Jo, the playworker, that she would prefer her daughter, Frankie, not to take part in any physical activities today, because she has been a little wheezy in the night.

During the day some team games are organised, and one of the playworkers asks Jo whether Frankie should be playing. Jo simply laughs and says that her mother tends to be a bit of a fusspot, and that Frankie wants to play.

1 *Why is Jo's attitude wrong?*
2 *How might the parent feel when she finds out that her instructions have not been respected?*
3 *How would you have handled this situation, if you felt during the day that the child was feeling better?*

## Respecting confidentiality

Parents and carers often pass on information that is confidential. They do this to help staff understand the needs of their children, or to explain the reasons behind their child's behaviour. Often the information that they give you will be personal and in some cases painful for them.

Unless the child's welfare is at stake, therefore, this information must remain confidential and be passed on only to those who really need to know.

If you are given information that you feel indicates that a child's welfare is at stake, seek help either from your line manager or from social services. Occasionally, you may be given information about parents and carers from other professionals, such as a social worker. This type of information is equally confidential, and again should not be passed on to anyone else.

## Key to good practice

### Confidentiality

✎ When parents or carers are sharing information which is personal, find a quiet and private area so that others cannot overhear.

### Case study

Jodie is the mother of Hugo, who attends your after-school club. You have noticed that she is looking pale and drawn recently, and she asks if she can have a word with you. You ask her if she would like to pop into the office. Once there, she bursts into tears and says that she has just found out that she will need an operation in the next few weeks. She wants you to know because she is concerned that her son will probably react quite badly.

1 **What would you say to reassure her?**
2 **With whom will you need to share this information?**
3 **Why is it important to provide a place where parents can share information privately?**

## Avoiding disagreements with parents and carers

Most play settings that maintain good relationships with their parents and carers rarely have disagreements with them. Disagreements can produce bad feeling: if left unresolved, the parent or carer may withdraw the child.

In many cases, disagreements can be avoided by having clear policies and procedures, and making sure that parents are aware of these when the child starts in the setting. Disagreements can also be avoided by involving parents and carers when planning, and by not making assumptions about their needs and wishes.

## Managing disagreements with parents and carers

In some cases, disagreements with parents and carers may be unavoidable. When they arise, handle them carefully and tactfully, and remain polite and courteous.

## Keys to good practice

### Managing disagreements

**Do:**

⚒ remain calm and friendly

⚒ find a private area to discuss issues with parents and carers

⚒ try to find out any relevant information beforehand

⚒ apologise if the setting has been in any way partly to blame for the disagreement

⚒ listen to what is being said and investigate further if necessary

⚒ try to work out a compromise solution

⚒ thank parents and carers for coming in to talk with you

⚒ consider arranging a way of keeping in contact, or following up on the discussion

⚒ record details of what has been said or agreed

⚒ consider referring the disagreement to your line manager for guidance.

**Don't**

⚒ become angry and defensive

⚒ make any promises that you cannot keep

⚒ refuse to listen to what parents and carers are saying

⚒ pass any comments about situations unless you have investigated first

⚒ breach confidentiality.

## Case study

Read the following scenarios.

- Mr James has come into the setting. He is angry because for the second day running his child has not had a turn on the computer game. This is partly due to the game being out of action, and also because there are many other children wanting to use it. He says that you should not be putting out equipment if there is not enough of it.
- It is policy that children should not bring mobile phones into the setting, for many reasons including the setting's unwillingness to take responsibility for the phones. Jasmine's mum feels that this policy is wrong, and has sent her child in with a phone which was one of her birthday presents.

- As part of the playscheme, the children go on several organised trips. Parents and carers are told that the children should bring only a maximum of £3 on these trips, as everything is provided for them. Becky's granny, who brings her to the playscheme, often gives her a £10 note. The granny has come into the setting to complain that yesterday Becky was not allowed to spend this money.

1 **Work out how you would handle each of these cases. (You can role-play them with a partner, or write down what you would do.)**

2 **Why is it important to try to understand parents' and carers' points of view?**

## Responding to complaints and suggestions

In Unit A55 we looked at the importance of gaining feedback in order to improve individual performance and the organisation's practice. Some feedback will be provided by parents and carers, and it is essential that you listen to it and respond well. Parents and carers will sometimes have a different perspective from your own: by listening carefully to their suggestions, you might find ways of improving your service for the future.

Complaints are often harder to handle than suggestions – it is not easy to take on board criticisms. Try hard to see any complaint from the parent's or carer's perspective. Remember that they will often have come into the setting having rehearsed in their own mind what they are going to say: this may make them seem aggressive, when in fact they are apprehensive. If you can see that there has been some mistake, misunderstanding or poor practice, apologise and explain that you will ensure that this will not recur. Most parents and carers react well if they feel that what they are saying is being taken seriously. In some cases, you might need to refer a complaint to your line manager, or tell the parent or carer that you will report back to them once you have found out more.

## PC12 unit test

1 Why is it important to welcome and greet all children in a setting?
2 Outline three ways in which you could help children to communicate with you.
3 What is meant by the term 'ground rules'?
4 Why is it useful to involve children when working out ground rules?
5 Why do ground rules need to be reviewed regularly?
6 What is meant by the term 'role model'? Why is it important to be a good one when working with children?
7 Why is it important for settings to have an agreed behaviour management policy?
8 Outline three strategies that can be used to manage children's unwanted behaviour.
9 Explain why it is important to provide opportunities for children to express their negative feelings.
10 Why is it important that playworkers build a positive relationship with parents and carers?
11 Outline three types of information that parents might wish to be given.
12 Give an example of the type of information that a parent might pass on to you that would be confidential.

# Provide a child-centred play environment

As well as providing suitable and interesting play opportunities, playworkers also need to provide a good environment in which children will want to play. A good play environment is one that meets the needs of all the children within it, is attractive, and promotes positive images.

The elements for this unit are:

PC13.1  Provide a play environment which meets the children's needs
PC13.2  Promote positive images through the play environment

## Element PC13.1 Provide a play environment which meets the children's needs

Play environments vary enormously from setting to setting. Some play settings are housed in premises that were not designed for children, while others are purpose-built. This means that every setting has its own 'feel', along with strengths and difficulties. This section looks at ways of providing a good play environment which is child-centred and makes children feel welcome and involved.

### WHAT YOU NEED TO LEARN

- Ensuring that the play environment is physically suitable, friendly, attractive, stimulating, and challenging
- Fostering children's sense of ownership, and welcoming their ideas
- Reviewing and updating the play environment
- Reporting any resource problems

### Providing a good play environment

The term 'environment' is a wide one. It covers not only what you see, but also what you can feel. The layout, the furniture and the equipment of a setting are important, but so too is the atmosphere created by the staff. Children are very sensitive to their environment and quickly distinguish between environments that they like and those in which they feel uncomfortable.

Providing a good play environment is like doing a jigsaw: several pieces must be put together for it to be complete.

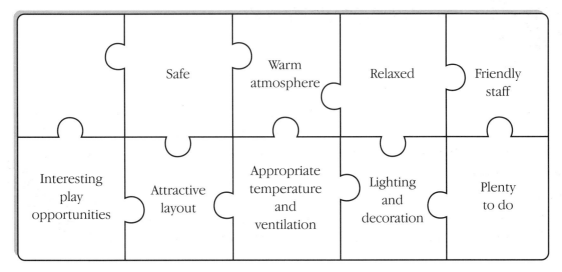

**Characteristics of a good play environment**

There are many benefits to settings from spending time making a good child-centred play environment. Parents and carers are more likely to consider using a play setting where they are sure that their children will be happy and enjoy coming, so such settings are more likely to flourish. A good environment for children is also a good one in which to work, so recruiting and retaining staff and helpers becomes easier. The list below summarises the benefits:

- children are more likely to enjoy coming to the setting
- the setting is able to appeal to a wide range of children, of differing ages and backgrounds
- children are less likely to be bored
- children's social and overall development is promoted
- parents and carers feel more confident about using the setting
- new children are more likely to be attracted to the setting
- accidents are avoided
- staff enjoy their work more
- the reputation of the play setting is enhanced
- registration and funding are more easily gained.

# Making sure that the environment meets children's needs

To be able to meet children's needs, you need to understand what these needs might be. This means looking at four levels of needs:

- children's basic needs
- age/stage-related needs
- the needs of specific groups of children
- the needs of individual children.

## Meeting all children's basic needs

There are some basic needs that *all* children need to have met. These can be categorised into three main areas, as the table below shows.

| Area of need | Examples | Ways in which playworkers can meet the need |
|---|---|---|
| Physical comfort | Food and drink<br>Warmth<br>Cleanliness<br>Safety<br>Rest<br>Exercise | Provide suitable food and drinks for all the children.<br>Find out about children who have specific dietary requirements.<br>Ensure that the setting is clean and safe.<br>Make sure that the lighting, heating and ventilation are appropriate.<br>Check that children are appropriately dressed.<br>Make sure that the play opportunities allow both exercise and rest. |
| Emotional | Respect<br>Attention<br>Care<br>Sense of belonging | Make sure that children are welcomed into the setting.<br>Praise and value children.<br>Provide play opportunities for children to make friends and join in with groups.<br>Show children that you enjoy being with them.<br>Provide support during play opportunities.<br>Give children individual attention.<br>Listen to children's ideas and comments.<br>Make the parents and carers feel welcome. |
| Stimulation | Opportunities to be creative<br>Opportunities to solve problems<br>Opportunities to explore | Provide play opportunities that are varied and plentiful.<br>Make sure that play opportunities are of interest to the children.<br>Provide play opportunities that are challenging and stimulating.<br>Make sure that play opportunities are not too difficult, or children will become frustrated and bored. |

## Meeting age/stage-related needs

In addition to the basic needs, children will also have needs that relate to their stage of development. Children develop at slightly different rates, but a pattern of development can be seen. Knowing this general pattern in key areas will help you to make sure that you can meet children's play and other needs.

Although looking at age-related information can be helpful in giving a guide as to what you might expect, you should be very cautious: not every child you work with will show behaviour and skills generally expected at that age. Treat children as individuals, and concentrate on meeting the needs for their stage of development as shown opposite.

| Age | Stage of development |
|---|---|
| 5–7 years | • Need some adult input and support<br>• May want adults to provide starting points for play<br>• Beginning to enjoy playing games and can cope with rules<br>• Will enjoy praise<br>• May be unsure in the presence of older children at first. |
| 7–11 years | • Friendships are becoming increasingly important and children may play in tighter friendship groups<br>• May enjoy being given some ideas for play activities, but should be quick to develop and think of their own play activities<br>• May enjoy developing games that have rules<br>• Becoming more independent, but may seek help and support from adults at times<br>• May be competitive and compare 'performance'. |
| 11 years + | • Friendships are very important and approval of peers is highly prized<br>• May start to become self-conscious<br>• Will want to take control of their play and may have clear ideas about what they want to do<br>• May become more interested in taking on responsibility for the day-to-day management of the setting<br>• Behaviour may be changeable with older children showing a mix of immature and mature behaviour<br>• May find it harder to play in mixed gender groups unless encouraged by adults<br>• May perceive support from adults as being 'interference'. |

## Meeting the needs of specific groups of children

In addition to being aware of the needs of individual children, you should also be aware of the needs of *groups* of children, especially to make sure that they are not being discriminated against. Examples include refugees, children living in care, and those who have a different culture or religion from the majority in the setting.

The keys to providing an environment that is non-discriminatory are not to make any assumptions, and to be questioning in your attitude. For example, do not assume that all children will be able to afford to go on expensive outings, or that English will be their home language.

In addition, your setting will need to be pro-active in order to counter the stereotypes to which children will be exposed in our society. Play opportunities need to be provided that will appeal to both boys and girls, and also opportunities that help children become aware of other cultures, religions and lifestyles (see also page 173).

## Active knowledge ✔

Do not assume ...

• that all children live in houses
• that all children are living with both natural parents
• that parents and carers can afford outings, pocket money and extras
• that all children speak English at home
• that all children celebrate Christian festivals such as Easter or Mothers' Day
• that all children eat and enjoy the same foods.

*Can you add to this list?*

## Meeting the needs of individual children

As well as looking at the overall needs of *most* children, settings also need to be able to meet the needs of *individual* children. The range of needs will vary from setting to setting, but may include children who have specific dietary or medical requirements, as well as children with special needs. Some children will also have some short-term needs, such as children who have recently moved area and need time to adjust, or children whose parents have recently separated who might need extra attention and support. The range of individual needs can be very wide.

*Settings need to be able to meet the needs of individual children, such as those with special needs*

### Gaining information from children

Most children with particular needs, especially older children, are very keen to be involved with any decision-making. Whenever possible, talk to them about their needs and how you can best meet them. They may have strong views about the help that they do and do not want. A child with diabetes, for example, may want the other children in the setting to know about why their food is different; while a child who speaks another language at home may not want any reference made to this. Listening to children is therefore vital in making sure that you can meet their needs.

### Gaining information from parents and carers

You will also need to work closely with parents and carers, who will be able to give you background information and sometimes advice as to how best to meet their children's needs. For example, the parents of a child who has epilepsy will be able to tell you about the signs that their child shows before an attack, or the side-effects of the medication; and the carers of a child with learning difficulties might tell you about the play opportunities that this child enjoys and the types that they find it harder to take part in.

### Gaining information from other professionals

You may also work with other professionals in finding out how to meet children's needs. This is particularly important when working with children with special needs, as the support and equipment required can be very specific – for example, a standing frame might be used to help children paint or stand for an activity.

Professionals will also have advice as to how best to support children and promote areas of their development – for instance, physiotherapists and speech therapists might ask a setting to do some daily exercises with a child. In many cases other professionals will be able to lend you equipment and resources, or put you in contact with organisations that can help.

# Organising the play environment

The layout and organisation of the environment is crucial. A good layout will allow children to move from activity to activity easily and in safety, and will give children enough space to play in. (Conflicts may occur if one group of children's play overlaps with and interferes with another group's.)

A good layout also helps towards the smooth running of a setting. Play opportunities are put near to the facilities and resources that will be needed. Accidents and spillages are then less likely to occur, and tidying away becomes easier. Good access to resources also helps children to be self-reliant as they can get out the items that they need.

## Effective settings

Many factors should be considered when thinking about the layout of the play setting. Wherever possible, care should be taken to make sure that play opportunities are put in appropriate places within the setting: for example, play opportunities that require small fine movements and hand–eye co-ordination should be near good lighting, whereas 'messy' play activities such as water and sand need to be housed near a sink. Some activities require plenty of space if children are to benefit fully – a game of rounders needs a great deal of space, for example, while children devising their own play might need a more secluded area in which they can rehearse 'privately'.

Most play settings find that they have to make many compromises because their setting is not perfect – there may be a shortage of space or storage, for instance. It is easy to fall into the routine of putting out certain play opportunities in the same places, just because it has become a tradition. Take time every so often to look afresh at the space available – new ideas may spring to mind.

# Keys to good practice

## Organising the play environment: checklist

- Will there be enough space for each play opportunity?
- Is the play opportunity situated near the resources and equipment that will be required?
- Can exit points be kept unobstructed?
- Is there enough room for children to move between play opportunities safely and easily?
- Will staff be able to supervise children?
- Are there quiet areas where children can 'rehearse', read, or simply chat?
- Are electric sockets near appliances, to avoid trailing flexes?
- Are activities that need good lighting near windows or sources of light?
- Are 'messy' activities near sinks and away from carpeted areas?

## Active knowledge ✔

1 *Draw a diagram of the layout of the play opportunities in your setting on one day.*
2 *Explain the benefits and disadvantages (if any) of this layout.*

## Making the play setting friendly, attractive and stimulating

As well as making sure that the physical environment is safe and interesting, it is also important that the general atmosphere in the play setting is a welcoming one. Children are particularly sensitive to atmosphere, and this will often determine whether or not children want to return.

## Creating a good atmosphere

Creating a good atmosphere is a little like cooking a cake – it needs a mix of several ingredients. One of the main ingredients is the staff themselves. Staff who are warm, friendly and genuinely interested in working with children will help to create a good atmosphere, although it is important that they also work together as a team.

Another essential ingredient is the way in which the physical environment is maintained. A messy and grubby environment indicates that staff take no pride in their workplace, while an attractive environment sends out a very positive message.

A third essential ingredient is the children themselves! If children are happy and enjoying being in the environment, they will create a lovely atmosphere. This will happen only if they enjoy the play opportunities and feel that they are being valued.

## Keys to good practice

### Creating a good atmosphere

⚒ Make sure that children, parents and carers are warmly greeted when they enter the setting.

⚒ Consider creating a reception area with plants, posters and photographs.

⚒ Make sure that equipment that is not being used is properly stored away.

⚒ Prioritise finding storage solutions that will allow children to access resources easily.

⚒ Make sure that the setting is properly cleaned.

⚒ Ask children for ideas on how they would like their environment to look.

⚒ Put up display boards and encourage the children to create colourful displays.

⚒ Work with the children to produce programmes of play opportunities, activities and outings.

⚒ Encourage parents and carers to be involved in the setting, for example helping with play opportunities.

⚒ Look for ways to strengthen teamwork, such as a communications board, nights out, and staff meetings.

## Encouraging children to 'own' the play environment

While it is important that staff take pride in the play setting, it is also important that children feel that it is theirs. Making sure that children have a stake in the play environment contributes to their development, as it encourages them to work co-operatively, considering not just their own needs but those of other children also. Having access to a setting that they feel is 'theirs' is also very important for children who are feeling insecure in other areas of their lives, for example if they are not enjoying school or if their home life is unsettled. The benefits are summarised in the diagram below.

## Sharing responsibility

If children are to feel that the play environment is their own, they must be given opportunities to take responsibility for it. They must be involved in decisions, encouraged to make suggestions, and allowed to improvise and adapt equipment, providing that safety is maintained.

Helping children take responsibility for their environment does not mean that playworkers take a back seat and leave everything to the children, however! This would not work, particularly in settings with very young children. What it does mean is that playworkers need to find ways of working alongside children, listening to them, and giving them opportunities to contribute. This is quite a skill: children may need to be guided as to how to make fair decisions, how to listen to each other, and how to consider what is practicable.

*Children can be encouraged to share responsibility*

There are many ways of encouraging children to contribute, and most settings use several. Common strategies include:

- holding meetings with all the children
- encouraging groups of children to hold their own meetings, to discuss specific issues
- giving children choices, wherever possible – for example, using preference sheets
- having a 'suggestions' box
- carrying out surveys and evaluations
- having a 'comments' noticeboard for the children.

For children really to feel that their suggestions are valued, it is important that you act upon them whenever you can. If this is not possible, explain why – for example, there may be financial or health and safety restraints.

## Consolidation

Think of a recent occasion when you encouraged children to make suggestions about their play environment.

◆ *Explain the circumstances, and how you did this.*
◆ *Were you able to act upon their suggestions?*
◆ *If not, write about how you explained this to the children.*

# Making the best use of resources

Most play settings have limited resources and limited budgets, so staff have to make the best use they can of the resources they have available. This sometimes means thinking about individual pieces of equipment and considering other ways in which they might be played with or used. A slide, for example, could become a good den if a sheet were draped over it, and a basketball net might be used for devising a new team game.

Below are some practical ideas for making the best use of resources.

## Visiting other play settings

Visiting another play setting may spark off new ideas – another setting might have different games, for example.

## Making an audit of equipment

An audit of equipment from time to time helps everyone in the setting to remind themselves exactly what resources are available. Items sometimes get forgotten in cupboards.

## Combining resources

Sometimes resources can be combined to make a new play opportunity – for example, toy cars can be combined with the sand area to make a safari race track, or rollerblades and balls can be combined to produce a new game of dodgeball on skates!

## Sorting and repairing equipment

Sort out equipment that is no longer safe or that is broken. Before throwing away any resources, check with the manufacturer whether spare parts are available. These are quite often free, or very inexpensive.

## Reporting and acting where there are resource problems

Where there is a clear shortage of resources, take action. A poorly resourced setting will find it hard to provide stimulating opportunities for children. In some settings a clear case will need to be made for new equipment, for example if a management committee needs to be persuaded. If this is the case in your setting, consider using the equipment audit to show that there is an identifiable problem. Be very clear about what you are requesting. Instead of simply complaining about equipment, offer ideas about what you need and how much it would cost. Before going ahead and either buying in equipment or fund-raising, check out any policies with your line manager. There may be a policy about accepting secondhand toys, for example.

# Reviewing and developing the play environment

One of the keys to a successful play setting is continual reflection upon what is happening. It is very easy to get into a comfortable 'rut', and for routines and activities to be carried on because they have become 'tradition'. This is dangerous: new children may come into a setting and find that their needs are not met; and staff may become less motivated and challenged. It is often harder for permanent settings to realise that they need a change of routine or layout unless review becomes part of a regular process, yet the benefits of developing the play environment are enormous. Such reviews can help the team:

- motivate staff and volunteers
- make sure that equipment and resources are up to date
- make sure that the play environment meets all children's needs
- provide variety and stimulation
- prevent children from feeling bored
- keep up to date with health and safety regulations.

## Ways of reviewing and developing the play environment

There are many ways of making sure that the play environment remains interesting and challenging. These might include the following.

### Staff training

Staff might go on training courses, which will give them new ideas and help them keep up to date with current good practice.

### Visits to other play settings

Many staff find it very helpful to visit other settings. Local networks can be formed to facilitate this type of exchange.

### Looking at new resources and products

Looking at brochures and visiting exhibitions may make staff aware of new products and equipment. Introducing some of these can help to develop a play setting.

### Encouraging children to bring forward suggestions

Children can often contribute useful suggestions, provided that they are given the opportunities and encouragement to do so (see also page 169).

### Involving others

By bringing in visitors, holding open days and actively encouraging parents and carers to be part of the setting, you can develop the setting further. Involvement and interaction like this helps everyone to feel motivated and energised.

---

## Consolidation

Think about a play opportunity that you have provided recently.

- ◆ *How did you make sure that it looked attractive and stimulating?*
- ◆ *What equipment or resources did you use, and why?*
- ◆ *If you were to repeat the same play opportunity, how could you vary it to make it more interesting?*

# Element PC13.2 Promote positive images through the play environment

The children we work with will be the next generation of citizens, voters and perhaps decision-makers. Research has shown us that children learn their values – and prejudices – from the adults who are close to them. This means that the children you are working with may be influenced by what they see, feel and hear when they are with you. Whenever possible, try to show them what it means to respect others and be tolerant of lifestyles and experiences which they do not share. This section looks at ways in which we can promote positive images through the play environment.

## WHAT YOU NEED TO LEARN

- Monitoring for negative images
- Selecting equipment and materials that promote positive images
- Discussing positive images with children
- With colleagues, modelling positive images

## The positive images that need to be promoted

It is generally recognised that various groups of people living in society are often discriminated against because society has preconceived ideas or prejudices about them. Prejudices can sometimes be born out of direct experience, but most come from stereotypes, often formed by the media. Prejudices against groups of people tend to mean that these people receive less than fair treatment, and this in turn can lead to segments of our society feeling rejected and resentful.

The list of people who are discriminated against is sadly quite long. It includes:

- disabled people
- people whose skin colour is not white
- people whose religion is not 'mainstream' Christian, such as 7th day Adventists, Muslims, and Jews
- travellers, gypsies and others who have not chosen a 'conventional' lifestyle
- people who are over 60
- people who are obese
- people who are homosexual or bisexual.

The above list is quite short – it would be impossible to list in detail *all* of those people who are discriminated against. The list could even include men who have become bald, as recent research shows that they are less likely to be selected for interviews!

To counter the prejudices that children might absorb, it is important that all play settings try to show in positive ways groups of people who are usually stereotyped – for example, an elderly person who is fit and active, or a disabled person who is able to be independent.

## Using visual images

Visual images are powerful. A single picture or moment in a film can often be reawakened by our memories because the brain encodes visual information effectively. Posters, films and photographs are therefore important ways of promoting positive images and challenging the usual stereotypes. You could put up posters in the settings that show men working as cooks, or disabled children playing happily alongside able-bodied children. Where you come across images that are *not* promoting positive images, you could use these as talking points with the children.

### Selecting positive visual images

When choosing photographs, posters or cut-outs from magazines, be sure that they do not reinforce stereotypes. Look particularly at images from other countries and cultures. For instance, there is a tendency to show all families living in India as being poor, whereas although there certainly is poverty there, there are also some very wealthy people living in India.

Select images that challenge everyday stereotypes. Do not show all women as nurses or carers, or all disabled people as helpless.

As well as selecting positive visual images, it is also important to maintain them. A torn and scruffy poster may convey a negative impression to visitors.

## Active knowledge ✔

1  *What impression does this poster create?*
2  *Why is this a stereotype?*

# Choosing play equipment and materials

If we are buying equipment, we have a strong responsibility to think about any hidden messages or stereotypes that might be promoted with the equipment – for example aggressive fighting soldiers or very 'twee' care toys. Where possible, we should try and look for toys that can be played with by all the children in the setting in a variety of ways. We can also look out for equipment and materials which will give children more understanding of a range of lifestyles, cultures and religions. This might mean buying in specific equipment – for example cooking implements, dressing up clothes and toys that are made and are popular in other countries. We can also enhance the physical environment by using objects and fabrics that are popular and reflect other cultures – for example using batiks and strong colours for curtains.

## Active knowledge ✔

Look at and consider the play resources in your setting.

1 *Which ones promote positive images?*
2 *Using a catalogue, choose five items that you think would promote positive images in your setting. Explain the reasons for your choice.*

*Remember that girls play football too!*

# Playing in non-stereotypical ways

Some play materials and equipment are targeted by their manufacturers at boys or girls. Whilst it is not always possible to avoid these in a setting completely, playworkers can attempt to make sure that both genders try playing with them. Once children begin to play stereotypically, they lose out on developmental opportunities as their range of activities is reduced.

An example of this is imaginative play. This type of play can encourage children to express their feelings and to develop communication skills, but often boys, in particular, come under pressure to reduce this type of play. To counter this, try to look at ways of ensuring that play activities that are usually thought of as 'boyish' or 'girlish' are made attractive to both genders. Making an activity attractive is usually the most effective strategy – unless children *want* to play, they will resist well-meant attempts to get them to join in.

The table shows some of the activities which have traditionally appealed only to one gender and ways in which they might be made more appealing.

| Activity | Ways to make the activity attractive to both genders |
|---|---|
| **Music-making** | (This activity has often appealed more to girls than to boys.)<br>Use positive images of famous stars of both sexes.<br>Encourage mixed music-making, for example form a band for the setting.<br>Encourage children to think of a title for the band, taping tracks and performing. |
| **Cooking** | (This activity has been seen as 'women's work'.)<br>Get children to taste something delicious, then see if they can make it.<br>Try competitions like those on television, such as *Ready, Steady, Cook*.<br>Try making contact with local restaurants and see whether one of the chefs will demonstrate, for instance making naan breads or sushi. |
| **Imaginative play** | (Older boys often feel that they can no longer dress up or role-play.)<br>Look for a wide range of costumes, such as clowns, clothes, or uniforms.<br>Encourage children to put on their own mimes or other performances.<br>Encourage the use of puppets and masks that can be made. |
| **Football and outdoor games** | (As girls get older, many tend to play less physical games.)<br>Consider having mixed competitions.<br>Make fun outdoor activities such as obstacle courses for *It's a knock-out*.<br>Encourage mixed team activities.<br>Look for fun materials, such as balloons or bouncy castles. |
| **Sewing, weaving, knitting, etc.** | (This area has been thought of as a 'girly' by boys.)<br>Try some communal weaving projects using interesting materials.<br>Look out for projects that require some sewing, such as making a kite using fabric, or making costumes for shows.<br>Look at design aspects of clothes, including famous designs such as for sportswear. |

## Using conversation to promote positive images

Children can also learn about respecting others from playworkers. Make use of informal opportunities. Watch out for opportunities as they arise – for example, if you were planning an open day, you might raise the issue of making sure that people with limited mobility could still enjoy the day; or when looking at ideas for cooking activities, you could suggest trying recipes for traditional food from other cultures.

Show children that you yourself are always interested in finding out more about the way people live, and that you enjoy trying new foods and listening to new ideas. It is useful if you have some background knowledge about other cultures and religions as well as your own, because you can then pass this on in conversation with children. When cooking, for example, you might say, 'Did you know that many Jews keep separate saucepans for cooking dairy products and meat products?' or 'Of course, tea in this country used to be considered to be very valuable, and was locked away in little boxes.' Snippets of interesting information given in this way can encourage children to think more and find out more about the different ways in which people live.

The table below shows types of opportunities that can be created.

| Opportunity | Types of issues that can be discussed with children |
| --- | --- |
| **Preparing food and snacks** | Talk about food that they enjoy or dislike.<br>Talk about the way in which every culture has its own food traditions.<br>Encourage children to taste new foods. Make sure that you show that *you* are ready to do this. |
| **Listening to music** | Talk about the singers. Male singers might be positive role models for boys who think music-making is 'sissy'.<br>Bring in different types of music and musical instruments.<br>Talk about how people can have different musical preferences.<br>Make sure that you show that you are interested in different types of music and enjoy listening to new things. |
| **Talking about local or national events in the news** | Try to talk about the background to events that are in the national news, such as why refugees are trying to leave their countries, or why disabled people feel that they should have more rights.<br>Encourage children to think about different points of view, and listen to what they think. |
| **Reading books** | Use books as discussion points. For example, if a book has very stereotypical behaviour in it, ask the children what they think about this.<br>Ask children if they think that the books are a fair reflection of what is really happening.<br>Find books that challenge assumptions. |
| **Trips and outings** | Talk about what you are seeing, for example people's behaviour 'Why do you think that person swore?', or 'Why is it wrong for people to park in disabled spaces if they don't need to?'<br>Use opportunities for children to look at the environment around them, for example the architecture of buildings. |

As children are quick to pick up hidden messages from tone of voice and expressions, it is important that you are able to show respect and tolerance when speaking about others. There is little point in trying to promote positive images if in conversation you use phrases such as 'They have a really strange way of eating' or 'They seem to speak in a funny way'.

Be ready also to challenge promptly inappropriate remarks by children to each other. (See also page 145.)

## Modelling

Your own behaviour will set an example to children, so you must be a good role model. Children often learn by watching and imitating behaviour. (This theory is called the social learning theory.) Not only your words but your behaviour and your reactions will shape children's behaviour as they 'model' themselves on the adults around them.

### Ways in which we can be good role models

Children need to see through our actions that we respect and are accepting of others. Small actions such as holding the door open for others, or listening carefully to parents, are all ways in which children will see how adults respect one another. Try to challenge assumptions and stereotypes through your behaviour. For example, traditionally women have been seen as good at cooking, but helpless when it comes to fixing things. To challenge these stereotypes, women in play settings can show that they know how to use a screwdriver or wire a plug; and men can show that they can cook, clean and tidy.

## Keys to good practice

### Being good role models

- Staff should show how to work together.
- Tasks in the setting should not fall into traditional stereotypes.
- Staff should show that they are good listeners, and ready to take on different points of view.
- Staff should be respectful to each other.
- Women can lead and join in traditionally 'male' games such as football and rugby.
- Men can lead and join in activities such as music-making, sewing and weaving.
- Staff should avoid creating teams that are sex-segregated (boys versus girls).
- Staff should show that they are knowledgeable about other cultures.
- Staff should show that they are interested in trying out new skills and activities.

## Case study

Marilyn is a playworker in a holiday scheme. She has organised a camping break on a farm for the children, and is accompanied by Jack.

When they arrive at the campsite, she suggests to Jack that he takes a group of children to put up the tents, whilst she concentrates on preparing the food with another group. There are several tents to put up and she says that she's not very good at 'technical stuff'.

1  *Why is this approach unlikely to promote positive images to children?*
2  *Suggest a way in which the tasks of preparing food and putting up tents could be done in a less stereotypical way.*
3  *Can you think of ways in which the camping break on the farm could be used to promote and make children aware of different lifestyles?*

# PC13 unit test

1 Why is it important for a play setting to offer a good environment?
2 Explain some of the ways in which adults can meet children's basic needs.
3 How might playworkers be able to find out about particular children's needs?
4 Why is it important for children to take ownership of their play environment?
5 List three ways in which playworkers can encourage children to make suggestions.
6 Why is it important for playworkers to promote positive images actively in the play setting?
7 Why are visual images powerful ones?
8 Give an example of a play activity that has been traditionally stereotyped. Explain how you might encourage *all* children to participate.
9 Why is it important that playworkers act as positive role models?
10 List two ways in which playworkers might act as positive role models.

# Unit PC 14

# Promote and maintain the health and safety of children

All adults working with children have a responsibility to keep them healthy and safe. In playwork settings this means that we have to be aware of potential hazards, develop emergency and health and safety policies, and be able to respond appropriately in the event of an accident or emergency. Playworkers also have a role in helping children to maintain their own health and safety outside the setting. The elements for this unit are:

PC14.1  Maintain children's safety during play
PC14.2  Ensure the safety of the play environment
PC14.3  Respond to injuries and signs of illness
PC14.4  Follow emergency procedures
PC14.5  Promote children's personal safety outside the play environment

## Element PC14.1  Maintain children's safety during play

Whilst children are in your care, you have a duty to keep them safe. As part of this role, you must help them play in safety and be able to supervise them carefully. This section looks at the ways in which you can maintain children's safety as they play. It also looks at the legal duty that you have in relation to health and safety.

### WHAT YOU NEED TO LEARN

■ Monitoring children during play
■ Dealing with hazards and incidents

## Legislation relating to health and safety

### The Health and Safety Act 1974

The main piece of legislation that affects the day-to-day provision of health and safety in workplaces is the Health and Safety Act 1974. Settings have a duty to comply with this Act, and any further regulations that have been added since. Work settings cannot plead that they did not know of the regulations: it is essential that senior staff keep up to date in their knowledge of this Act. You can check current regulations by contacting the government agency responsible, which is the Health and Safety Executive. (Their address is given in Useful addresses on page 325.)

The Act gives duties both to employers and to employees.

### Duty of employers

Essentially the Act requires that employers ensure that they are providing a safe work environment, and that they provide training and equipment, and produce health and safety policies.

Employers employing more than five people must also carry out a risk assessment on their premises, and write a safety policy that explains how the risks are to be minimised.

### Duty of employees

The Act makes it clear that employees must follow the setting's health and safety policies, and use the safety equipment and protection provided. It also makes it clear that employees must not place either themselves or others at risk of harm as a result of their actions.

## Other legislation

The table below shows other regulations that affect the provision of health and safety in settings.

| Regulation | Duty of the setting |
|---|---|
| **Control of Substances Hazardous to Health Regulations (COSHH) 1994** | Many settings use chemicals or materials that are potentially hazardous, such as bleach and cleaning materials. The COSHH regulations require settings to list the hazards and consider how they will minimise the risks. For example, cleaning materials should be stored in a locked cupboard. |
| **Reporting of Injuries, Diseases and Dangerous Occurrences Regulations (RIDDOR) 1995** | Workplaces must provide an accident report book. All accidents must be recorded in the book. Most settings keep separate books for staff and children. Any injuries to an employee that means that he or she cannot work for three or more days must be reported to the Health and Safety Executive. |
| **Fire Precautions (Workplace) Regulations 1997** | Settings should have plans for evacuation and procedures in the event of a fire. Alarm systems should be in place and fire drill should be carried out regularly. Signs showing what to do in the event of a fire should be placed in every room. |
| **Health and Safety (First Aid) Regulations 1981** | There is a legal duty for employers to keep a first-aid box and to appoint at least one person to be responsible in the event of an accident. |
| **Children Act 1989** | This Act was wide-ranging and gave several duties to local authorities. Under the Act, settings that care for children under 8 years old for more than 2 hours must be registered and inspected. As part of the inspection, health and safety arrangements must be checked. |

## Supervising children during play

One important way in which we can help children be safe is by supervising them as they play. This is a way of preventing accidents and incidents that might be potentially dangerous. There are different ways of supervising children, depending on the play situation; these might be seen as levels of supervision.

*General supervision tends to be low-key monitoring*

### General supervision

This tends to be low-key, and in some ways could be thought of as monitoring rather than supervising. Children remain free to explore their environment, take 'safe' risks, and be active in their play.

### Close supervision

This type of supervision is more focused as the playworker is nearer to the children. Most playworkers find that if they are not involved themselves in an activity, they can walk around and talk to children as they play. This allows them to assess the potential risks and hazards, while still allowing children to control their play.

### Constant supervision

This type of supervision is often used when there are particular dangers to be monitored, or children who need extra support. Constant supervision should not make children feel 'watched', but they should feel supported. This will often mean that you will be involved in the play activity alongside the children.

However closely involved you are with a particular child or group of children, you should still be aware of other play activities and children around you. This is especially important if there are many children in the setting, and if the other adults are also directly involved with children. One practical way of doing this is to consider your body position: try to put yourself where you have the best possible view of what is happening around you.

## Supervision ratios

The supervision ratio is the number of adults relative to the number of children. Supervision ratios can vary from local authority to local authority, and play settings will be advised of ratios when they apply for registration. It is common to have a 1:6 or 1:8 ratio with children aged over 5 years but under 8 years.

Play settings that only look after children over 8 years, or that provide less than two hours of care, do not have to register with the social services, and this means that they do not have to work to fixed ratios. It is advisable, however, to adhere to a minimum ratio of 1:8. The supervision ratios will need to be altered if children are taken out of the setting, and although a ratio of 1:6 is normally considered acceptable, it is advisable to work on a ratio of 1:4.

There should also be a minimum of two adults at any time, so that if an emergency occurs, one adult can seek help while the other remains with the children.

## Active knowledge ✔

1  *What is the staff ratio in your setting?*
2  *Is your setting registered with social services?*
3  *When outings are organised in your setting, what staff–child ratio is used?*

## What to look out for when supervising play

Most playworkers develop a sixth sense when supervising children. They can often tell by the noise level or the quality of sound when there might be a potential problem. Play that is working well is generally noisy and lively but purposeful, whereas loud, angry voices or very excited voices might indicate the need for close monitoring. By being able to recognise the indications of potential hazards and checking on children's play, you should be able to prevent accidents or incidents of unwanted behaviour simply by walking over and talking to the children.

Below are some of the key indicators that a closer look at the way children are playing might be needed.

### Equipment being used inappropriately
Many children will think of ways of using equipment creatively in their play, for example they may choose to go down slides on their stomachs, or to use benches as home bases. Using equipment creatively should generally be encouraged, provided that children are not damaging the equipment or putting themselves or others at risk. It is always a good idea to look closely at the ways in which equipment is being used, however, in case there is a potential danger. Common dangers include using ropes as harnesses in play, or using sticks as weapons.

### Loud, angry voices
These might indicate that children are finding it difficult to co-operate and need some adult input to solve an immediate problem. It is always a good idea to react quickly: angry voices can lead to aggressive behaviour.

### Over-excited cries
When children are very excited, their bodies produce more adrenaline. This extra adrenaline can make it harder for them to evaluate any risks that they are taking, or to

consider how their actions might affect others. This means that it is wise to interpret cries of excitement as a possible danger signal – go over to see what the children are doing. In many cases children will be playing safely and you will not need to intervene, but you might decide to stay nearby.

### Children's expressions and body language

Playworkers are sometimes able to pick up on a potential problem by looking at children's expressions. Furtive or secretive looks can sometimes mean that children are about to do something that might be harmful in some way, for example an older child might be thinking about going off to have a cigarette. As well as monitoring the activities that children are engaged in, it is also a good idea to think about their body language and their facial expressions.

*Furtive behaviour can conceal harmful activities*

### Consolidation

Think about a time recently when you supervised children's play.

◆ *What type of supervision was needed?*

## Encouraging children to be responsible for their own and others' safety

One of the skills in supervising children's play is to avoid giving the feeling to children that they are being 'watched'. This feeling inhibits children's play, and can cause older children to feel very resentful. One way of avoiding this is by involving children and encouraging them to be responsible for their own and others' safety. As in other contexts, you can involve them in setting some ground rules.

## Ways in which ground rules can be set

Depending on the circumstances, ground rules can be set in different ways, for example at the start of an activity, or when new children join the activity. (See page 138 for further information about the benefits of ground rules.)

There are different ways of setting ground rules with children, including:

- discussion in small groups
- discussion with all the children in the setting.

And there are different stages at which such rules may be set:

- at the start of an activity
- during an activity, if children are playing in unexpected ways
- after an incident
- when new children join the activity
- when new children come into the setting.

## Helping children to take responsibility

There might be times when an older child will be interested in monitoring and organising the play of younger children in a setting which will allow them to take on some responsibility.

You can also help children to feel responsible during a play activity by asking them if they can work out for themselves the potential dangers of the activity that they are engaged in. This means that they can think about what they are doing and devise their own strategies for making it safe.

## Case study

The children at a holiday playscheme have asked if they can make a water slide, as the weather is hot. Look at these two different responses.

*Response A*
PLAYWORKER:  Well, I suppose you can, but I warn you that if you are not playing safely, I will have to ask you to stop. That means no messing around, no pushing, and no waving the hosepipe around. If I see any of that, I will turn the water off and you will have to go inside. Is that agreed?

*Response B*
PLAYWORKER:  That sounds like a good idea, but before we can get out the equipment, we will have to think about how we can make this a safe activity. I have known children get quite bad bruises and knocks unless there are some rules. If I tell you what the main dangers are, can you think about how we can manage these fairly?

1 **Which response is more likely to help children take responsibility for their safety and actions?**
2 **Why is it important to explain the potential safety hazards to children before an activity starts?**

# Risks and hazards

A *hazard* is a situation which creates a 'real' risk, for example a hole in the floor is a hazard, which creates the risk of a fall. Most hazards need managing immediately – in this case, the floor will have to be mended.

A *risk* is a potential danger which might or might not happen. There are different levels of risk: for example the risk of falling through a hole in the floor is high, but the risk of an aircraft falling onto the setting is low.

Playworkers need to be able to identify hazards and deal with them while children are playing. They also need to look at the way in which children are playing, and consider the risks.

## Anticipating potential problems

Accidents and incidents of unwanted behaviour can happen very quickly: you must be able to identify hazards rapidly. In many cases this means being able to predict the likely outcome of a situation – for example, if you can see that a group of children are shouting encouragement to a child who is climbing over a fence to collect a ball, you might predict that the child might fall, or run into the road, or damage the fence. In some cases, you may also recognise that the use of certain pieces of equipment, if not carefully supervised, might be hazardous, including paddling pools, skipping ropes, and bats.

Hazards can also come from the environment. In order to spot these type of hazards promptly, it is useful if you have a good understanding of the risks unique to your setting. Is there a main road nearby? Are there dustbins? Is there an access gate? Be aware also of the general state of the equipment being used.

Places where the general public have access can pose potential risks, too, for example in a public park there might be danger from dogs, or litter that has been dropped, as well as from strangers.

### Identifying hazards correctly

You need to be able to identify hazards correctly. It is frustrating for children to have their play stopped if they are actually playing in a safe way. To avoid this happening, if you are not sure whether there is a hazard or not, go over and watch how the children are playing for a moment. Loud, excited voices may just indicate that the children are having fun, rather than being in danger.

### Dealing with hazards

Once a hazard has been identified, it is essential that quick action is taken. This might mean stopping the children's play temporarily while you deal with the hazard (see also the table on page 191). If individual children's behaviour is putting either themselves or others in danger, you might need to talk to them about the risk they are posing (see page 192).

## Reporting incidents

It is always a good idea to report incidents to colleagues or in some cases to your line manager. If an incident needs following up later, or if there is a possibility of the hazard recurring, they will know about it. (For example, there might be several wasps around a waste bin in the park, or a particular child might be acting rather aggressively.) When reporting incidents, say how you dealt with the situation and if any further action is needed. Minor incidents will be reported verbally, but major incidents must be recorded.

You should *always* report and record *accidents*, and the setting should keep an accident book. Other incidents that need noting down might be kept in a log, or in a way that has been agreed by the setting. Writing down incidents provides a record for the future, which may later prove very useful.

---

### Consolidation

In the summer, Smiley's Playscheme uses the local park to provide opportunities for outside play. Recently the playworkers have had to keep moving the children away from one of the play areas, because there are wasps around an overflowing litter bin. The manager has phoned the council to complain about this, and has been told that the litter bins are regularly emptied and checked. The manager has decided to start recording each time the bins are full and there is a hazard from the wasps.

◆ *Why is it a good idea to keep a note of this information?*
◆ *How might this information be used?*
◆ *Design a form that staff could use to record this information.*

---

## Element PC14.2 Ensure the safety of the play environment

As well as supervising children as they play, we need also to look at the risks within the play environment and make sure that we can minimise these.

*What hazards can you spot here?*

- Monitoring the play environment for risks
- Carrying out health and safety checks
- Taking action to prevent harm

## Types of hazard

There are many different types of hazard that we need to be aware of in the play environment. Some hazards are visible, such as broken equipment; others are less obvious, such as a blocked fire exit or the risk of food poisoning from food that is not stored properly. Although you can carry out some checks at the start of sessions, many hazards and dangers emerge as sessions proceed, so you need to pay constant attention to possible hazards.

The table below shows some of the main dangers that might be present in play environments and looks at ways of preventing them.

| Danger | Causes | Ways of prevention |
|---|---|---|
| **Falls** | Falling off equipment<br>Slipping on floors, mats or off equipment | Keep the setting tidy<br>Make sure children know the ground rules before they use equipment<br>Check that equipment is safe and secure |
| **Cuts and bruises** | Broken equipment<br>Overcrowding in areas<br>Children engaged in unsuitable activities | Supervise children well<br>Regularly check equipment for faults |
| **Poisoning** | Cleaning fluids or other chemicals being left out<br>Children experimenting with drugs and other substances | Store cleaning materials and other hazardous substances correctly<br>Supervise children well<br>Help children to be aware of ways to keep themselves safe |
| **Food poisoning** | Food being served at incorrect temperature<br>Poor hygiene when preparing food<br>Incorrect storage of food | Make sure that staff who handle food have been on food-handling courses<br>Ensure good overall cleanliness in all areas of the setting, especially in kitchen and toilet areas |
| **Burns and scalds** | Temperature of water in taps too high<br>Poor supervision in kitchen areas<br>Children experimenting with lighters or matches | Ensure regular maintenance of central heating and water systems<br>Supervise children well<br>Help children to be aware of ways to keep themselves safe |
| **Infection** | Poor hygiene procedures, especially in the toilets or the kitchen<br>Lack of ventilation | Use posters to remind children and others to wash their hands<br>Help children to become aware of ways to keep themselves healthy<br>Dispose of tissues and other products safely<br>Use disposable gloves when handling bodily fluids<br>Check ventilation in the setting |

## Assessing risks

No environment will ever be risk-free. You need to strike a balance between the needs of the children to play and their right to be safe.

When thinking about the activities that you provide and that the children choose, you should consider the risks and decide how these can be minimised. Children will inevitably be taking some risks in order to be able to explore and play freely – for example, climbing up a tree has an element of risk: the child might fall! A playworker needs therefore to be able to assess the risks and provide a safe environment, without being over-protective. This allows the children to learn to take 'safe risks', and to gain confidence and independence.

### Active knowledge ✔

Look at the following list, and consider what the potential risks might be:

- a visit to the local park
- children playing rounders
- putting out a paddling pool for splashing around in
- going to the local swimming pool.

1  *How high are these risks?*
2  *How can the risks be managed?*

### Routine health and safety checks

One way in which we can minimise unacceptable risks is by carrying out regular checks on the environment and the equipment. This should also include looking at the cleanliness of areas such as the toilets and the kitchen. Some settings devise checklists in order to help staff remember what areas in particular they should be concentrating on.

#### *Outdoor checks*

Any outdoor play area should be checked before it is used, on a session by session basis. It is often harder to maintain cleanliness and safety outside; for example animals such as dogs and birds can easily enter such areas and foul them. Some settings also have problems with vandalism or misuse of property, which again means that outdoor areas have to be checked.

The table below shows the types of checks that might need to be carried out.

| Area | Checks to be made |
|---|---|
| **Grass areas** | Look out for evidence of animal faeces, litter, broken glass, and areas of the grass that might be slippery. |
| **Concrete areas** | Look out for litter, and uneven areas which might cause children to fall over. |
| **Large equipment** | Check for signs of rusting, metal fatigue or cracking plastic. Make sure that the equipment is stable, especially climbing frames. |
| **Bikes and other equipment that moves** | Check brakes, steering and overall condition. Make sure that protection such as knee and elbow pads is available for activities such as rollerblading or skateboards. |
| **Litter bins** | Make sure that these are not overflowing, and that there is no litter dropped around them. Empty them if necessary. In summer, look out for wasps |
| **Fencing** | Consider whether there are any gaps which might pose problems, either by children leaving the site or by strangers entering. Check that fencing is secure as children are likely to lean against it. |

### Indoor checks

The indoor setting should be carefully checked at the start of each session. In most settings, staff take equal responsibility for making sure the environment is suitable for children's play. Some settings are able to pay cleaners and caretakers, which means that the routine cleaning and maintenance is done for them.

| Area | Checks to be made |
|---|---|
| **Flooring** | Make sure that floors are clean. Look out for rugs or carpets that are not firmly attached to the floor. |
| **Electrical appliances** | Make sure that these are checked annually. Look out for overloaded sockets, and for trailing flexes – these might cause children and others to fall over |
| **Kitchen areas** | Kitchens should be clean. Check regularly that the temperature is correct inside fridges and freezers. Throw away any food that has been incorrectly stored. |
| **Toilet areas** | These should be cleaned and checked regularly during sessions. Make sure that soap and paper towels are provided. Make sure that waste bins are provided and are regularly emptied. Check that there are bags and bins for the disposal of sanitary towels. |
| **First-aid kits** | A first-aid kit should be placed in the kitchen, and another in an area such as the staff room or the office. Check the first-aid kits regularly. |
| **Temperature, ventilation and lighting** | Check that the room is well ventilated. Never block ventilation vents: they prevent potentially dangerous build-up of gases. Check the lighting and temperature of room. Acceptable temperatures are between 17° C and 22° C. |
| **Equipment** | Ensure that equipment is clean and in good repair. Store equipment carefully at the end of sessions. |

## Encouraging children to identify and report hazards

Encourage children to identify and report hazards in their environment. They will gain from doing this: sharing responsibility boosts their confidence, encourages them to be responsible for their own and others' safety, and makes them aware of health and safety. Children may also be able to spot hazards more quickly than you, because it is they who are actually using the equipment and playing in the environment.

To help children learn to identify the hazards in the environment, you will need to be a good role model. When you see a hazard yourself, talk about the way in which the hazard might cause a risk.

## Taking action to deal with hazards

Although you should always try to look out for hazards before children arrive in the play environment, there may still be times when you need to deal promptly with an unexpected hazard – for example, a glass might break on the floor.

Once a hazard has been recognised, quick action must be taken. In working quickly, you might be able either to prevent an accident or incident, or to limit the extent of it. In some cases, you will need to move children away from the area, in others you will need to remove the hazard.

| Hazard | Type of action that might be required |
|---|---|
| **Broken or damaged piece of equipment** | Immediate removal of piece of equipment if possible, or 'section off' the area or equipment |
| **Children's behaviour** | Intervene quickly but sensitively, using strategies outlined on page 145. |
| **Suspicious stranger** | Evaluate the risk. Consider moving the children away, or stay with the children. |
| **Weather** | Move children to shelter or shade. Avoid children being exposed to extremes of temperatures or being soaked. (Never shelter under a tree in a storm.) |
| **Dangerous item,** such as a hypodermic needle, a condom, broken glass, or dog faeces | Steer children away. If it is within the setting, you should arrange for it to be cleared away. (Always wear appropriate protection, wrap dangerous items up, and dispose of them appropriately.) |
| **Fire** | Evacuate the building according to your setting's procedures. |
| **Accident** | Follow the procedures of your setting (see also page 200). |

## Encouraging children to manage risks for themselves

Children need to learn how to manage risks – for example, when they are climbing, they need to be aware of how to minimise the risk of falling. Being able to manage risks gives children confidence and develops their independence.

One way in which you can help children to manage risks safely is by talking to them about the potential risks in the environment and encouraging them to think of strategies to manage the risks. For example, you might ask children what the risks are when they are cooking, and how they could minimise these. Playworkers need to be quite skilful in deciding to what extent a child is mature enough to minimise a risk, as the overall responsibility for the safety of children still rests with the playworker. Playworkers therefore need to spend time getting to know the children they are working with, and observing them in the play setting.

### Consolidation

◆ *Write down an example of how you encouraged children to think about risks in the play environment.*

◆ *How did you help them to think about ways of managing these?*

◆ *Why is it important that children learn to manage risks 'safely'?*

## Element PC14.3  Respond to injuries and signs of illness

As well as knowing how to avoid potential dangers and accidents, playworkers also need to know how to respond if children do have accidents or feel unwell. As you never know when or where a child might need first-aid treatment, it is a good idea for *all* adults working with children to attend a first-aid course and then keep their skills up to date. This section looks at the basic ways of responding to injuries and signs of illness.

### WHAT YOU NEED TO LEARN

- Protecting casualties and others from harm
- Summoning qualified assistance
- Providing reassurance and comfort
- Reporting incidents

### Responding to an accident

In situations where you are the first adult to arrive on the scene, it will be important that you are able to keep calm and respond appropriately. The flow chart below shows the steps involved in responding to an accident.

1. **Keep calm**
   - This reassures children and helps them to follow your instructions.
   - It prevents further accidents.
   - It allows you to assess the situation more accurately and make the right decisions.

2. **Look out for any further dangers**
   - What was the cause of the accident? Is this still a danger?
   - Do other children need to be evacuated?
   - Does the casualty need to be removed to prevent further injury?

3. **Assess the extent of the injury**
   - Is the child breathing, talking?
   - Can you see bleeding?
   - Is the child in great pain?

4. **Decide on the type of help required** (see tables on major and minor injuries)
   - Is emergency help required?
   - Is a first-aider's assistance required?

5. **Summon help**
   - Is it safe to ask one of the other children to get help?
   - Can help be summoned by calling out?
   - Is there a telephone or other means of getting help?

*Responding to an accident*

## When emergency help is required

You may need to seek emergency help as a priority, unless the first-aider is present with you; ideally you should summon both, as the first-aider may be able to take some immediate action.

The list below shows situations in which emergency help *must* be summoned.

- the child has stopped breathing
- you cannot find a pulse
- the child has difficulty in breathing, or is turning blue
- the child is vomiting blood
- the child is unconscious
- the child is bleeding profusely.

## Summoning help

At times, a child needs medical attention. This might mean getting help from the first-aider in your setting, or summoning the emergency services. If you cannot leave the casualty, call out for help or, if safe, ask another child to seek assistance. In most cases, another adult should be with or near you.

### Active knowledge ✔

1  Who are the qualified first-aiders in your setting?
2  Where is the first-aid kit?
3  Where is the nearest telephone in the setting?

## Providing reassurance and comfort

When children are feeling unwell or have had an accident, you can help by giving them plenty of reassurance and by providing a calm atmosphere for them. Remember that other children in the setting who have witnessed the accident, or who have noticed that the child is ill, will also be worried. They too need reassurance, and praise for remaining calm.

It may be helpful to explain to the casualty and the other children what exactly is going to happen. For example: 'What we have to do now is just wait for a minute or so, to see whether you are going to be sick again. Sometimes being sick is nature's way of telling us that you need to slow down or that you have eaten something that doesn't agree with you.' Explaining in a positive way helps children understand the situation, which can make it less frightening.

Young children may also need some physical comfort: you can offer this by holding their hands or sitting near them. Unless absolutely necessary, you must stay with the casualty, or the child who is feeling unwell, so that she or he feels less frightened.

## Reporting to the qualified assistant

When help arrives, it is important that you provide clear, accurate information. The type of information required will depend on the accident or illness. If you are unsure about any aspect of the information you are giving, always say so.

### Information that might be needed

You will need to be able to supply information such as this:

- the cause of the accident
- the location of the accident
- the time of the accident
- the symptoms of the illness
- any obvious signs of injury
- the age of the child
- any known allergies or existing medical conditions, such as diabetes or asthma
- the emergency contact number of the parent or carer
- the doctor's name and address.

## Keeping calm and following the organisation's procedures

It is important that you keep calm throughout the incident, and follow your organisation's procedures. Time can be wasted and children can be left feeling insecure if these procedures are not followed. For example, if a child's parents need to be contacted, to avoid confusion the right person from the setting needs to do this. In some settings this will be the manager, in others it might be the person who is attending to the child.

## Active knowledge ✔

1  In the event of an emergency, who has responsibility for contacting parents?
2  Where are the emergency contact numbers stored?
3  What emergency procedures are in place in the event of a medical emergency?

## NEWTOWN PLAY CLUB
**Emergency contact sheet**

**Emergency Contact Sheet**

Name of child ................................................................. Date of birth ....../......./.................

Name of family doctor ..........................................................................................

Address and phone number ...................................................................................

..............................................................................................................................

Allergies/Medication...............................................................................................

**Contacts**
Please write below the names of 3 people who could be contacted in the event of an emergency.

| Name.............................. | Name.............................. | Name.............................. |
|---|---|---|
| Address ............................. | Address ............................. | Address ............................. |
| ........................................ | ........................................ | ........................................ |
| Phone number ...................... | Phone number | Phone number |
| Relationship to child | Relationship to child | Relationship to child |
| ........................................ | ........................................ | ........................................ |

*An emergency contact sheet*

## Informing parents and carers about accidents or illnesses

As well as being good practice to keep parents and carers informed about the health of their children, most children in emergencies want to see their parents or carers. This shows how important it is that emergency contact numbers for all the children you work with are accurate and up to date.

When telephoning parents or carers, it is important to stay calm. Tell them carefully about what is happening to their child, and what they need to do. Tell them where their child is, and the telephone number either of the setting or the place to which the child has been taken.

Minor injuries also need to be reported to parents and carers. Most settings do this at the end of the day. Many settings have prepared slips which tell the parents and carers briefly about the incident, and the treatment if any that has been given. Giving parents and carers this information is essential in case the child's state of health deteriorates later on – for example, a bump on the head could later bring on concussion.

## Reporting accidents

All settings are required to have accident books. To conform with the Health and Safety Act 1974, there should be a separate one for staff and visitors into the setting. Settings also have a duty to notify the Health and Safety Executive of any accidents that result in a member of staff requiring time off work or medical attention. Accident books are also checked annually when registration is renewed.

It is a good idea to look at the accident book regularly, in case a pattern of accidents can be detected. It might be that accidents tend to occur around the same time of day or in particular areas of the setting. If so, this could indicate a hidden hazard, or that there needs to be a change in the amount of supervision or in the layout.

---

### Accident/Incident Report (child)

Name of child: *Ben Lewis*

Date of birth: *11·2·89*

Date of accident: *24·8·00*   Time of accident: *9·10 am*

Brief details including any injury sustained:
*Ben tripped over the door step whilst coming in from the garden, causing him to topple over and bump his chin on the ground causing redness and a graze to his chin.*

Action taken by member(s) of staff:
*Cold compress and reassurance*

Signed (staff): *L. Largoni*   Signed (parent): *A Lewis*

Date: *24·8·00*   Date: *24·8·00*

RIDDOR Form (F2508) completed:   Yes/No

Signed off by a member of staff: *S. Cox*   Date: *24·8·00*

---

*An accident book*

## Types of minor injuries that children might have

The table below shows the types of common injuries that children might sustain, and the suggested treatment for these. Wherever possible, always get a qualified first-aider's assistance. If you are concerned that the injury might be serious, seek emergency help.

| Injury | Treatment | Check for |
|---|---|---|
| **Bump to the head** | Apply cotton wool squeezed in cold water. If the bump is bad, apply wrapped crushed ice. | Drowsiness, vomiting or headaches: these might indicate concussion. *Seek emergency help immediately.* |
| **Nosebleed** | Tip the head forward. Pinch the bridge of the nose and apply a wet or cold tissue. | Continued bleeding or blood mixed with clear fluid. *Seek emergency help immediately.* |
| **Grazed skin** | Rinse the wound with cold running water. Allow it to heal in the open air. | Check for any debris, such as broken glass. *Seek medical help if the debris is difficult to remove.* |
| **Bruises and trapped fingers** | Apply cotton wool squeezed in cold water | Gently feel the area to check for bumps that might indicate a fracture. *If necessary seek emergency help.* If a child feels unwell and shows you bruises, consider whether this could be meningitis. Test bruises by putting a glass on top of them: if the marks still show under the glass, *seek emergency help urgently.* |
| **Vomiting** | Do not leave the child unattended. Try to work out the cause of vomiting. Give small sips of water. | Get help if the vomiting is persistent or if it occurs after a bump to the head. *If there is any blood in the vomit, seek help.* |
| **Insect stings** | Reassure the child. Do not squeeze the sting. Seek help to remove the sting. | If the sting is in the mouth or if the child starts to have difficulty in breathing, *seek urgent emergency help.* Some children are allergic to stings. |

# Identifying illnesses

As well as being able to respond to accidents, you also need to be able to identify children who are feeling unwell. Knowing children well is an advantage: you will often tell from their behaviour or skin colour that they are 'not themselves'. In many cases, you will see the signs that children are incubating an illness before it actually emerges.

The diagram below shows some of the signs that children might show if they are becoming unwell.

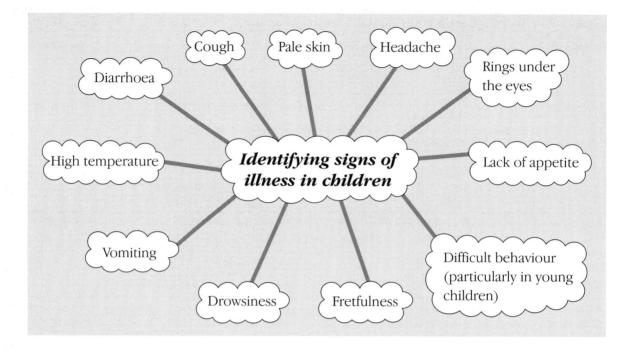

## Infectious diseases

When a child is identified as having an infectious disease, take steps to prevent any infection from spreading, and give the child necessary treatment.

The table below shows ways in which you can help to prevent a spread of infections in settings.

| Action | Reason |
|---|---|
| Move the sick child away from other children | To prevent infections from spreading in the air or through physical contact |
| Use tissues and paper towels | To prevent cross-infection |
| Carefully dispose of tissues, paper towels or other materials containing bodily waste | To prevent cross-infection |
| Keep the setting well ventilated | To prevent infections from spreading – bacteria and viruses flourish in warm stale air |
| Use disposable gloves | To avoid infection and cross-infection |
| Cover any open cuts and grazes | To avoid infection entering the skin |
| Wash and sterilise any equipment that is used, such as buckets | To avoid cross-infection |

## Common illnesses

It is helpful if playworkers are aware of some common illnesses, as shown in the table opposite. It is particularly important to be able to recognise those, such as meningitis, for which children might require emergency treatment.

| Illnesses | Incubation period | Symptoms | Action | Treatment |
|---|---|---|---|---|
| **Common cold** | 1–3 days | Running or blocked-up nose, headache, tiredness, temperature | If a child feels unwell, contact the parents/carers. Make sure that disposable tissues are being used. | Rest; plenty of fluids. |
| **Chicken pox** (varicella) | 10–14 days. Children can return to the setting once the scabs have all dried | Groups of red spots with raised white centres that become itchy, on trunk and limbs. Slight fever. | Contact parents/carers immediately. Separate the child from other children. | Rest; calamine lotion. |
| **Ear infection** | | Pains (earache and/or headache), sometimes vomiting. | Contact parents/carers immediately, as the child will need to see a doctor. | Antibiotics; rest. |
| **Food poisoning** | 30 minutes–36 hours. | Diarrhoea, vomiting. | Contact parents/carers immediately. Separate the child from other children. Try to find out the source of the food poisoning. Everyone should wash their hands scrupulously. | Fluid only. |
| **Gastroenteritis** | If caused by bacteria, 7–14 days. If caused by a virus, 30 minutes–36 hours. | Nausea, diarrhoea, vomiting. | Contact parents/carers immediately. Separate the child from other children. Pay great attention to hand-washing and hygiene procedures in setting. Disinfect toys and equipment. | Rest; increased fluid intake. |
| **German measles** | 14–21 days. | Mild symptoms, including a pink rash on the head, a sore throat, and slight fever. | Contact parents/carers immediately. Separate the child from other children. Make sure that there is no contact between the child and pregnant women. | Rest if needed. |
| **Measles** | 8–14 days. | Koplik spots appear on the mouth and on the inner cheek before the main rash appears. Fever, runny eyes and a cough are followed by a red blotchy rash. | Contact parents/carers immediately. Separate the child from other children. | Rest; plenty of drinks. |
| **Meningitis** (viral and bacterial) | 2–14 days (variable) | Fever, severe headache, nausea, stiff neck, and a blotchy skin rash that can look like bruises. Drowsiness and dislike of light. Symptoms appear very rapidly and the child quickly feels very unwell. | Press a glass against the bruise-like marks. If they do not blanch or fade with the pressure, seek urgent medical help. *This disease is life-threatening!* Contact parents/carers immediately. Separate the child from other children. | Urgent hospitalisation; treatment with antibiotics. |
| **Mumps** | 14–21 days | Fever, headache, difficulty in swallowing; swollen face and glands in the neck. | Contact parents and carers immediately. Separate the child from other children. | Rest; plenty of fluids. |
| **Tonsillitis** | 14–21 days | Fever, headache, difficulty in swallowing, and a very sore throat. | Contact parents/carers immediately. Separate the child from other children. | Antibiotics; rest. |
| **Whooping cough** (pertussis) | 7–21 days | Spurts of violent coughing with the child taking deep breaths and making the 'whoop' sound. | Contact parents/carers immediately. Reassure the child, as this is very frightening. Separate the child from other children. | Antibiotics; rest; reassurance. |

## Case study

May keeps complaining of a headache. She is looking very pale and is becoming more upset, losing energy and looking generally unwell. She is also complaining of feeling sick.

1 *What action should be taken?*
2 *What could be the possible causes?*
3 *Why is it important to take immediate action when children complain of feeling unwell?*

## Element PC14.4 Follow emergency procedures

All settings need procedures to be used in emergencies. Procedures help everyone in the setting to react calmly and efficiently in the event of an emergency. In some cases, being able to follow procedures quickly might be life-saving. It is important that everyone in the setting is aware of procedures, and that practices are carried out from time to time.

## WHAT YOU NEED TO LEARN

- Informing others of emergency procedures
- Following procedures, and maintaining others' safety
- Reporting incidents, and recommending necessary changes to procedures

## Informing people of emergency procedures

Ideally everyone in the play setting, including the children, should be aware of the emergency procedures to be followed in the event of the building needing to be evacuated, if there is a security incident, or if a child or adult is missing.

Most settings use three main methods to make sure that people are aware of what they should do:

- signs and notices
- verbal explanations
- drills and practices.

### Signs and notices

Good signs and notices help people to know what to do if a building needs to be evacuated. To be useful, signs should be well displayed and eye-catching. The language used should be simple and easy to understand. It is good practice to put instructions about evacuation in every room.

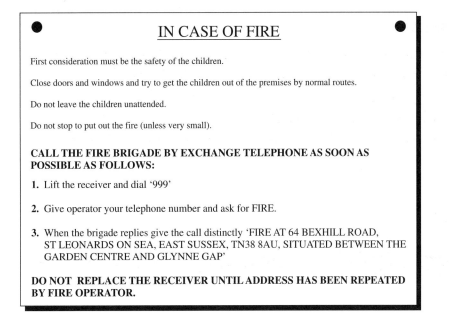

IN CASE OF FIRE

First consideration must be the safety of the children.

Close doors and windows and try to get the children out of the premises by normal routes.

Do not leave the children unattended.

Do not stop to put out the fire (unless very small).

**CALL THE FIRE BRIGADE BY EXCHANGE TELEPHONE AS SOON AS POSSIBLE AS FOLLOWS:**

**1.** Lift the receiver and dial '999'

**2.** Give operator your telephone number and ask for FIRE.

**3.** When the brigade replies give the call distinctly 'FIRE AT 64 BEXHILL ROAD, ST LEONARDS ON SEA, EAST SUSSEX, TN38 8AU, SITUATED BETWEEN THE GARDEN CENTRE AND GLYNNE GAP'

**DO NOT REPLACE THE RECEIVER UNTIL ADDRESS HAS BEEN REPEATED BY FIRE OPERATOR.**

*An evacuation notice*

## Fire signs

Special signs and symbols are used to indicate fire exits and the route to be taken when evacuating. If you are responsible for these signs, make sure that your setting is using the latest symbols – text-only signs have been replaced. The fire safety officer is a good source of advice and can help you consider where signs should be placed.

*Signs indicating fire exits*

## Verbal explanations

As well as signs and notices, you should pass on verbal explanations. These are important, especially when there are new members of staff or adults in the setting. A verbal explanation can help people take in the information easily.

You can also tell *children* what they should do in the event of an emergency. This might be done at the start of a holiday playscheme, when children first come into a setting; or before a particular session, for example before children go out to the local park. It is important that children are given very clear messages about what they should do in the event of an emergency, and that you remind them from time to time.

## Consolidation

What would you tell the children to do in each of the following situations:

- if they heard a fire alarm while they were indoors
- if a stranger approached them while they were playing outdoors
- if they became separated from the rest of the group while on a trip.

*Write down what you would say in each case, and explain why these instructions are appropriate for your setting.*

### Drills and practices

Most settings hold regular fire drills and emergency procedure practices. This is one way of checking that the procedures would work well in the event of an emergency (see also page 206). When a procedure has been practised, it is followed more automatically in the event of a real emergency. Adults and children are less likely to panic, as they have already rehearsed the actions that they need to take. It is a good idea to hold a drill when there are several new members of staff, or when there are many new children in a setting.

If you are taking part in a drill or practice, show the children that you are taking the procedures seriously. Let them learn from your example that procedures are important. If you are responsible for arranging emergency procedure practices, try to simulate real life as much as possible. This might mean beginning the practice when one or two children are in the toilets, or when everyone is in the middle of an activity.

### Informing parents and carers

Parents and carers too should be aware of the emergency procedures in the setting. They will then know how their children would be cared for in the event of an emergency, and where they would be taken to. Parents and carers will also need to know whom they should contact and where they should go if an emergency occurs.

Many settings provide this information in a handbook or an information pack about the setting.

### Following emergency procedures – correctly, calmly and safely

Until a real emergency occurs, it is hard to know how one will react. If you are aware of and have practised emergency procedures thoroughly, however, you should be able to stay calm and act appropriately.

Staying calm allows you to assess the situation rationally, and to take decisions that are safe and appropriate. It is also essential that adults stay calm so that children see that someone is taking control of the situation: this will reassure them. The diagram below summarises the benefits of staying calm.

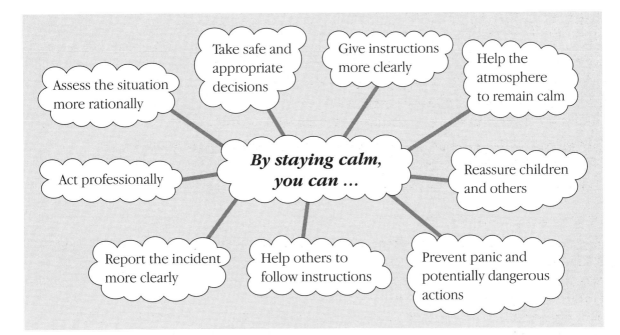

By staying calm, you can ...

- Assess the situation more rationally
- Take safe and appropriate decisions
- Give instructions more clearly
- Help the atmosphere to remain calm
- Act professionally
- Reassure children and others
- Report the incident more clearly
- Help others to follow instructions
- Prevent panic and potentially dangerous actions

*Following emergency procedures calmly can save lives*

## Active knowledge ✔

Look at the following situations.

- You are sitting down with the children, having a picnic lunch in the park. A man walks towards the group, stumbling and using aggressive language.
- The children are watching a video on the television. All of a sudden there is an almighty bang, the screen goes off and smoke pours from the set.
- At the swimming pool, you realise that you cannot see one of the children. You ask her friend, who says that when she last saw her she was going out to get some sweets.

1 *How would you deal with each of these situations? (Assume that there is another adult with you.)*
2 *Write down, in order, the actions that you would take.*

## Maintaining the safety of others

Throughout the emergency, you need to maintain the safety of the children and others while you are dealing with the incident. If a child has gone missing, for example, you still need to consider how to keep the rest of the children safe; or if there is a fire in the building, how to ensure that once outside the children will not be in any further danger during the arrival of police, ambulance and fire vehicles.

You need to think clearly about how to keep others safe while managing the incident. In most cases, you will have another adult with you, so one adult can supervise the children while the other manages the incident, for example reporting the fire or finding a colleague.

If you are *alone* in an emergency situation, making sure that the children are out of danger must be your first priority, however tempting it might be to try to deal directly with the incident.

## Getting help during the emergency

In many emergencies, you will need further assistance, either from colleagues or from others such as the fire or ambulance service. You will need to report accurately what has happened and to say what assistance is required.

In an emergency, some people find that their minds go 'blank'. To make this less likely, practise the reporting procedure. The key skills in reporting an emergency are these:

- Stay calm.
- Provide instructions so that the emergency services can find the location.
- Provide an accurate account of what has happened.
- Give details of the current state of incident, such as injuries, and the extent of any damage.
- Explain what assistance is needed.

## Contacting the emergency services

The emergency services have specially trained operators who guide callers through a series of questions in order to provide the right type of assistance quickly. They also want to establish the identity and location of the caller. The quickest way of getting help is to listen to the questions you are being asked and to respond to them carefully.

Details that are usually asked for include:

- your location
- your phone number
- your name
- the type of service required – police, ambulance, fire service, mountain rescue, coastguard, etc.
- the location of incident
- what has happened.

### Reporting a fire

When reporting a fire, in addition to the general questions that will be asked, you should also be ready to tell the operator more about the fire and its location, and whether there are still any people who have not been accounted for.

This information will help the fire service to know how they should approach the incident. (For example, if chemicals were involved, the crew would use breathing apparatus.) It is also helpful if you are able to tell the operator about the type of building, such as how many storeys it has, and where the fire has broken out. This will help the fire crew attack the fire efficiently.

### Reporting a security incident

A security incident may need some form of police assistance, although the police may also bring in back-up support such as an ambulance or the fire service. In addition to the general questions, the emergency operators might also ask for further information: for example, if the incident involved an intruder, you might be asked to provide a description of the person and details of this person's behaviour. If you have received a bomb threat, you might be asked to provide details about the call or message that you have received.

### Reporting missing persons

An incident involving missing persons might require the assistance of the police or a specific service such as mountain rescue, the coastguard, or the river police. In addition to the general information, you will also need to provide details about the person who is missing, including a description of his or her clothing, age and general appearance. You will also be asked when this person was last seen, and what arrangements had been made before she or he went missing.

## Contacting colleagues in the setting

During an emergency you might also have to summon help from or warn colleagues. This might mean using a telephone or simply calling out for help. In either case, you must be able to pass on information accurately. This is harder than reporting to the emergency operators – your colleagues will not be trained in handling emergency information! Speak clearly, and check that they are taking in the information you are giving them.

You might also need to give colleagues clear instructions, so that they know what they need to do.

For example, you might need a trained first-aider to stay with the injured child while you phone for the ambulance, or you might need someone to look after the other children while you look for a missing child.

## Following instructions in an emergency

You too will need to be able to follow instructions carefully. Those to whom you report the emergency may ask you to do something specific. For example, in the event of an intruder on the premises, you might be asked to observe the intruder at a distance, in order to report the intruder's current location. Similarly, in the event of a fire you might be asked to move the children to a different evacuation zone.

Listening to instructions is not always easy when you are under stress. One way of helping yourself to remember instructions is to repeat them back; another is to write them down.

## Evaluating emergency procedures

Most settings carry out practices from time to time, to check that their procedures are effective. Practices also help the adults and children in the setting to get used to reacting quickly and appropriately.

After a practice, review how effective the procedure has been. Are there any ways of improving upon it? During a practice, you may have noticed potential difficulties, or thought of a better way of carrying out the procedure – if so, make a note of this and then talk to your line manager, or the person responsible for the health and safety procedure in the setting.

It is also helpful to be aware of the types of difficulties that can reduce the effectiveness of emergency procedures.

## Potential difficulties

The tables below show some potential difficulties that might come to light during a practice of emergency procedures.

### *Evacuating a building (e.g. a fire or a bomb alert)*

| Problem | Possible causes | Potential danger |
|---|---|---|
| **Exits are obstructed** | There is furniture against the fire exits<br>The exits are locked<br>The exits are blocked by objects such as coats or pushchairs | This could cause a crush at an exit<br>This might expose people to danger for longer<br>People might become trapped within the building |
| **Alarms are not easily heard** | The alarm system's bells are not loud enough<br>Alarms are not installed throughout the building | Groups of children and adults might be slow to respond |
| **Evacuation is not very fast** | Children and adults in the setting need more practices<br>Children and adults are not taking the practice seriously<br>The procedures are not highly developed<br>The evacuation signs are not clear<br>Children and adults are unsure where to assemble<br>There is poor communication and instructions are unclear<br>The alarm is not being heard | Children and adults might become trapped in building |
| **Uncertainty about whether everyone is out of the building** | Assembly points are not clearly signed<br>Registers have not been taken out and checked<br>The signing-in and -out books have not been filled in<br>Adults and children are unsure of what to do when they reach the assembly point<br>The assembly point is unsuitable | A person might be left behind in the building |

## Missing persons

| Problem | Possible causes | Potential danger |
| --- | --- | --- |
| **A missing person is not quickly identified as being missing** | Registers have not been taken frequently enough<br>Children have not been counted<br>Signing-in and -out procedures have not been used<br>There is a breakdown in communication, with some staff assuming that others had responsibility for the child | It might be harder to find the child or adult after a time lapse |
| **No description of a missing person is available** | There is no photograph in the child's record<br>Staff have not fully observed the child or adult and have not noticed what she or he was wearing | Police and others searching will find it harder to identify the missing person |
| **An emergency contact is unavailable** | The emergency contact numbers have not been kept up to date<br>Only one contact number has been put down | The missing person might be trying to find emergency contact |
| **A missing person does not know what to do** | The missing person has not been told what to do in the situation<br>No meeting point has been arranged<br>A missing child does not know how to use a public telephone box to seek help | The missing person might put herself/himself in danger |

## Security incidents

| Problem | Possible causes | Potential danger |
| --- | --- | --- |
| **An unbadged visitor gains access to children in the building** | Doors have been left unlocked<br>There are too many access points into the building<br>Signing-in and -out procedures have not been used<br>Visitors have not been given badges<br>Staff did not challenge an 'unbadged' visitor about the purpose of her/his visit | The unbadged visitor could be a potentially dangerous intruder, or a parent who has not been given access to her/his child |
| **A stranger approaches children, either in a public place or in an outdoor area** | The setting's outdoor area has gaps in its fencing<br>Gates to the setting have been left unlocked<br>The adult–child ratio is not sufficient for the activity<br>Children have not been adequately supervised<br>Children have not been advised about talking to strangers<br>The children are wearing name badges | The stranger might persuade a child to go with her/him<br>The stranger might assault the child, verbally or physically<br>The stranger might be selling drugs |

## Element PC14.5 Promote children's personal safety outside the play environment

As well as maintaining children's safety while they are in your care, you also share some responsibility for keeping them safe when they are *outside* the play setting. There are many ways in which we can do this, including giving children advice, acting as a good role model, and being aware of the potential dangers in the vicinity of the setting.

### WHAT YOU NEED TO LEARN

- Identifying risks to children outside the play environment
- Seeking advice and guidance in evaluating possible risks
- Offering advice and guidance to children

### Finding out about possible risks

In order to be able to talk to children and to take active steps to prevent dangerous situations from arising, it is essential that you understand the nature and severity of the risks outside the play setting. Some risks are always prevalent, such as dangerous roads; but others depend on the area where the setting is located, for example a setting may be near to a layby used by drug leaders.

In addition, some risks are occasional ones, and to be aware of these you may need to keep in regular contact with other professionals and organisations, in order to keep up to date with possible dangers. Encouraging other professionals and organisations to keep in contact with us is good practice: it allows for an exchange of information and views. Some organisations are often quite keen to talk directly to children; they may employ education officers and liaison officers to work with other organisations that work with children. Contact with external organisations and professionals also allows playworkers to make sure that the advice and guidance they are giving is up to date and effective. Finally, it means that in an emergency, help and advice can be sought easily.

The table opposite shows types of risks that might face the children you work with, and ways in which you might be able to keep yourself informed of these dangers.

| Possible risks | Possible sources of information |
|---|---|
| **Extremes of weather conditions** | Local radio and television |
| **Suspicious strangers** | Police; child protection officers; other organisations such as schools |
| **Drug dealers, and availability of drugs in the local area** | Police, drug awareness officers |
| **Empty and disused buildings and houses** (children might have accidents if they played there) | Fire brigade; police; local council |
| **Railways** (children might play on the tracks or be tempted to throw objects onto the line) | Transport police; manager of local railway station |
| **Roads** (children might have to cross them or might wish to cycle along them to the setting) | Road safety officer |
| **Child abuse** | Kidscape; NSPCC helpline; local social services; child protection team |
| **Rivers, canals and sea** (children might be tempted to play near these) | Coastguard; water services |
| **An outbreak of an infection in the area** (such as meningitis) | Health visitor; local hospital |

## Evaluating the risks

Once you are aware of the risks that children in your setting might face, you will then need to consider how much of a threat each might pose. This should be done with other colleagues at a team meeting, or spontaneously if the risk comes suddenly to your attention.

Evaluating risks is not always easy, but factors that you might consider include the age of the children, and the distance between the setting and the source of the risk. Below is a list of questions to help you assess risks.

### How old are the children?
The age of the children will influence their ability to make appropriate judgements. Young children might be more at risk when crossing roads than older children, while older children might be more likely to use bicycles or be targeted by drug dealers.

### How well do you know the children?
If children are new to the setting or if you do not have much contact with them, it will be harder to know whether they have good common-sense or whether they are impulsive. Even so, knowing where they live and a little about their lifestyle might help you to assess the risk. For example, if there are reports of a suspicious person loitering, and if a child has a long walk alone from home to the play setting you might decide that this represents a sizeable risk, whereas a child who is dropped and picked up by a parent would be much less at risk.

### How well do you know the area?

If you are familiar with the area where children live and play, and know the local 'history', you will be better able to assess whether some risks are likely to be serious. For example, if you know that the local reservoir is an area where children have always played and that there is a warden nearby, you might see this as less of a risk than a stretch of canal where several accidents have taken place.

### How reliable is your information?

It is important to consider the sources of your information. You will need to make sure that your information is reliable, and this might sometimes mean checking further with other professionals. For example, a child might say that some of the older children are planning to play by the railway line. You might like to check first with a colleague where the railway line is, and then decide how to handle the situation.

If you consider that the risks are great, you should take some action, such as contacting an outside organisation, other professionals, or parents or carers. Playworkers have a professional duty to ensure the safety of children while *in* their care, but also a moral one to take reasonable care to protect them *outside* the setting.

## Obtaining guidance and advice

With some type of risks, it will be important to seek further guidance and advice. The table on page 209 shows organisations and other professionals who might be able to warn you about potential risks, and they might also be called upon to give you some professional advice. For example, if there were an outbreak of meningitis in a local school, you might need to consider the overall risk to children. This might mean telephoning the local hospital or medical services to find out more about how meningitis can be spread.

It is essential to call upon professional advice in some situations, to avoid the distress and anxiety caused by misinformation and rumour. If the children have heard that there is a suspicious person hanging around an area, it will be essential to contact the police to gain up-to-date advice and information.

## Sharing advice and guidance with others

If there is a potential risk to children, it is essential that everyone working in the setting knows what it is, and the advice that is being given to minimise it. This ensures that the advice given by different members of staff is always the same, so that children and parents receive a clear message. This helps to provide some reassurance. It also prevents a staff member from inadvertently causing a further problem, such as by allowing a child to go home when the parents are expecting to come to the setting to collect the child.

If it is not possible to pass guidance directly to others, look for other ways to pass it on, such as using a noticeboard in the staff area, or, in an emergency, telephoning staff members.

## Case study

During a routine visit to the play setting, a visitor mentions to the manager, Mandy, that later on in the afternoon there is to be a large demonstration outside the council offices nearby. She says that groups of people are already gathering, and that the police are beginning to close the roads.

Mandy talks to the other playworkers in the setting to discover whether anyone else has heard about this demonstration. It is decided that the demonstration could cause some parents difficulty in coming to get their children at the end of the day, and also that it would be unwise to allow children who normally walk to the setting to go home when there is a risk of them getting lost in the crowds or being frightened by the number of people.

1　*Where should Mandy get further information and advice about the demonstration?*
2　*Why is it important that all members of staff are kept informed of the situation?*
3　*Why might parents need to be contacted?*

## Making children aware of risks outside the play environment

Although you can take some steps yourselves to minimise the risks to children outside the play environment, this will not be enough in itself. One way in which you can help children to protect themselves is by encouraging them to learn about the risks in their environment. When they know about the risks, they can adopt strategies either to avoid them or to minimise them.

The diagram below shows some of the benefits to children of making them aware of the risks in their environment.

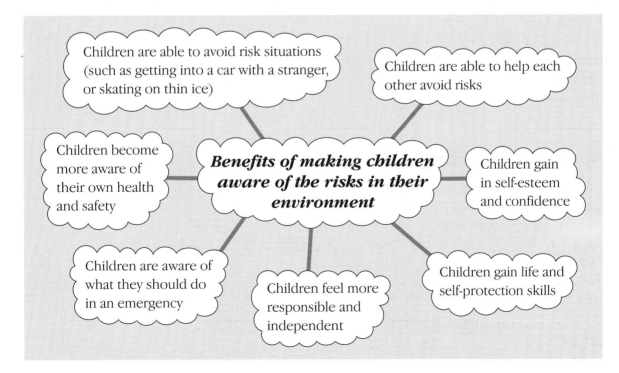

Children are able to avoid risk situations (such as getting into a car with a stranger, or skating on thin ice)

Children are able to help each other avoid risks

Children become more aware of their own health and safety

***Benefits of making children aware of the risks in their environment***

Children gain in self-esteem and confidence

Children are aware of what they should do in an emergency

Children feel more responsible and independent

Children gain life and self-protection skills

## Helping young children learn about strategies and risks

Although it is important to talk with children about the risks outside the play environment, it is also important not to frighten them or cause them to lose confidence. You need to be aware of how much information to give, and to make sure that it is appropriate to the children's age and stage of development.

Younger children may need very 'black and white' advice about what to do in a situation where a stranger approaches them or if they become lost. Young children can become confused if they are given different guidelines, so you might also consider talking to their parents or carers to make sure that the advice they receive is consistent.

The work you do in helping children to keep themselves safe should be ongoing: regular reminders often work better than occasional activities. This is particularly true for younger children.

## Encouraging older children to think about risks

When working with older children, it is a good idea to encourage them to take an active part in learning about the risks. Some settings do this by asking the older children to help the younger ones learn about the risks. They can produce songs, plays and posters, and contact and visit organisations involved with safety. Older children also need to be given opportunities to talk through any aspects of the risk that worry them, and to think about their own strategies to avoid them. Simply telling them about risks will not be effective.

It is also important to understand that some older children will be under peer pressure to join in activities that they know to be potentially dangerous, such as hanging around on railway lines, taking drugs, or under-age sex. Coping with peer pressure is not easy, so you need to help them identify strategies they can use to be assertive and resist pressure. You may help children by using role-plays or by simply listening and giving support. You can also help by making sure that they are aware of counselling services and advice lines such as Kidscape and Childline.

## Ways of making children aware of risks

There are many ways of making children aware of the risks in the environment. You may for example use posters, or invite in visitors to talk to the children. You could use:

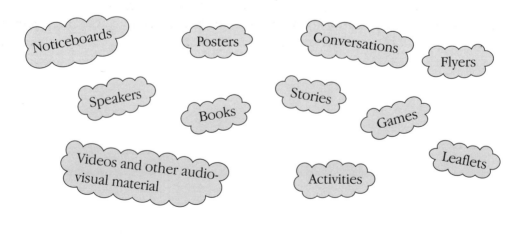

## Support from other organisations

Many organisations produce leaflets, stickers and posters designed to make children aware of the particular risks. The fire service, for example, produce packs for different age ranges, and will provide speakers to talk to children about fire prevention. Organisations are keen to work with play settings, and will often provide resources to help us make children aware of the risks and dangers.

There are also short courses in first-aid designed for young children, basic life-saving, and cycling proficiency. Such courses can provide children with interesting ways of learning about risks, whilst also gaining some useful life skills.

---

## Consolidation

Plan an activity that will help children learn about keeping safe.

◆ *Explain why you have chosen this topic.*
◆ *How will you make sure that it is suitable for the ages of children in your setting?*
◆ *How will you make sure that the information is up to date and relevant?*
◆ *If you are able to carry out the activity, explain what you learnt from doing this with the children.*

---

## PC14 unit test

1 What are the three different levels of supervising children?
2 What are the main pieces of legislation that affect health and safety requirements in settings?
3 Why is it important to set ground rules with children to ensure their safety?
4 Describe five checks that might be carried out in the play setting to ensure children's health and safety.
5 In the event of an accident in the play setting, what is the first thing that an adult arriving on the scene should do?
6 Why is it important to remain calm in an emergency?
7 Explain why regular practices of evacuation procedures are important.
8 Give one example of a potential difficulty during each of the following emergency procedures: fire; security incident; missing person.
9 Why is it important to have emergency contact numbers for parents and carers?
10 Describe three ways in which you might help children learn about risks outside the play environment.

# Unit PC 23

# Contribute to the protection of children from abuse

A sad but necessary part of working with children is keeping them safe from abuse. As a professional working with children, you need to recognise the signs of abuse, as well as knowing how to help children protect themselves from abuse.

The elements in this unit are:

PC23.1  Help children to protect themselves from abuse
PC23.2  Identify signs of possible abuse
PC23.3  Respond to a child's disclosure of abuse
PC23.4  Report possible abuse

You need to find out about your setting's child protection policies and procedures, and you should also consider attending child protection workshops.

## Element PC23.1  Help children to protect themselves from abuse

A good starting point when looking at child protection is to understand who the likely abusers of children are. Most cases of abuse against children are committed by people known to the children – often family members, including older siblings. In some cases, children are abused by people working with children, for example teachers, playworkers, or social workers.

It is important to understand that child abuse is not limited to particular 'types' of families or children. Abuse can occur in rich and poor families, to children in stable family structures as well as those whose family backgrounds are unsettled. All adults working with children in *every* setting need to help children keep safe.

This section looks at the way in which you can help children to protect themselves from abuse.

### WHAT YOU NEED TO LEARN

- Encouraging children to assert themselves
- Promoting children's sense of self-worth and self-esteem
- Encouraging children to feel good about and respect their bodies
- Informing children about potentially abusive situations
- Telling children how to respond to abuse

# Helping children to protect themselves from abuse

You and your colleagues can make sure that while children are with you, they are in a safe environment. But you need to think also about how you can help them keep themselves safe when they are *not* with you. This means looking at ways in which you can teach children to be confident about themselves, to know where they can get help and advice, and to avoid being in potentially dangerous situations.

The list below outlines the knowledge and skills that children need in order to help keep themselves safe from abuse:

- strategies to cope with bullying
- knowing how to deal with strangers
- understanding that they have a right to privacy
- learning to trust their own feelings and instincts
- learning to respect and value their bodies
- being aware of 'good' and 'bad' secrets
- knowing what to do if they are or someone else is being bullied or abused
- learning that it is all right to say 'no' to an adult.

To develop these skills and this knowledge, and to use them, children need to be confident and assertive.

# Helping children to be assertive

Victims of child abuse often say that they tried telling someone about what was happening to them, but no one seemed to listen to them or act on what was said, and they did not try and speak out again. It can take children great courage to speak out: abusers often exert terrific power and control over their victims. They may tell them that they will not be listened to, for instance, or that if they speak out, terrible things will happen to them. The only way in which we can help children protect themselves against this type of pressure is to give children enough confidence and strength to find a voice. This means that part of our role is to help children be assertive.

## What is assertive behaviour?

Assertiveness does not mean being aggressive, or constantly challenging authority or the system. What it *does* mean is having enough confidence to challenge adults or others if their behaviour is inappropriate, and feeling able to seek help. Children who are assertive are able to respect themselves and others. They are aware that they have 'rights', such as the right to privacy, the right to protection, and the right to good care.

### Assertiveness is linked to self-esteem

In order to be assertive, children first need to feel confident about themselves. Inner confidence is often referred to as *self-esteem*. Children who have *high* self-esteem value themselves, and therefore have enough confidence to put their ideas forward or, in the case of abuse, either to challenge the abuser or to seek help.

Children who have *low* self-esteem are more easily bullied and controlled because they lack the confidence to speak out. Victims of bullying or child abuse often have low self-esteem: they are often made to feel responsible or guilty for what is happening to them. By helping children to feel more confident, you can help protect children from abuse, and also encourage children who *are* being abused to seek help.

'I feel good about myself...'

'Arthur, could you help me with the computer?'

*Children who are respected by others will develop high self-esteem*

## Self-esteem is a process

Building confidence and self-esteem takes time. Children gather signals about themselves from a variety of sources, including their families, friends, teachers, and others around them. These signals are often hidden ones. Do people listen to them when they are talking? Are they praised? Do they have plenty of friends? Signals such as these lead children to judge themselves, and contribute either positively or negatively to their confidence. Children also judge themselves according to their achievements, often in comparison with their peers or friends.

As children are always taking in information about themselves and judging themselves, it is essential that you and your colleagues must help children feel confident.

## Ways of raising children's self-esteem

You can help children's self-esteem by showing them that you value them for who they are, not what they can do or how they behave. This can be referred to as *unconditional positive regard*. In practical terms this means actively welcoming children, listening to their ideas, and showing them through our facial expressions and body language that you enjoy being with them. The signals that you send out in this way must be sincere: children are quick to sense when people do not really mean what they are saying.

### Helping children with low self-esteem

Showing children unconditional positive regard is not always easy, as in many cases the children who really need to experience this are the ones who are most difficult to work with. Previous experience may have left them with low self-esteem, and in consequence they may at times show attention-seeking or unwanted behaviour. You need to deal with their behaviour, but at the same time you need to show them that you sill value them as people. You could look for particular ways of making them feel special and wanted – examples might be asking them if they would like to help set up a game, or asking for their advice or opinion.

## Helping children to be self-reliant and independent

You can also help children's self-esteem by encouraging them to be independent and self-reliant. Taking control, making choices and feeling responsible all help children to feel good about themselves and thereby raises their self-esteem. The playwork environment should be an ideal place for children to be able to make choices, put forward views, and take on some responsibility, as these reflect the underlying play values.

The diagram below shows how in practice children might be given opportunities for self-reliance and dependence.

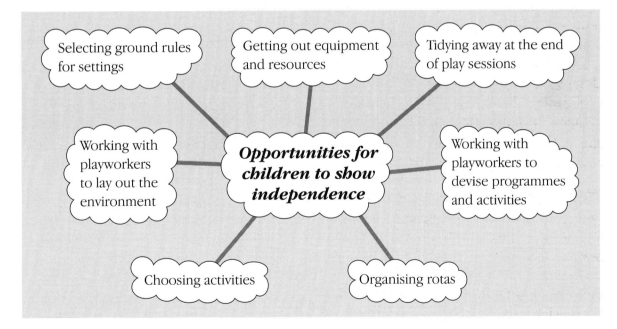

When children are taking responsibility and showing initiative, encourage them and praise their efforts, but make sure also that they have not taken on more than they can manage successfully. You may need to monitor a situation and ask children sensitively whether they need any help: this allows children to feel still that they are achieving something, and also that they are in control of the help.

## Case study

A group of children have decided to plan a treasure hunt. They have worked out some of the clues, but are struggling to think of places to hide them.

The playworker senses that the children are running out of ideas and asks them if they would welcome some help. They explain what they are doing, and show him what they have done so far. He praises their ideas and asks whether they would like some suggestions for hiding places. He gives a couple, which trigger off further contributions from other children. One of the children writes them down, and the playworker says, 'When you are ready or need a bit more help, come and get me. This should be fun and you've got some great ideas.'

1  *How did the playworker allow the children to stay in control of the activity?*
2  *Why is it important that children are encouraged to take the initiative?*

## Ways to help children make choices and express their feelings

Two important skills that children need in order to be assertive are being able to make choices and being able to express their feelings. There are many ways in the play environment that you can help children do both of these. For example, you can invite children to be involved in the planning of play activities, you can provide choices of activities and equipment for them, and you can encourage them to voice their feelings.

## Consolidation

Think about a recent activity that was child-led and that allowed the children to make choices.

*Write about this activity, explaining why it might have helped children's self-esteem, and how you helped them to be assertive.*

## Secrets

One of the ways in which some abusers gain control over children is by telling them that the abuse is a secret, and that they should never tell anyone about this secret. In some cases children are also told that if they break the secret, terrible things will happen to them or their families, or that they will not be believed by others.

You can help children keep safe from abuse by making it clear that it is all right to break a secret if it is making them unhappy. Sometimes children are taught to think of secrets as 'good; and 'bad'. *Bad* secrets are ones that make them unhappy in any way; whereas *good* secrets are ones that make them happy and that they know that they can break.

The case study below shows how one playworker helps children to think about secrets.

## Case study

It is Farah's birthday next week and one of the children has asked Jo, the playworker, if they can plan a party for her. This seems like a good idea, and Jo asks the children what they would like to do. One of the older children says that everyone must keep the party a secret from Farah, and that no one is allowed to talk about it. One of the younger children looks a little concerned and Jo quickly decides to take this as an opportunity to talk about secrets.

JO:    'I can see that it would be nice if this turns out to be a real surprise for Farah, but perhaps we should remember that this is a *good* secret. That means that if you want to tell your parents or someone else about what we are doing, you can. *Good* secrets always make us feel happy and excited in this way; but remember that if you are keeping a secret that makes you feel uncomfortable or unhappy, you can always tell someone. It'll be good if we can make this party a surprise for Farah – do you know what kind of games you might want to play?'

1   *How has Jo managed to make a point about secrets without scaring the children?*
2   *Why is it important that the word 'surprises' rather than 'secrets' is used when planning this type of activity with children?*

## Helping children to feel good about and respect their bodies

In order for children to feel confident, they also need to value their bodies and reach an understanding about 'ownership' of their bodies. You can help children learn that they can protest or seek help if an adult or another child touches them in a way that makes them feel uncomfortable. Children also need to acquire a sense of personal space and privacy – in some cases the children themselves do not realise that the way they are being treated is not appropriate.

Below is an outline of some of the ways in which you might help children to develop a sense of 'ownership' over their bodies, and the right to privacy and personal space.

### Touching and gestures

Children need to develop an awareness of what are and are not appropriate touches from adults and others. For example, a pat on the arm in a situation where a child needs a little encouragement would generally be considered to be appropriate, but stroking the arm is likely to be an *inappropriate* gesture.

Most children have a natural instinct about being touched, but they need to learn to trust their instinct and to be confident enough to say 'no' if someone is touching them in a way that makes them feel uncomfortable.

This is a sensitive area to approach with children and there are some structured materials that have been produced by organisations such as Kidscape which can be used to help discussions.

Children eventually need to learn that they have control over their bodies and that if someone touches them in a way that makes them feel uncomfortable, they can say so. It is, of course, essential that you act as a good role model and are consciously aware that you do not touch children inappropriately.

*Adults working with children need to empower them. If children feel confident, they are more likely to report abuse*

## Touching children – being a good role model

Playworkers should make sure that they only touch children in appropriate ways, according to their ages and needs. For example, a young child might wish to hold your hand for reassurance, but this might not be an appropriate gesture with a 14-year-old unless there were special circumstances.

This does not mean that you should make *no* physical contact, just that you should be sure that it is appropriate. In some situations it may be a good idea to check that the child is happy with the contact, and feels in control. Look at the two case studies opposite.

## Case study

- Michael is 12 years old and has suddenly burst into tears whilst talking about his father, who died recently. The playworker feels that some physical reassurance would be helpful and says, 'I think you need a hug – would that help?' Michael nods his head and, arms outstretched, he reaches out for a firm hug. He then releases the playworker.
- Simone is 10 years old and is next to the playworker as they are crossing a busy road. The playworker says, 'This is a busy road – I think that it might be a good idea if you grab either my elbow or my hand as we cross. What do you think?' Simone holds onto the playworker's elbow as they cross the road.

*How in each of these cases has the playworker helped the child to remain in control?*

## Respecting privacy

As children develop, they tend naturally to wish for more privacy when they change and go to the toilet. This should be encouraged and respected. If children need to change out of clothes, therefore – for example, if they have got wet – they should always be given access to a safe changing area. If for some reason, you need to give some assistance, always knock on the door, or find a way of making the child feel comfortable about your presence and in control of the situation.

### Case study

Clare, who is 12 years old, comes to a female playworker looking worried. She whispers that she thinks that she has started her first period, and does not know what to do. The playworker asks if she would like her to telephone her parents, but Clare says that she would prefer not to because she knows that they are both busy and she wants to try and be 'grown up'.

The playworker asks Clare if she knows what is happening to her body, and Clare says that she has had lessons at school and also that her mum has told her about periods. The playworker gets out a pack of sanitary towels, and asks Clare if she would like to use them. Clare says yes but asks if the playworker could come with her. The playworker goes with her and stands outside the closed toilet door, giving her reassurance. Clare says that she thinks she will be fine now and the playworker tells Clare that she can come and find her if she wants any more help.

1   *Why did the playworker suggest that she might wish to telephone her parents?*
2   *How did the playworker help Clare to feel reassured, whilst respecting her privacy?*
3   *Should the playworker tell Clare's parents at the end of the day what has happened?*

## Helping children value their bodies

From around the age of 10 years, many children begin to develop a strong awareness of their bodies as the process of puberty begins. In some cases, children also develop low self-esteem about their bodies, believing themselves to be too thin or too fat. This means in practical terms that you should avoid making remarks about children's weight, height or size, and make sure that you act as a good role model by taking good care of your own body – for example, by not smoking in front of children.

### Case study

It is lunchtime on the playscheme, and the playworkers sit outside in the sun and have their packed lunches with the children. The playscheme has a policy that playworkers should not accept food and drink from the children, to prevent children from giving their lunches away and also to avoid any feelings of inadequacy in children who cannot bring in extra treats.

One child offers playworker Andrei a chocolate bar and some crisps. He smiles and says that he would love to have it, but points to his stomach and says that he would get too fat.

1   *Why should this type of remark be avoided?*
2   *What could Andrei have said to the child instead?*

## Taking a structured approach – using specialist materials

There are different ways of approaching 'keeping safe'. It is important that this area is handled sensitively, according to the age of the children you are working with and the setting you are in.

In some settings, playworkers might consider taking a structured approach to helping children keep safe. This may be most successful if children are attending the setting regularly and staff have built up long-term relationships.

There are books and specially designed packs that tackle the area of abuse. The packs focus on positive strategies for 'keeping safe'. Most packs have materials that can be used with different ages of children. There are many advantages in using this type of pack, as they have been professionally written and the supporting materials are of a high standard. One leading charity producing such materials is Kidscape.

---

**SIGNS AND SYMPTOMS**
(from Stop Bullying! KIDSCAPE)

A child may indicate by signs or behaviour that he or she is being bullied. Adults should be aware that these are possible signs and that they should investigate if a child:

- is frightened of walking to or from school
- is unwilling to go to school
- begins to do poorly in schoolwork
- becomes withdrawn, starts stammering
- regularly has books or clothes destroyed
- becomes distressed, stops eating
- cries easily

- becomes disruptive or aggressive
- has possessions go 'missing'
- has dinner or other monies continually 'lost'
- starts stealing money (to pay bully)
- is frightened to say what's wrong
- attempts suicide or runs away
- has nightmares.

These signs and behaviours could indicate other problems, but bullying should be considered a possibility and should be investigated.

---

*Material from Kidscape*

## Taking an informal approach – using play opportunities and guidance

In many settings, playworkers will need to adopt an *informal* approach to helping children learn to protect themselves from abuse, either because they do not see the children frequently, or because it is not appropriate to the type of play environment that is being provided – for example, a drop-in play session. The informal approach means looking out for opportunities that will help children to show assertive behaviour, and taking opportunities to talk to children about potentially risky situations.

A good way of helping children is to ask them to think about strategies they could use if they were feeling uncomfortable. This means that discussions can be opened up, and ideas explored; and information given in a relaxed and safe atmosphere.

# Element PC23.2 Identify signs of possible abuse

Although you can help children to protect themselves, and encourage them to come forward if they have any problems, you still need to be vigilant on their behalf. You need to be aware of the possibility of bullying, and understand the different types of abuse and how to recognise signs that abuse may be occurring. This section looks at how to detect bullying and abuse, and what to do if you suspect that a child is being, or has been, abused.

- Observing children sensitively and unobtrusively
- Noting any indications of abuse
- Maintaining confidentiality

## General signs of abuse and bullying

There are some general indicators that children might be being either bullied or abused:

- significant changes in children's behaviour
- changes in children's moods
- reluctance to go home
- unwillingness to attend school
- reluctance to be near certain children or adults
- attention-seeking behaviour
- verbal or physical aggressiveness
- unpredictable attendance
- implausible explanations of injuries or implausible reasons for not attending school or the play setting, or for wanting to go home
- behaviour that is not appropriate for the child's age.

### Implausible or changing explanations

A child whose explanation keeps changing or who is very vague may be trying to think of an excuse for trying to avoid her or his attackers, or for covering up injuries.

### Fearful and withdrawn behaviour, or changes in normal behaviour

Any dramatic changes in children's normal behaviour and mood may indicate that there is a problem (although this is not necessarily related to abuse). A child who seems particularly frightened or worried may be a victim of abuse.

### Unwillingness to go home or to school

If children are having a good time, they are often reluctant to go home, but a child who is being abused at home may think of excuses for staying a little longer. Similarly, children who are avoiding going to school might do so because they are being bullied, or because the abuser is in the school.

### Unpredictable attendance

Sometimes children do not attend settings after they have been abused, to prevent people from asking about their injuries. Their attendance might become unpredictable. You might notice that one evening a child was talking about the games and activities he wanted to do the next day, but that the next day he did not actually attend. If this occurred frequently, you might consider whether there was another, underlying reason.

## Aggressive behaviour towards others

Children who have been abused or bullied may show aggressive behaviour themselves. They might suddenly 'explode' and lash out or they might bully other children, particularly younger children.

## Inappropriate behaviour for the child's age

Children who show behaviour inappropriate for their age – such as an 8-year-old who has a tantrum, or a 12-year-old girl who keeps inviting boys to kiss and touch her – may be doing this because they are being bullied or abused.

# Using observations to help you build up a picture of a child

The general signs that may indicate that a child is being either bullied or abused may not in themselves give you enough evidence to be sure that there is a problem. Some children may show these signs because of some changes in their lives.

Keep an eye on the child and share your concerns with someone else, and then you could carry out some observations.

*A reluctance to go home may indicate an underlying problem.*

# Keys to good practice

## Observing for signs of abuse

Some questions to consider:

- Is the child reacting in a way that you would expect for their age and stage of development? (For example, a 5-year-old might still have the occasional toileting accidents, but most 8-year-olds do not.)

- Is the child interacting in his or her usual way with adults and other children? (For example, might change from joining in a lot to isolating herself.)

- Does the child seem happy to be collected by her or his carer? (For example, does the child's expression change dramatically when the carer arrives? Does he seem reluctant to be alone with the carer?)

- Does the child seem to have noticeable changes in mood? (For example, a child may on some days seem very at ease, and on others seem quite different.)

- Are there any recurring themes in the child's play or language? (For example, is the child's language very abusive, or is her play very aggressive?)

- Does the child show any signs of physical discomfort? (For example, a child might look stiff, or rub parts of his body.)

---

Where you are collecting evidence – for example, you might have been asked by another professional to carry out some observations over a week – it can be a good idea to record these in a book rather than several pieces of paper, as this shows that they are consecutive. It is important that records are written up as soon as possible, or small details might be forgotten. Do not record your judgements or opinions; stick only to what you have heard, seen or done. For example, if you saw a small circular burn, write 'He has a small circular burn'. (To write 'He has a cigarette burn' would be to introduce your own interpretation.)

Most settings have written guidelines that you should read and follow. Date and sign your observations. Record accurately what the child or the parents have said to you.

Be careful when carrying out observations that you do this discreetly and sensitively: if children feel that they are being watched, they might start to avoid coming to the setting. Store your written records in a secure place, where only staff who need to know have access to them.

## Case study

André is 8 years old, and has been coming to the after-school club for over a year. Hazel, one of the workers, realises that he is not as enthusiastic and happy as he used to be. She talks to the deputy, who on reflection also thinks that he seems a bit 'down'.

Watching him that day, Hazel notices that although he settles quickly into the games, he keeps an eye on the clock, and from time to time he looks across to the door. At home time, he is one of the last children to be ready and then spends a few minutes 'looking for something' which later he says doesn't matter. His father extends his arm to him and tries to pat him on the shoulder. Hazel notices that he avoids this contact and tries to walk behind his father.

1 **What would you do if you were Hazel?**
2 **Why might it be a good idea to carry out some observations on André?**
3 **What should happen to these observations once they have been carried out?**

## Bullying

Bullying used to be thought of as inevitable in schools, but this attitude is now changing as people are beginning to understand the damage that bullying can cause. Bullying is any act of deliberate hostility that causes the victim distress. This includes verbal abuse and emotional intimidation such as 'sending someone to Coventry', as well as physical acts of violence.

According to Kidscape, a leading charity in preventing abuse and bullying, persistent bullying can cause:

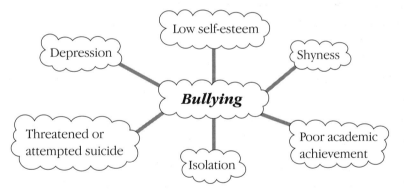

As well as looking out for signs of abuse, therefore, you should also be looking out for signs of bullying, especially if you are looking after children who come straight from school.

Watch for:

- children who do not take the shortest and most convenient route to the setting
- children who do not want to use the school bus
- children who come in looking frightened and dishevelled
- withdrawn behaviour
- unexplained bruises or scratches
- unexplained changes in behaviour
- children who say that they are not enjoying school.

Bullying can do untold emotional damage to children. It is essential that bullying is not allowed to occur in play settings. Be aware of children who might dominate others and put others down, by calling them names or by not listening to their ideas. When drawing up 'ground rules' with children, you may like to ask them to consider bullying as an issue.

## Types of abuse

Abuse is usually classified into four main areas:

- Physical
- Sexual
- Neglect
- Emotional.

### Physical abuse

Years ago, physical abuse was tolerated, and even in some ways encouraged, by a more violent culture: 'Spare the rod, spoil the child'. Today, physical abuse and assault have no place in children's lives. Physical abuse means inflicting physical harm to a child – for example burning them with cigarettes, or whipping, shaking or beating them. It also includes encouraging children to harm another child, or giving a child substances that are poisonous, such as alcohol and drugs.

Physical abuse generally produces very different injuries from minor accidents – for example, many children bump their heads or graze their knees, but they do not in general have burn marks on their backs.

#### *What to look out for*

| Indication | What to look for |
|---|---|
| **Bruises** | Notice if these are in unexpected places, such as at the top of the arms, the backs of legs, or the neck.<br>Look out also for bruises that show fingermarks or the outlines of shapes.<br>Consider whether children *frequently* have bruises, however small. |
| **Burns and scalds** | Burns and scalds might be in unexpected places, such as on a back or on the upper arms.<br>Look out for untreated burns, or that burns occur frequently.<br>Consider whether burns have particular shapes – an iron shape might indicate that an iron was held against the child, for instance, or a round small circle might indicate cigarette burns. |
| **Fractures** | Does the child often seem to have 'accidents'?<br>How detailed is the explanation of how the fracture occurred? |
| **Head injury** | Look out for bumps to the back and sides of the head, or for recurrent black eyes or sore ears.<br>Does the child often have head injuries?<br>How detailed is the explanation? |
| **Cuts and other wounds to skin** | Look out for injuries in unexpected places. Many 'normal' cuts are to the hands, and are generally superficial.<br>Are the injuries being treated?<br>Are there any bite marks or scratches?<br>Look out for any other unusual marks to the skin that might indicate that the child has been hit or pinched. |

### Unusual reluctance to show the body

Older children often need privacy when changing, but total reluctance to change – for example, to take off a jumper – might indicate that the child is trying to keep herself or himself covered to avoid injuries being seen.

### Frequent injuries

Many children have minor accidents from time to time, but take notice if a child is constantly having small injuries, especially if within the play setting you perceive the child to be quite sensible and careful.

## Case study

Tom did not come to the playscheme on Wednesday, although the day before he was saying how much he was looking forward to having his turn on the computer and taking part in the inter-league table football that the children had designed. He seemed very well and staff are a little puzzled.

Two days later, he reappeared and when Gorgi said that he was missed on Wednesday, he just shrugged his shoulders and said that he had to go away that day. It was clear that he does not want to discuss it.

This has since happened twice more during the holiday, and staff have also noticed some yellow bruising on his back, and that at sometimes he tends to take himself off and just sit alone.

1  *Do you think that there is any cause for concern? Explain your reasons.*
2  *Could there be alternative explanations for his behaviour?*
3  *What other signs might the playworkers look out for?*

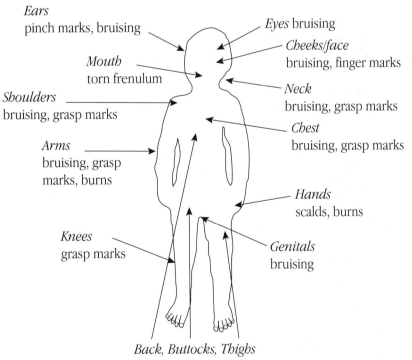

*Ears*
pinch marks, bruising

*Eyes* bruising

*Cheeks/face*
bruising, finger marks

*Mouth*
torn frenulum

*Neck*
bruising, grasp marks

*Shoulders*
bruising, grasp marks

*Chest*
bruising, grasp marks

*Arms*
bruising, grasp
marks, burns

*Hands*
scalds, burns

*Knees*
grasp marks

*Genitals*
bruising

*Back, Buttocks, Thighs*
linear bruising, outline of belt
buckle, scalds, burns

*Injuries caused by abusers*

## Sexual abuse

Sexual abuse can be defined as any act that is used to gratify an adult's sexual desires and includes fondling and touching as well as sexual intercourse. Most people working with children find it hard to believe that other adults would exploit children in this way, so in previous years there was little awareness that some children were victims in this way.

### *What to look out for*

| Indication | What to look for |
|---|---|
| **Physical signs** | Look out for unusual bruising, for example to the inner thighs or the back. Note frequent urinary infections, or children finding it painful to go to the toilet or being very afraid of doing so.<br>In older girls, look for early signs of pregnancy, such as nausea, putting on weight or wearing particularly baggy clothes. |
| **Self-destructive acts** | Sexual abuse can lead older victims into showing self-destructive behaviour. Examples are:<br>• under-age drinking<br>• taking drugs<br>• promiscuous sexual behaviour (from older children)<br>• tattooing, or cutting themselves. |
| **Behaviour** | Watch for sudden changes in normal behaviour patterns – for example, a child who becomes very clingy or withdrawn. In some cases children become very aggressive as a way of coping with their anger and humiliation. |
| **Sexual knowledge** | Consider whether children's behaviour and sexual knowledge is appropriate for their age. For example, some children act out in their play parts of the abusive scenario. Others might show precocious and inappropriate sexual knowledge. They may also show affection towards adults in a sexual way – for example, trying to kiss a play worker. |

## Neglect

Some parents can find it difficult to provide adequate parenting for their children. They may love them, yet be unable to give them the basic care that children need, such as food, clothes, and cleanliness. Parents neglect their children through extreme poverty, due to feeding a drug or alcohol habit, because of depression, or through ignorance, amongst other reasons. In severe cases of neglect, children are under-nourished and left very much to fend for themselves: this makes them very vulnerable to bullying at school, as well as being potential prey for paedophiles.

## What to look out for

| Indication | What to look for |
|---|---|
| **Physical signs** | Watch out for children who seem always to be hungry, who look pale, and who are in generally poor health (due either to being poorly fed or from having too little food). Consider whether children often have accidental injuries (which might be a result of being poorly supervised). Look out for children who are inadequately dressed, such as a child wearing shoes with holes in, or arriving in the setting with no coat in extreme weather conditions. |
| **Hygiene and appearance** | Consider whether a child's hygiene and general appearance are often poor – for example unwashed clothes, teeth that need brushing, hair that has rarely been combed. |
| **Emotional signs** | Older children will often have developed a coping mechanism that means that they appear to be unfazed by remarks from other children. They may appear to lack trust and have very much a 'day to day' feel about life. Look out for children who seem to be on the 'edge' of a group, and who avoid discussing their home backgrounds and families. |
| **Behaviour** | In some cases, children might take other children's possessions, or seem to be quite hard and not prepared to share. Older children might even turn to shoplifting in order to get food or other items. Watch for children who tell lies about their circumstances, or older children who have acquired things which ordinarily you would not have expected them to be able to afford. Be aware of children who do not seem to have a place to go to, or who seem to be hanging around the streets. |

### Other signs

Attendance at school and at other settings by neglected children may be irregular: they may be called to look after younger siblings, or even their parents.

## Emotional abuse

Until recently, emotional abuse was not really recognised as being as important as other types of abuse. The effects of continual emotional abuse are, however, as devastating as any other type of abuse, and can haunt the victim in later life.

Emotional abuse occurs when children are ridiculed, repeatedly criticised, and not allowed to develop their self-confidence. They may also be deprived of love, affection and warmth. Children who have been emotionally abused are easy targets for other abusers such as paedophiles, who seem to offer them the 'friendship' and 'love' that they crave.

*What to look out for*

| Indication | What to look for |
|---|---|
| **Physical signs** | In younger children there will be few physical signs; but older children, especially girls, may harm themselves. Look out for self-destructive behaviour: for example, self-mutilation by tattooing themselves, denying themselves food, or taking harmful substances. These attention-seeking devices are ways of crying out for help. In severe cases, older children might even try to take their own lives. |
| **Emotional signs** | Children who are emotionally abused have very low self-esteem and confidence. They may be attention-seeking and look for popularity in inappropriate ways. Look out for children who seem very lonely or who act as the 'clown' to gain popularity. Consider whether children are particularly needing attention and are clingy. Look out for children who are very worried and anxious, and who fear making mistakes. Consider whether children are very sensitive to criticism, or seem to have developed a 'don't care' attitude. |
| **Behavioural signs** | Children with low self-esteem might be extremely attention-seeking and 'needy', wanting a lot of adult time and support. Look out for children who burst into tears for no particular reason, or who seem very tense and anxious. |

## Accuracy in evaluating suspected abuse

Professionals working with children must put the child's welfare and protection first. If you have any doubts or niggles about a child's behaviour, you should take them seriously and start evaluating whether abuse is the cause. Think carefully about what has made you suspect abuse, and then share these concerns with a colleague or supervisor: this person may also have had some background concerns about the child.

In some cases, you may be able to probe the child carefully for a little more information. For example, if a child comes in with a black eye, you might be gently able to ask the child what happened; or if a child seems particularly depressed, you might make a comment such as 'You look a little down today – what's up?' Most children will be ready enough to answer this type of question in an open, natural way. If you get a very negative and surprising reaction, or if the child's reply is unconvincing, you should start to follow your setting's procedures.

You might also be able to gain some more information about a child from the parents. Most parents put their child's welfare first, so a comment such as 'He seems a little down lately' is generally taken positively, as a sign that the play setting staff care about their child. If parents seem particularly anxious, defensive or even aggressive about your general comments or questions, this might be a sign that there is an underlying problem.

## Case study

Look at the following three cases.

- Oliver has come into the setting with a black eye and bruises to his cheek. He smiles at Simon and says that he fell off his bike and knocked himself on the handlebars. Simon asks him if he has had any medical attention and Oliver says no, because his mum's friend is a nurse and she looked at him and has told him to tell someone if he feels drowsy or sick. Oliver says that his mum won't let him ride his bike again for a few days until he's better.

- Mark always looks a bit scruffy, but today Jane notices that his trainers have holes in them and that he seems particularly tired and low. He asks when snacks are going to be served and Jane asks him if he is feeling hungry today. He replies that he is starving and he hasn't had anything since breakfast, then changes his tone to add, 'I just wasn't hungry earlier.' Jane watches him at snack time and spots that when no one appears to be looking he stuffs some biscuits into his pockets. Jane offers him a sandwich and notices that Mark is wolfing it down. She decides to ask whether everything is all right. Mark doesn't reply, but changes the conversation. At the end of the session Mark disappears, but Jane spots him later on in the evening hanging around the streets.

- The children have decided to put on a play at the club, and today they were meant to be rehearsing it. One of the children, Angie, has said that she doesn't want to do the play any more, which seems strange because she had been so keen and had enjoyed dressing up. Chris asks her if everything's all right, and she just nods her head and then asks if she could put her costume on over her clothes. This seems strange, so Chris decides to watch her a little more closely. She looks as though she is in some kind of pain and she is less talkative with her friends than usual. At home time, when her parent comes in, she visibly pales and her body language becomes stiff and defensive.

*Consider each situation, and decide whether you would seek help or advice.*

## Recording indicators of abuse

If you suspect that a child is being abused, you should keep a note of the signs that have caused this suspicion. Be accurate in your recording, and note down only what you have either seen or heard. Be aware that this might be used in a criminal court, as evidence: write in pen, and sign and date the paper. It should be stored in a secure place. If you are not sure what to write, refer to your setting's procedures.

## Following procedures is essential

If you suspect abuse, you should always consult a colleague or supervisor and follow the procedures of the setting. Most settings follow their local authority guidelines and build these into their procedures. By following these procedures, you will be helping the child; you will also be protecting yourself against accusations of maliciousness. In cases where procedures have *not* been followed, abusers have sometimes not been convicted because of 'contamination of evidence'. In other cases, parents have been angered because cases have been badly handled, and it emerged afterwards that no abuse had been evident.

## Confidentiality

In some cases of suspected abuse, children are actually showing signs of stress not caused by abuse, but by family upheaval or changes at school. People's lives can be ruined by gossip and false accusation: at every step of a suspected abuse case, confidentiality *must* be maintained. Victims of abuse have not only a right to protection, but also to their privacy. If you have needed to report a case of suspected abuse, do not talk about it to anyone, including colleagues, unless called upon to do so. This confidentiality must be maintained permanently, even after the case has been resolved. Any documents that are linked to the case should be securely handled, and kept in a place where only those directly involved have access to them.

## Element PC23.3 Respond to a child's disclosure of abuse

In some cases of abuse, it may be the children themselves who come to you for help. This may happen in a variety of ways – a child might have made a conscious decision to talk to you about what is happening, or the child might during the course of an activity say something that is very revealing.

When a child tells someone else about being abused, this is often referred to as a *disclosure*. The way a child's disclosure is handled is very important: if it were *badly* handled, the child might not get the protection that he or she needs, or the abuser might be free to carry on abusing.

### WHAT YOU NEED TO LEARN

- Responding calmly and promptly to disclosures of abuse
- Telling the child that what is said must be passed on
- Providing reassurance and support
- Recording what was said, but maintaining appropriate confidentiality

## Degrees of disclosure

There are different levels of disclosure:

- A *full disclosure* is where a child gives you the 'whole' picture of what is happening, including the name of the abuser or abusers.
- A *partial disclosure* is where a child tells you only some of what is happening. The child might become reluctant to say who is responsible for the abuse, or might change her or his mind about saying anything.

## Children often find it hard to disclose abuse

Most victims of abuse and bullying find it very hard to tell someone about what is happening to them. Often the abuser has gained terrific control over them, through threats or by gaining the child's loyalty and friendship. Paedophiles, in particular, target lonely children and spend a lot of time building up a friendship before actually beginning to abuse the child. Children often feel that they cannot speak out.

In some situations, children may be unsure that they are being abused – the abuser may have suggested that this type of behaviour is normal. In other cases, children can be led into thinking that they are in some way to blame for the abuse, for example, 'If you were a good boy, I wouldn't have to do this to you.' Children who are being bullied by other children are often made to feel that they are in some way inadequate, and therefore responsible for their own abuse.

These types of conflicting messages and loyalties make it hard for children to know whom to trust and what they should do. This is why it is essential that you believe a child who comes forward for help.

The diagram below summarises some of the reasons why children can find it hard to talk about what is happening.

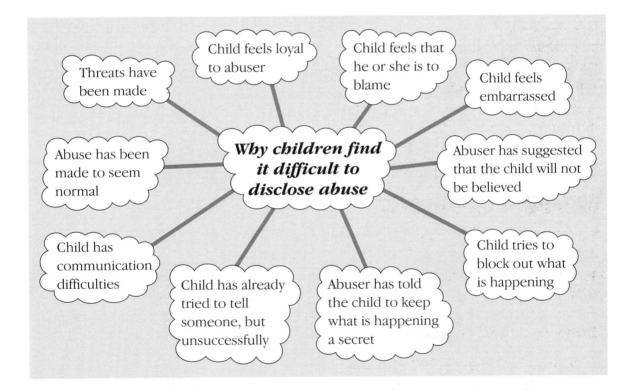

## When children might make a disclosure

Disclosures often happen quite unexpectedly, so it is important to be aware of how to handle disclosures should they arise, so that you can respond appropriately.

Children who have decided to speak about what is happening to them have probably decided that they can trust you. They may then speak on the spur of the moment, having suddenly found the courage and the circumstances to speak out. They may start by telling you about other problems that they have, so it is vital that children see playworkers as people who will listen to their problems.

Finally, some disclosures follow on from recent activities, discussions or items in the news.

## What to say to the child

It is essential that children know that what they have said will not get them into any trouble, and that they were right to talk about it. This reassurance needs to be emphasised: by doing this, you are often breaking the primary control that abusers have over children.

Children may well ask that you do not tell anyone else. This is a promise you cannot make. You alone are unable to help such children and protect them. If you make a promise that you cannot keep, breaking that promise will break the child's trust. This means that you should tell abused children that in order to help them you will have to tell other people, but that these people will understand what the child is feeling, and will sort out the problem.

Some children may have mixed feelings about their abusers, and may ask what will happen to them. These type of questions have to be handled truthfully, so it may be best to be vague in your answers – for example, 'I'm not really sure, but other people will look at what has happened and work out what should be done.'

### Ways of showing support to children

One of the best ways in which you can help children is to show that you are actively listening to what they are saying. You can do this by nodding your head, by making eye contact, and by making comments such as 'That must have been hard for you' or 'You have done the right thing in saying something'. It is also important to help children feel that they were not to blame for what has happened to them, as this is another hold that some abusers have over their victims. It is generally a good idea to let children say as much or as little as they wish, and avoid questioning them.

### Case study

Harry is 10 years old, and has been hanging around asking Isabelle the playworker if he can help her. They sit together sharpening crayons, and he says that he likes helping like this. Isabelle says that she enjoys having someone around like this to chat to, and she is pleased that he wants to help her. They talk about school and then Harry says 'I don't really mind school, it's better than being at home.' Isabelle says simply, 'What don't you like about being at home, then?' Harry says that he's always getting into trouble at home and that his stepdad gets cross with him. He carries on, 'Sometimes when I've done something really bad, like wet the bed, he has to get the belt out and it hurts and then that makes my mum cry.' Harry says, 'I try not to be bad, I really do, it's just that I'm not very good at being good.' (Harry then starts to cry.)

1   *Write about how you would handle this situation. What would you say to Harry?*
2   *Why is it important that Harry does not feel guilty about what has happened to him?*
3   *How has the abuser managed to make Harry feel that he is to blame?*

# Evidence

## Avoid contaminating the evidence

In some cases of child abuse, the child's disclosure to you will be used as evidence against the abuser in a court of law. This means that it is crucial that you do not ask questions or lead the child in any way – if you did and if a case came to trial, the defence team might say that ideas were put into the child's mind. It is probably a good idea just to listen to children, letting them tell you what has happened in their own words.

Evidence can also be seen as invalid if children repeat what they have said to many different people, so it is essential that the child protection team is called in as soon as possible, to give advice and guidance on how both to support the child and to follow procedures.

## Record what has been said

It is essential that you write down a summary of what the child has said as soon as possible afterwards – preferably within an hour, although it is legally admissible as evidence provided it has been recorded with twenty-four hours. Write clearly what was said, your comments to the child, and what action you then took. You should also note down what was happening before the disclosure took place, and who else was nearby.

As this record might be used in evidence at a later date, it is essential that you record only what has actually happened: this must be an accurate record. Note down the time and the date of the disclosure, and sign the record. If you make a mistake, cross it out but do *not* obscure it with correction fluid. This record will be confidential, and you should put it in a secure place.

If the child goes on to say anything further about the abuse, or if any incident relating to the child takes place subsequently, you should make a further record.

---

# Keys to good practice

## Responding to a child's disclosure of abuse

- Remain calm.
- Allow the child to say what has happened, without interruption.
- Show the child through your body language that you are listening.
- Avoid asking questions or challenging.
- Reassure the child.
- Tell the child that she or he has done the right thing in saying something.
- Tell the child that you will need to tell someone else, so that the child can be helped.
- Explain to the child what is going to happen next.
- Report the disclosure immediately.
- Write a report as soon as possible afterwards.

---

# Element PC23.4  Report possible abuse

If you suspect that a child has been abused or bullied, either because the child has made some form of disclosure or because you have recognised some indicators, you must take some action promptly. In this section we look at reporting abuse and bullying separately, as often different people need to be involved.

## WHAT YOU NEED TO LEARN

- Collecting information about possible abuse
- Following organisational procedures
- Supplying information promptly and appropriately
- Making reports and maintaining appropriate confidentiality

## Reporting bullying

If you suspect that a child is being bullied by other pupils at a school, you should report this to the parents or carers of the child, and if necessary directly to the school. You may be able to talk over with the child the range of support options that exist – most schools have a 'bully box', for instance, in which children can anonymously record the names of bullies; or the child may wish to phone a helpline such as Childline.

If children decide to report the bullying at school themselves, you should always follow this up by asking what happened, and assess whether the child really has been able to report the bullying. Although most schools now have an active approach to counter bullying, you should continue to look out for indicators of bullying, in case it persists.

## Keys to good practice
### Helping a child who is being bullied

- Talk to the child's parents or carers.
- Make contact with the school.
- Encourage the child to talk to her or his teachers.
- Make sure that children know the Childline number.
- Contact Kidscape for advice.

## Reporting abuse

Every setting should have its own policy on child protection, and this should include a detailed procedure of what should happen. If you are responsible for the setting, it is important that you read the policy, make sure that staff understand it, and review it regularly. If you need to alter your policy or draw up a new one, it is a good idea to contact your local authority social services team, as guidance can vary from authority to authority.

The chart below shows the process that most settings follow.

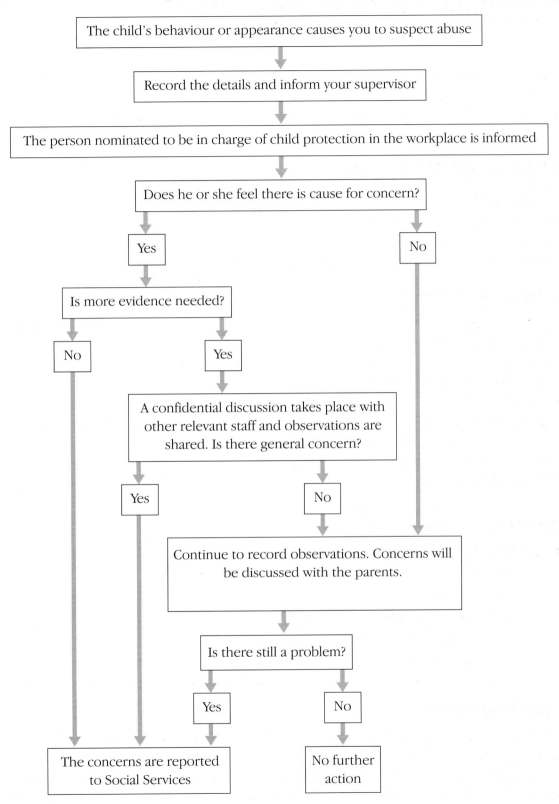

*Reporting abuse*

## Active knowledge ✔

Look at the procedure in your setting for reporting suspected abuse.

1 *To whom would you need to report suspected abuse?*
2 *What would happen if this person were absent?*
3 *Where should any records relating to the children be stored?*

## What you should do if you cannot follow set procedures

In most cases, you should be able to follow set procedures within your setting, but if for some reason you feel unable to do so – for example, if you suspect that a co-worker is an abuser – you should contact either your local child protection team or the NSPCC helpline.

## Writing up a report

When abuse is reported, you might be asked to put together a report. This report will be highly confidential, and in some cases might provide some evidence for a prosecution. It is therefore essential that you are careful in the language you use. Most reports contain the following types of information:

- name and date of birth of the child.
- the child's address
- parents' or carers' names
- the date and time of the report
- concerns (note down whether these are your own, or those of someone else in your team)
- detailed descriptions of any behavioural changes or physical indicators, with dates when these were noted
- details of what the child, or parents or carers have said
- action that has been taken so far (who has been contacted, and who knows about current situation).

## Register of injuries

In some settings, a log is kept of all injuries with which children come into the setting. This is partly done as a safeguard for the setting, so that staff cannot be accused later of injuring children or supervising them poorly. It also means that if a child were to require medical attention, the staff would be aware of any injuries that might have triggered it.

The register of injuries also provides a way for staff to ask parents gently about how the injuries occurred, and whether there is anything that they should be looking out for – for instance, if a child has a bruise on the head, it would be sensible during the day to look out for any signs of concussion.

## The process of investigating abuse

It is useful to understand what will happen after social services have been contacted, especially as colleagues or even older children might ask you.

## Preliminary enquiry

Once social services have been contacted, they have a duty to carry out an investigation. This means that they will make initial enquiries to find out more. They will start by gathering information from a range of people, including the family, as the list below shows:

- the child's parents or carers
- the child's health visitor or doctor
- the child's teacher
- the person who reported the original concerns
- the police might also be involved early on, and they may also approach the alleged abuser.

## Case conferences

Case conferences are meetings where key people involved are brought together. The main aim of the case conference is to decide whether any further action needs to be taken, and if so what needs to happen. Parents or carers or their representatives are often invited to be present at the case conference, as the Children Act 1989 encourages agencies to work alongside parents.

## Removal of children from their families

In the 1980s there was widespread concern after some high-profile cases in which children were thought to have been taken away needlessly from their families. This meant that some of the general public viewed social workers with fear and suspicion, and this might have prevented some reporting of suspected abuse.

The Children Act 1989 made it clear that wherever possible children should remain with their families. In some cases, an emergency protection order might be sought following a case conference, in order to remove the child from his or her family, but this is quite rare. Emergency protection orders have to be obtained from a court, and are only granted if it is feared that the child is in imminent danger. Generally the approach taken is to try to work with families, although the alleged abuser might be asked to leave the family home.

## The child protection team

When an incident of suspected abuse is reported to social services, a team of people will be involved. There have been some well-publicised cases where children did not receive the protection that they needed, because of a breakdown in communication between the different agencies. To avoid this many areas have developed area child protection teams, in which a range of people from different agencies work together on cases. This approach is sometimes referred to as a multi-disciplinary approach.

Some of the people who might become involved once alleged abuse has been reported are:

- the GP (family doctor)
- a health visitor
- a paediatrician – a specialist in children's medicine
- the child protection officer, from the police
- a social worker specialising in child protection
- a teacher or headteacher
- an education welfare officer.

## Finding help for yourself

Many professionals working with children find that reporting and being involved in child abuse cases is emotionally draining and potentially disturbing. Child abuse exposes us to a side of life that many of us would prefer not to see. If you are involved in such a case, you might need to talk with someone else about what has happened. In some cases a supervisor or a colleague who is also involved will be able to offer you support.

If you feel that you need more professional help, many child protection teams will be able to offer support directly, or they may point you in the direction of a counselling service. It is important to remember, however, that if you are talking to someone who is not directly involved in the case, you must respect confidentiality. You should not mention the child's name, or the abuser's name, or indicate where you work.

## Resources

### NSPCC

The National Society for the Prevention of Cruelty to Children (NSPCC) is strongly involved in protecting children. It employs its own social workers and child protection officers. It also has a helpline for people to use if they suspect that abuse is taking place.

### Childline

This is a charity which runs a freephone line for children to use. This freephone line takes around 3000 calls a day from children who need someone to listen to them. Children know that they can talk in confidence to an adult and remain anonymous, although the specially trained counsellors encourage children to seek further help from people in their home area.

### Kidscape

This organisation was founded to help children learn the skills of keeping safe. It produces many resources to help schools, parents and organisations caring for children teach children strategies for protecting themselves. Kidscape also runs training programmes, and a bullying helpline.

## PC23 unit test

1 Why is it important that playworkers build up a 'listening' relationship with children?
2 Why should children be given opportunities to make choices and be assertive?
3 If you wanted to help a child who was being bullied, where would you get advice?
4 Outline the different types of abuse.
5 What signs may there be that a child is being bullied?
6 Why is it important that all staff read the child protection policies in your setting?
7 Describe some ways in which you might be able to help children learn about keeping themselves safe from abuse.
8 What are the general indicators that might show that a child is being bullied or abused?
9 In what circumstances might you decide to carry out some written observations on children?
10 Outline the ways in which adults should act if a child discloses abuse.

# Support the efficient use of resources

The effective use of resources is an issue for every organisation – no organisation has infinite resources! This means that the resources that *are* available have to be carefully monitored and managed. Resources that need to be managed in a playwork setting include money, stock, equipment and consumables. The smooth running of most settings will depend on these resources, so they need to be managed wisely.

The elements in this unit are:

A21.1   Make recommendations for the use of resources
A21.2   Contribute to the control of resources

## Element A21.1   Make recommendations for the use of resources

The allocation and use of resources within organisations can cause conflict between staff, so it is important that they are carefully managed. In order to be able to do this, it is important to know exactly what is required and why. This makes it easier to make a case to others for the provision of resources, and also to allocate them fairly and wisely.

### WHAT YOU NEED TO LEARN

- Involving others in identifying necessary resources
- Considering past use of resources, and current trends and developments
- Identifying benefits from additional resources
- Making recommendations on time and in a helpful way

## What is meant by 'resources'

The word 'resources' is a very broad term. In playwork settings common resources include:

- finance
- administrative assistance
- staffing
- training
- specific equipment, such as computers, televisions or videos

- play equipment and toys
- consumables, such as paper, paint and crayons, cleaning materials, and disposable gloves
- furniture.

In general, the resources in organisations assist people in their work and help to maintain the smooth running of a setting – where a setting has an administrative context, for example the manager may find more time to support staff and be with the children. Unfortunately, as resources in all organisations are limited difficult decisions must be made about how resources should be allocated. In the small setting, for example, if funds are used to pay an administrative assistant, savings may need to be made in other areas, such as buying new toys.

## What resources are required?

A good starting point when managing resources is to find out what the main needs are in the setting or amongst the team. Resources are then more likely to be directed into areas which really need them, and staff are less likely to become frustrated because they do not have what they need to carry out their work, or because they feel that resources are being wasted.

Begin by consulting team members and other people involved about their resource *needs*. When doing this, make it clear that their resource needs will not necessarily be completely met (unless you have an unusually large budget!). Most managers consult using a range of methods, depending on the situation – if the setting has been donated a sum of money, for example, staff might be asked at a team meeting to suggest possible ways of using it, whereas if a manager has a training budget, she or he may wish to talk to individual staff members about their needs.

The table below shows how you might find out about the resources that staff feel they need.

| Method | Comments | Advantages and disadvantages |
|--------|----------|------------------------------|
| **Team meeting** | Team members can be invited to talk about any resources that they require. This is useful when thinking about resources that are needed for the whole setting. | *Advantage* Allows for open discussion. *Disadvantage* Some team members may not contribute. |
| **Memos** | Memos can be sent out requesting information about resource needs. | *Advantage* Memos can be sent to specific people in the team. *Disadvantages* Not all members of the team may reply; and this is an impersonal method. |
| **Appraisal** | Staff appraisal is a good way of identifying particular staff's training needs. | *Advantage* Staff can talk about their needs in private. *Disadvantages* There may be a lapse in time between a staff member identifying that they need training and their appraisal interview. |

| Method | Comments | Advantages and disadvantages |
|--------|----------|------------------------------|
| **Informal consultations** | A simple chat about resources in the corridor or over coffee might be an effective way of getting feedback. | *Advantage* Staff are more relaxed.<br>*Disadvantages* Staff will not have had time to think about what they need. This can be a time-consuming approach in a large setting, and is open to criticisms of favouritism unless everyone is approached. |
| **Message book** | A simple book that allows staff to make a note of resources or other things that they wish to bring to the manager's attention. | *Advantage* Very useful for consumables when stocks are running low.<br>*Disadvantage* May not be appropriate for requesting other types of resources, such as training or large items. |
| **Forms** | Some settings use forms which they ask their staff to fill in to request resources. | *Advantage* This is a very straightforward method.<br>*Disadvantage* It does not give individuals the opportunity to explain the reasons behind their requests. |

## Active knowledge ✔

Consider the following types of resources:

- consumables
- training
- equipment that needs replacing.

1 *What will be the best ways of finding out your team's requirements for these?*
2 *Explain why these methods would work well in your setting.*

## Making recommendations

### Taking account of past experience

As well as gaining information from colleagues and team members, it is also a good idea to use information based on past experience, especially if the activities in the setting have remained similar. For example, last year's summer playscheme may have run with similar numbers of children, and the resources needed this year will therefore be similar. Information about the previous resource requirements can be gained from looking at past stock orders and resource audits, and from talking to members of staff. It is essential not to base everything around past experience, however, without talking to colleagues as well: in some cases there may not have been adequate resources. You should also note any changes or differences – for example, there may have been an increase in the number of children in one particular age group.

When making recommendations about the need for and allocation of resources in new settings, it can be useful to contact other organisations which have been carrying out similar work. They may be able to give some guidance as to the resources that they have found useful and the quantity required, such as the budget they set aside for maintaining and renewing toys and equipment.

## Taking account of trends and developments

One of the keys to managing resources is being able to predict accurately *future* resource needs. This requires a skilful analysis of what is likely to happen in the immediate term and also the longer term – for example, being able to predict that you will need to have more qualified staff in order to meet with registration requirements, or that more and more children will want access to a computer.

To be able accurately to predict what resources a setting is likely to need, you will need to be constantly aware of what is happening, both in and out of the setting. Trends outside the setting can often have a great impact – for example, the closing down of a local employer might have a major impact on the take-up of places. This means that both local and national developments need to be analysed.

The table below shows some examples of the types of developments that might have an impact on the resources needed by the setting.

| Trend or development | Potential impact | Resource implication |
|---|---|---|
| **Children wanting to use computers and the Internet** | Children may not be attracted to a setting that does not offer these facilities | More computers required Internet installations Training for staff on how to create play opportunities |
| **Working Families Tax Credit** | More places might be taken up | May need to take on more staff May need to expand facilities |
| **Steep increase in number of young families moving into the area** | May put pressure on places | May need to plan for expansion |
| **Setting is finding it hard to recruit suitable applicants who hold a qualification in playwork** | May not meet registration requirements May find it harder to expand or continue with current activities | May need to check that pay is competitive May need to train NVQ assessors so that training can take place in the workplace |
| **Another organisation in the area is considering setting up a similar service** | Level of demand for places might decrease | May need to invest in new equipment or resources to make own setting more attractive. May have to open for longer sessions, and so need more staff |
| **Homework policy** | Some parents may wish their children to do some homework while at the setting | May need to create a quiet area where children can do their homework Staff may need some training on how to assist children |

*Children may be attracted to a setting that offers computer facilities*

## Ways of finding out about trends that might affect the setting

The table above illustrates how both local and national trends might have an effect on the planning of resources in settings. The key to spotting trends that might be important is to gain information about what is happening. The diagram below shows some of the sources of information that might help you to keep in touch.

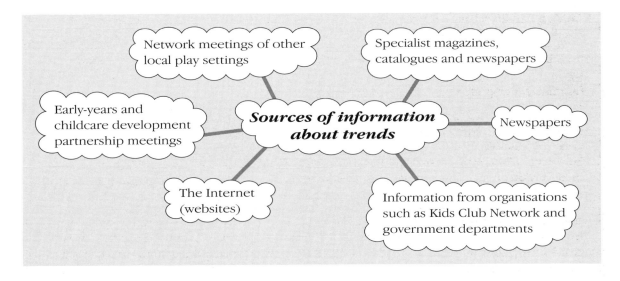

## Active knowledge ✔

1 *Give an example of a trend or development in your local area that might affect the resource requirements of your setting.*

2 *Explain what the resource implications might be for that trend or development.*

## Following organisational procedures

Many organisations develop internal procedures for requesting and allocating resources. Forms are often devised to help collate the resource requirements across the whole of the organisation. This allows the decision-makers – for example the owners, the management committee or the project officer – to see an overall picture of the resource requirements. When making any recommendations about resources, therefore, it is important to find out and use the organisation's procedures.

Organisational procedures also help settings to record the ways in which resources have been allocated. These records might be used for reasons such as monitoring equality of opportunity, or to refer to when making future budgetary forecasts.

## Active knowledge ✔

1 *Does your setting or organisation have any specific procedures which are used to request or recommend resources? If so, what are they?*

---

### Training request form

Name ............................................... Job title ...............................................

Course title ....................................... Date and length of course .....................

Cost .................................................. Anticipated travel expenses ..................

Aims and objectives of course:

How do you feel this training would be beneficial?

Attendance for this training has been approved      Yes/No

---

*A training request form*

## Taking account of team objectives and the organisation's plans

Any recommendations should be consistent with the team's objectives and the organisation's plans. Most organisations have a long-term vision of how they wish to develop their services, so it is important that any request for resources supports this plan. This prevents potentially expensive mistakes whereby resources are spent, and then later it is found that they have been badly used – for example, many small chairs might be ordered when predictions for the following year show an increase in the number of *older* children. Good communication is needed between those responsible for the longer-term plans of the organisation and those allocating or requesting resources.

There is often a need to balance short-term requirements of the team against the long-term plan of the setting, as the case study below shows.

## Case study

The Future Generation out-of-school club is currently operating in a small private hall. Although the hall is rented the team really feel that the management committee should spend some money decorating the hall, as it is shabby and unattractive. The management committee are keen not to spend anything, as at present they are trying to secure a lease on a larger and more attractive site.

This process seems to be taking forever, and the team are growing ever more depressed with their working conditions. The management committee have allocated some money for this year, and have asked you to make some recommendations as to how it could best be used.

1 *How would you decide on the recommendations?*
2 *Why might it not be a good idea to spend money on decorating the hall?*
3 *Why might you need to balance the needs of the staff against the needs of the organisation?*

## Indicating the benefits of the resources

There are many occasions – for example, as part of a bid to another organisation – when it might be necessary to make a case for having additional or new resources. When requesting resources, it is always a good idea to be able to explain why these resources are needed, and the immediate benefits of having them. The decision-makers who have to allocate resources are often looking at competing demands, and having to choose, for example, between funding a new toilet and replacing the outdoor play equipment. If you present arguments for the resources that you are recommending, the decision-makers will be able to prioritise more easily.

### RESOURCE REQUESTED:

#### Standing Frame

*Benefits*

1 Hughie will be able to stand and join in more activities unaided. This will increase his confidence and independence.

2 This equipment can be used in the future to help other children who come into the setting, and can be loaned out to other settings.

3 The standing frame will help the other children see a more positive view of a disability, as Hughie will be less dependent on others.

4 The purchase of the standing frame will help to demonstrate our *real* commitment to equal opportunities.

*Reasons for allocating resources*

## Presenting recommendations

There are many ways of presenting your recommendations: what is appropriate will depend on your situation. For example, if you are requesting resources as part of a bidding process such as the New Opportunities Fund (NOF), you might need to write down exactly what is required, the cost, and the reasons for your request. In other situations, you might be asked to present your recommendations verbally to a team meeting or management committee, and to explain your recommendations.

Whatever the situation, you need to be able to give clear reasons for your recommendations, and to express yourself clearly, whether in writing or verbally. If the request for resources is very important to the setting, or if the recommendations that you have reached are likely to be controversial, you might benefit from having a 'practice' run or read-through with a supportive colleague.

*A 'practice run' can help your presentation skills*

As well as being able to present the recommendations effectively, in some situations you may also need to be able to judge the *timing* of the presentation carefully. It may be important to put forward your case for resources to your line manager in time for a meeting of the management committee, for example, or just before the budget is due for review. You should also make sure that the actual moment you choose to present your recommendations is a convenient one, when your line manager has some time available to listen or to read your recommendations carefully.

## Element A21.2    Contribute to the control of resources

As well as identifying the requirements for resources, it is also important to control the way that resources are used in the play setting. Given that most settings have limited resources, using them wisely is crucial. This section looks at the ways in which you can contribute to the control of resources.

## Managing resources

It may seem surprising, but resources – or the lack of them – can affect everyone, as resources help towards the smooth running of an organisation. Resources need to be carefully managed, not just by controlling their use, but also by ensuring that they are used effectively. This might mean making sure that they were properly stored, for example, or that everyone in the setting is aware that the resources are available.

The table below shows four key ways in which resources might be managed in settings, and the importance of each of these.

| Way of managing resources | Benefits |
|---|---|
| **Good storage** | Prevents resources from being damaged<br>Allows staff and children to see what is available<br>Prevents resources from running out, as it is easy to identify when to re-order them<br>Prevents time being wasted looking for items |
| **Planning ahead** | Resources can be allocated according to need<br>Prevents limited resources from running out because too many have been used at the wrong time<br>Helps staff morale to know that resources will be available when needed |
| **Allocation and monitoring of resources** | Prevents staff from feeling that resources have been distributed unfairly<br>Allows staff to take responsibility for certain resources |
| **Record-keeping** | Makes it easier to carry out stock control<br>Provides evidence for audits that resources have been correctly used<br>Means that resources can be monitored and trends can be recognised |

## Sharing responsibility for managing resources

Managing resources should not necessarily be about keeping tight control of them – that could create situations in which team members felt resentful. Good management of resources includes making sure that those who need them can access them easily. This often means passing responsibility for these resources to those who will actually be using them. For example, if one member of staff is keen on music and often helps children to use musical instruments, it might be appropriate for this person to take on the responsibility for storing and maintaining them. Staff are more likely to take care of and use resources efficiently in this way than if they have no control over them. This is good management practice, and helps to create an atmosphere where everyone in the setting is working together to make the best of resources.

Controlling resources and restricting access to them often creates tensions and difficulties, as the case study below shows.

## Case study

Carol is newly in the manager's post. She has overall responsibility for monitoring the resources in the setting. She is concerned about the large expenditure on art and craft consumables. She is very keen to make sure that the next order lasts for the next three months, so she has decided to lock away the pens, paints, paper and the like. She tells other staff that if they want anything they should ask her.

This has created resentment in the team, who feel that they are no longer being trusted to take care and be sensible with the paper. It is also inconvenient because on some days children want to do a lot more creative activities than on others, and staff have to keep asking Carol to unlock the cupboard.

One day when Carol is on her break, one of the members of staff notices that the cupboard is unlocked. Carol returns to find that a lot of things have gone missing. She is very angry and hurt, and accuses the others of stealing her things.

1   *Explain why you think that the staff reacted as they did.*
2   *How could this situation have been prevented?*
3   *Why is it important that staff are able to have access to the resources they need?*

## Active knowledge ✔

*In your setting, are individual staff members responsible for any of the resources? Make a list of the resources, and explain who is responsible for them.*

## Monitoring the use of resources

Although it is good practice to pass on some responsibility for areas of resources to other people, it is important to understand that the ultimate responsibility for these resources remains your own. The people to whom you pass responsibility need your support. The amount of support will vary according to the levels of experience of the staff members and the extent of their responsibility – an inexperienced playworker might need to be shown the best ways of storing the resources under their control, for example, or how to order stock and note down the expenditure.

Ways of supporting staff include the following:

- training (for example, short courses on keeping financial records)
- devising record systems for them to use

- showing them ways of using resources effectively (such as how to store resources carefully)
- informally checking that they are comfortable with their role
- using staff-appraisal interviews
- regularly monitoring with them the resources for which they are responsible.

## Ensuring effective use

Monitoring use of resources is a key way of supporting staff, whilst also making sure that the resources are being used effectively. It means regularly working with staff to find out the current level of resources, and checking that these will meet the organisation's requirements. This can be done formally, using a record sheet, or informally, by asking for feedback about the current level of resources. Getting regular feedback from staff will avoid situations in which potential problems have built up to an unacceptable situation, thereby causing the organisation – and the staff member – serious anxiety. It is a good idea to make it clear when passing on responsibility that you will be monitoring the resources regularly: this prevents the staff member from feeling that they are being 'spied' on later.

## Ensuring efficient use

It is always a good idea to take a team approach to monitoring resources, although it is also important for you to have a good overview of how resources are being used. There may be times when resources are being used at an unsustainable rate – for example, the amount of petty cash being used might be such as to cause a budget shortfall, or the amount of paper towels being used might seem excessive.

When the way in which resources are being used needs to be addressed, it is important that you handle this sensitively. The wrong approach can make staff feel that they are being blamed, or that the organisation is being mean and unreasonable. It is therefore a good idea if it is raised as an issue at a team meeting, with suggestions as to how to proceed being invited from the team. For example: 'I've noticed that we seem to be ordering a lot of paper towels compared with last year – has anyone any comments or suggestions that might help us, as I must look at ways of bringing this under control?' This approach allows team members to take ownership of the difficulty, although the overall responsibility for resources will still be yours.

## Considering environmental impacts

Although organisations have to manage their own budgets and resources, they should also be aware of the impact of their actions on the environment. Resources such as electricity and paper may seem plentiful, but organisations should take a responsible attitude to their use and wherever possible choose materials that are recyclable and sustainable. Play settings should also look at ways of making resources go further, for example by developing a scrap-paper store or by using stickers to remind people to turn off lights. This is morally good practice, especially as you are working with the future generation and your own attitudes towards resources might affect theirs. The diagram below shows the sorts of resources in play settings that should be used carefully in the interests of the environment.

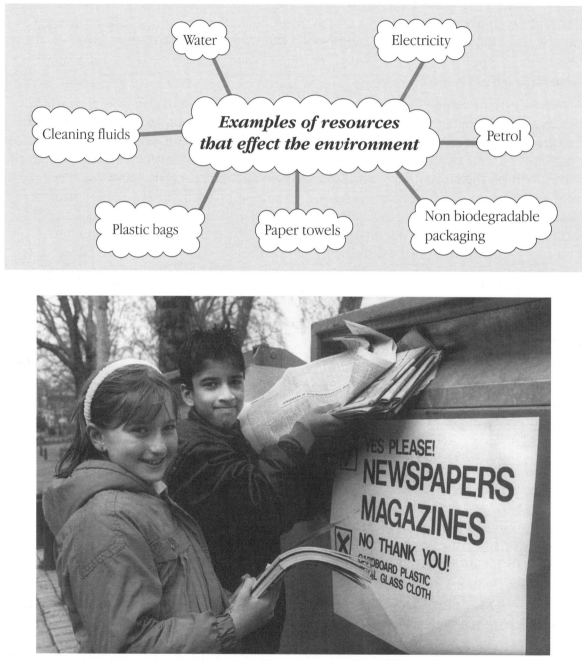

*Organisations, where possible, should choose materials that are recyclable*

## Active knowledge ✔

*Can you think of some practical ways in which your own setting encourages the responsible use of resources?*

## Monitoring the quality of resources

When resources are being bought from other suppliers, it is important to monitor their quality, as this may affect their safety and their use. Poor-quality paint, for example, may be less attractive to children and therefore wasted, while out-of-date food might cause food poisoning. It is particularly important to monitor the quality of resources when a new supplier has been chosen, or when a new product or service is being used.

As well as visual checks when products arrive in the setting, it might also be important to gain regular feedback from team members as to how they are finding these resources. A cheaper brand of washing-up liquid, for example, might prove to be more expensive in the longer term if a larger quantity is needed; and a more expensive glue might not necessarily be appreciated. Feedback from staff is very useful when ordering or re-ordering stock or resources.

### Identifying problems

It is important to deal with any problems with resources as soon as possible. For example, if the quality of resources bought in is poor, or if it comes to your attention that there is a problem with the sustainability of resources, you need to tackle this straightaway.

### Taking action when resources are unsatisfactory

Under consumer law, all goods should be of 'merchantable quality', which means that they should be of a reasonable standard, and should also be 'fit for purpose'. This means that settings that order goods that prove unsatisfactory should be able to return them promptly and gain a refund. To do this more easily, all receipts should be kept, as should records of supply or invoice numbers. Any complaints about services or goods should be put in writing, signed and dated, and a copy kept for future reference.

### Responding to concerns about the use of resources

Where there are concerns about the way in which resources are being used, you might choose to address these at a team meeting or with an individual member of the team (or, if more appropriate, this person's line manager). It is generally sensible to address any potential difficulties promptly, so that they do not develop into a major problem.

If you have any concerns that resources are being stolen, you need to talk first to your line manager and gain advice about how this should be dealt with.

### Active knowledge ✔

You are just walking through the main play area in your setting when you notice that a new member of staff is pouring away a large quantity of paint into the sink. This seems very wasteful.

1 *Explain how you would handle this situation.*
2 *Why is it important to address concerns promptly?*

# Using resources more effectively

In order to manage resources effectively, it is a good idea to keep looking at ways to improve their use and effectiveness. Some years ago, settings might not have thought about reducing their electricity or water consumption, but today this is important. Considering how resources are being used might enable you to identify improvements which might be made.

Making recommendations for any improvements can be thought of as a process.

> The first step is to make sure that you have a clear understanding of the current ways in which resources are being used, and *why* they are being used in this way. This means carrying out a fact-finding mission. This is important: although the reasons for the current use of resources might not be obvious, they might be completely justified.

> Once you have understood the current use of resources and the needs of the people using them, including children, you can start thinking about how the situation might be improved. Invite feedback about your ideas from the people who will be affected – they may have some suggestions of their own, or they may be able to see ways in which your ideas could be extended.

> After your proposals have taken shape, present your recommendations. This might be to your line manager, or to the team. It is important to be able to answer questions and to explain clearly the benefits of your proposals. Changes without good reason can demotivate teams, especially if they previously were content with the situation. Conversely, where teams *agree* to the changes, there is a greater likelihood of the improvement working.

## Case study

Naomi, a supervisor at a play scheme, has been concerned by the amount of paper that is being thrown away at the end of each day. She asks the team if there are any particular reasons why the paper needs to be thrown away, and finds out that often it has been used to put under paintings to protect tables because the setting had run out of newspaper. She asks staff how they would feel if a newspaper box were put in the reception area, to encourage parents and children to bring in newspaper; and also whether it would be possible to create a scrap-paper box.

At a team meeting, staff discuss how the scrap-paper box would be run, as similar things have been tried in the past and the paper has just built up and not been used. Everyone is happy with the idea of a newspaper box, and it is agreed that this will be introduced straightaway. Naomi proposes that she will research further how a scrap-paper box can be made to work, by asking other settings how they manage theirs.

1 *Why was it important that the issue of throwing away paper was looked at?*
2 *Explain why Naomi's approach is likely to be effective.*

# Keeping records of resources

Many types of records will need to be maintained in relation to resources. Records help play settings to run smoothly, and often provide evidence that resources are being used effectively. It is important that records are kept up to date, and that the staff who fill them in understand how to do so correctly. If there are any records for which you are directly or ultimately responsible, you should monitor these regularly.

Some records, such as financial records, are usually confidential: these should be shown only to authorised people, such as auditors or senior managers.

The table below shows the types of records that settings might keep, and the benefits of keeping these records.

| Type of record | Purpose |
| --- | --- |
| **Financial records** (such as petty-cash books) | To show how money has been spent. These may be requested by auditors, management committees, treasurers, or senior managers. To show that invoices have been paid. To provide evidence that the setting is meeting legal requirements – for example that it is paying VAT and National Insurance contributions. |
| **Order books** | To help when re-ordering stock. To make sure that invoices from suppliers match the orders. To monitor expenditure on services and goods. |
| **Booking forms** (such as for TVs or computers) | To make sure that resources such as computers are available for staff when they need them. To make sure that expensive items such as these are not left out or lost. To monitor how frequently these resources are being used. |
| **Stock-keeping records** | To keep a record of the amount of stock that is being used. To make sure that the stock level does not fall too low. |

## Consolidation

Consider how you manage the resources for which you are responsible.

◆ *How do you make sure that people in the setting have access to them, and that the resources meet their needs?*

◆ *Explain how you make sure that the resources are being used effectively.*

◆ *How do you keep records of these resources?*

# A21 unit test

1 What types of resources might need to be managed in play settings?
2 Why is it important that team members are consulted about resource requirements?
3 Give an example of a trend or development that might have resource implications for a setting.
4 Why is it important for those who make recommendations to have an understanding of the organisation's longer-term plans?
5 What are the benefits of controlling resources effectively in organisations?
6 Why is it important to pass on some responsibility for resources to those who need access to them?
7 Why is it important to support those who have responsibility for resources?
8 Explain why organisations and teams should consider the environmental impact of their use of resources.
9 Why is it necessary to monitor the quality of resources that come into the play setting?
10 What type of records related to resources might be needed in play settings?

# Unit A36

# Contribute to the selection of personnel for activities

The skills, experience and competence of staff are at the core of any effective play setting. Where staff are happy, motivated and capable of fulfilling their roles, the setting is able to run smoothly. Choosing staff is not an easy task, as it is important to match the needs of the setting carefully against the skills, experience and personalities of applicants, who may be people who already work in the setting or people who wish to do so.

This chapter looks at the process by which you might select staff. It is divided into two sections:

A36.1 Contribute to identifying personnel requirements
A36.2 Contribute to selecting the required personnel

## Element A36.1 Contribute to identifying personnel requirements

To be sure that staff are suited to the work activity that needs to be done, you need to think clearly about what skills and experience are required in order to do the work. This section looks at the importance of, and ways of, identifying personnel requirements.

### WHAT YOU NEED TO LEARN

- Considering work plans and targets within the area of responsibility
- Taking account of staff availability, financial resources, and other factors
- Complying with relevant legislation
- Presenting recommendations on time and in a helpful way

## Effective use of personnel

It is essential that you correctly work out what skills, experiences and qualities will be needed in a given job role, as well as how many hours will be needed. Among the many reasons for this are the following.

### Ensuring that staff are capable

It is essential that staff, whether they be full-time or part-time, paid or voluntary, are able to perform their tasks well and are motivated to do so. By identifying carefully the skills and experience that will be needed to carry out these tasks, you lessen the danger of asking someone to perform a task that they cannot manage.

## Ensuring that skills and experience are properly used

It is important to match staff and tasks carefully. Staff who are highly experienced and qualified may find it demotivating to carry out tasks in which they have little responsibility. By thinking carefully about the skills and experience required, you can make sure that each staff member's expertise is properly used.

## Monitoring cost, registration and safety

Play settings must be run cost-effectively, so paid staffing levels must be carefully worked out to make sure that the setting is neither over-staffed nor under-staffed. Over-staffing can have serious financial implications, as there might not be enough money in the budget to support the extra staff. Equally, when play settings find themselves under-staffed they are in danger of breaching the terms and conditions of their registration: settings will be running the risk of accidents if the adult–child ratio is not sufficient to allow proper supervision.

*Overstaffing can lead to financial problems so is not always a benefit*

# Identifying personnel requirements

To work out the personnel requirements accurately, you will need to analyse the task to be done. This might involve collecting information from colleagues. It is often a good idea to break a task down into areas, and consider each one separately. It is also helpful to distinguish between what is *essential* and what is *desirable*. For example, it might be desirable that a cook have experience of working in play settings, but this is not essential. It *will* be essential, however, that the cook has a Basic Food Hygiene certificate, and knows how to cook!

The table below shows some questions that might be important when thinking about personnel requirements.

| Area of information | Types of question to help analyse personnel requirements |
|---|---|
| Duties | What duties will the staff member be taking on?<br>To whom will they report?<br>Why is this member of staff required? |
| Time | How many hours should be allocated to this role?<br>Is this role a permanent role, or are staff required as a short-term measure (for instance, an outing might require staff just for one day)?<br>Is this a full-time or a part-time role? |
| Responsibility | What level of responsibility does this job entail?<br>Will staff need to manage others?<br>Will staff need to take responsibility for a specific area of work, or will they be supervised? |
| Complexity and skills | How difficult is the task?<br>What skills are essential in order to be able to complete the task?<br>What skills would be desirable? |
| Experience | Can this role be carried out by someone with no previous experience?<br>How much experience, and what type of experience, would be essential?<br>What type of experience would be desirable? |
| Qualifications | Are any formal qualifications essential for this post, in order to meet registration or other requirements?<br>What type of qualifications would be desirable? |
| Training | Is training needed in order for people to be able to do this task? |
| Voluntary/paid | Can this post be filled by a volunteer? |

### Job description: **Playworker**

**Job Title:** Playworker

**Reporting to:** Play Leader

**Purpose of job:** To work as part of a team delivering quality play opportunities to children aged 4–14 years

**Main duties:**
1. To maintain the safety of the children whilst they are playing
2. To plan and prepare play opportunities
3. To identify hazards and manage risks within the play environment
4. To liaise with other team members, parents and other professionals where necessary
5. To maintain confidentiality
6. To attend staff meetings whenever necessary
7. To attend staff training sessions

*Part of a job description*

## Using this information

Once you have defined your personnel requirements, this information may be used. You might use it to help argue a case for extra personnel, or you might be asked to write up a job description and a personnel specification. The job description outlines what exactly is required of the post-holder, while the personnel specification outlines the skills, experiences and qualities needed to do the job.

## Making a case for additional personnel

There may be times when you need to argue a case for increased staffing, typically with a management committee or with your line manager. To do this, you will need to prepare well so as to present a clear case. It is important to write down your arguments: this shows that you are taking the need seriously, and helps others digest the information. You should also show that you have carried out effective research, and any figures you cite must be accurate.

It is a useful strategy to explain what would be the potential consequences of *not* taking on the additional staff – for example, that the setting would no longer conform to registration requirements, or that staff morale will be lowered.

- Why do you think that extra personnel are required?
- What exactly would they do?
- How many hours would they be required for?
- How much is this likely to cost the setting?
- Can you suggest ways in which these costs be met (for example by having extra children or by getting a grant)?
- What are the consequences of *not* having extra personnel?

## Recognising work objectives and constraints

If you are responsible for thinking about personnel requirements, be aware of the possible constraints that your setting faces, as well as the longer-term objectives for the setting. For instance, you might prefer to recruit an experienced deputy play leader, but the management committee may have been given money to help train further an *existing* member of staff. Training internal staff might be a management objective of the setting; if so, this will affect the recruitment strategy. In the same way, a setting might want to recruit more playworkers who have experience of working with older children: this too would need to be taken into account when thinking about personnel requirements.

Most settings find themselves working against other constraints, too, such as the availability of staff within the local area, and tight finances. Although it might be desirable to find staff with a specialism in helping children with special needs, for instance, the setting might not be able to find someone at a cost that they could afford.

## Finding about organisational needs and legal requirements

If you are responsible for drawing up a job description or personnel specification, you will need to find out about your setting's needs and any internal policies about internal promotion and recruitment. You will need to consult your line manager or committee about any overall recruitment strategies that they have – for example, they may be hoping to find someone who has a second language, or who is interested in outdoor pursuits. How much are they prepared to pay? How many hours of work will be required? Where a new post is being created, to whom will the new post-holder be reporting? When filling an established post, it will be important to check whether any amendments are needed to the existing job role.

Seek advice too about the legal limits of what you can and cannot write when recruiting. It is illegal, for example, to advertise for 'men only' or 'women only', unless you have gained exemption, which usually happens only when an employer can prove that the *job* requires a person of a particular sex. Advice about employment legislation can be obtained from the Employment Services, the Department of Trade and Industry, and the Citizen's Advice Bureau.

Most settings look at the following policies when they are recruiting staff:

- Equal opportunities policy of the setting
- Staff development policy or 'Investors in People' documents
- Management plan of the setting
- Employment legislation, including the Equal Pay Act, the Disability Discrimination Act, the Race Relations Act, and the Sex Discrimination Act.

## Presenting your contributions

However great or small your contribution to identifying personnel requirements, you must deliver it on time and in the format asked for. Most recruitment processes are 'time-sensitive' – adverts may have to be in by certain days, or the management committee may meet only once a month. Working to deadlines is therefore important; it is no good complaining about being overworked and needing staff if you have failed to produce notes about personnel requirements!

It is also important to provide the information in the right format – this might mean presenting notes, or it might mean writing a full job description. If you are unsure about the format of a job description, look at another that the setting has used.

## Case study

Nelson works as the leader of the playscheme. The playscheme is run by the local parish church and gets some funding from the local council. Nelson is employed by the management committee, whose members are not playworkers.

Nelson has been approached by social services who would like to use the playscheme in the summer for two children who have moderate learning difficulties. Nelson recognises that this would mean an increase in staffing levels – she estimates that ideally another two staff would be needed. Nelson is meeting with the management committee tomorrow night.

1 **What information does Nelson need to find out before meeting with the committee?**
2 **Why has Nelson a good case for wishing to take on additional staff?**
3 **Explain the type of information that Nelson needs to present to the management committee.**

## Element A36.2 Contribute to the selection of required personnel

Once the personnel requirements have been worked out, the next step is actually to select people! This is not always an easy task; there may be several people interested in the post who have similar skills and experiences. This means that the selection process must be a fair and objective one.

This section looks at the skills needed to be able to contribute to the selection process, and the types of tasks that you might be required to do.

### WHAT YOU NEED TO LEARN

■ Helping to assess applicants
■ Making fair and objective evaluations
■ Communicating effectively with applicants and colleagues
■ Keeping records
■ Maintaining confidentiality

## The selection process

It is useful to have an overview of the selection process. Most settings find that several weeks pass between the decision to recruit someone and the person actually taking up the post. The flow diagram on the next page shows the usual steps in the selection process.

## Assessing the suitability of applicants

There are several methods often used, each of which has its own strengths and weaknesses. Most settings use a combination of methods, in order to make sure that they choose the person best suited to the post. The table on pages 266–7 shows a variety of methods.

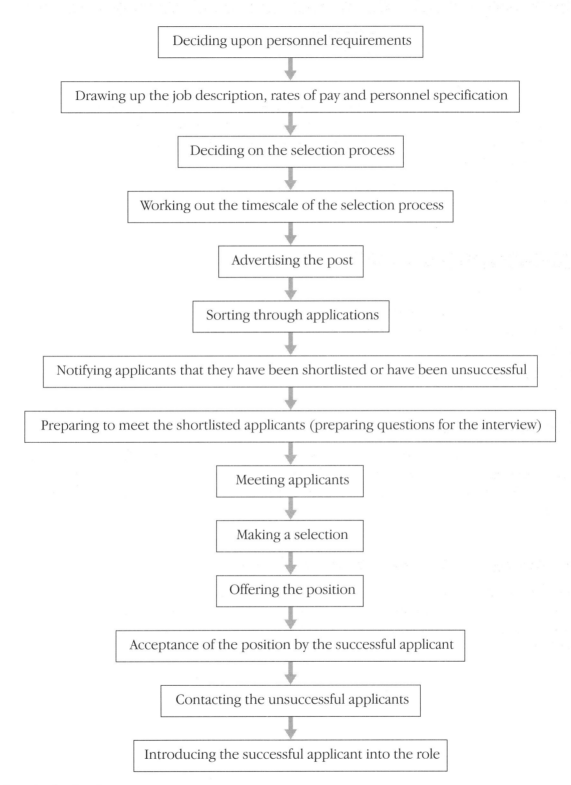

*A typical selection process*

| Method | Advantages | Disadvantages |
|---|---|---|
| **Letter of application** | Avoids having to design and send out an application form. Encourages the applicants to state why they think that they are suitable for the post. Applicants' writing or IT skills can be assessed. | Can be hard to assess, as every applicant is giving you different levels of information. Some potential applicants might not apply if they are unsure how to set out a letter of application. Some applicants who are capable might not 'sell' themselves well using this format. |
| **Curriculum vitae (CV)** | Allows the selection team to see someone's overall experience, qualifications and employment history. CVs are normally easy to read. Gives applicants the opportunity to record anything that they feel is important. Allows the selection team to see applicants' IT or writing skills. | Not all applicants have an up-to-date CV, so this may put off potential applicants. CVs may not give you enough in-depth information. |
| **Application form** | Allows the setting to ask questions that are important to the post. All applicants are being asked to provide the same information, so it is easier to compare applications. Allows the selection team to see applicants' ability to follow instructions, and their writing skills. | Application forms need to be carefully designed. Some settings use the same application form for several posts, parts of which might not be relevant to a given post. There might not be space, or a heading, for information that an applicant might think is important. |
| **Formal interview** | Allows the selection team to ask the same questions to each of the applicants, and compare their responses. Allows the selection team to see whether each applicant can cope with this type of stress. Can be time-effective, as interviews can be programmed in. | Some applicants might become very nervous, and not interview well. Applicants might not feel sufficiently relaxed to ask questions about the setting. |
| **Informal interview** | Makes applicants feel more relaxed, and their answers might give more information. | Different questions might be used for each applicant, thus making it seem 'less fair' as an interview. |
| **Observation of work** | Applicants might be asked to work for part of a session. This would help the selection team to see practical skills, and to assess the applicants' ability to relate to children and colleagues. | Applicants might have different situations to cope with, so they might not be able to show the same skills. Children may react differently if they sense tension. |

*Observation can be used to assess the suitability of applicants*

| Method | Advantages | Disadvantages |
|---|---|---|
| **Written exercises** | Written exercises or simulations can be used to find out what the applicant would do in a 'real life' situation. They help assess applicants' ability to read and act upon information. | Can be very daunting for applicants. |
| **Presentation** | Presentations ask the applicant to talk in front of others about a particular topic. This allows the selection team to see whether the applicant is good at speaking in public. | Can be very daunting for applicants, and is only usually used for 'key' posts in which giving presentations are going to be part of the role. |
| **References** | References are supplied by the applicant, and usually include one from the current employer. They can be taken up by telephoning, although written references should be asked for as documentary evidence. They give the selection team a further view of the applicant. | It is not unknown for former employers to give glowing references in order to 'lose' a member of staff with whom they are having problems. |

## APPLICATION FORM FOR EMPLOYMENT

PLEASE WRITE CLEARLY IN BLOCK CAPITALS                    **PRIVATE AND CONFIDENTIAL**

**Employment required**

| | |
|---|---|
| Position applied for: | |
| Where did you hear about this vacancy? | |
| Other employment interests: | |
| When could you start? | |
| Would you work full-time? | ☐ YES ☐ NO |
| If part-time, state days/hours: | |
| Have you previously worked for us? | ☐ YES ☐ NO    If yes, when? |

**Personal details**

Full name: Title:          Surname                    Forename(s):

Home address:



Postcode:

Home telephone:                    Work telephone:

Date of birth:

Are you legally eligible for employment in the UK?     ☐ YES    ☐ NO

Do you require a work permit to work in the UK?     ☐ YES    ☐ NO

*An application form*

## Choosing selection methods

The selection methods should be chosen to suit the post being filled. If a post requires good writing skills, it might be useful to ask for a letter of application; whereas a post that is essentially 'hands on' might be filled using an informal interview and observing the applicant in the setting.

Whatever system of selection is used, it must be fair and should be applied to all applicants. This means that applicants who send a CV when asked for an application form are not usually considered, as to do so would involve treating them differently from other applicants.

## Making a contribution

The way in which you might contribute to the selection of personnel within your organisation will depend on your role and the type of post that is being filled. There are, however, many skills that you will need to demonstrate, including these:

- confidentiality
- good organisation
- interpersonal skills
- honesty and accuracy
- analysis
- fairness
- objectivity.

## Honesty and accuracy

This is essential in any selection process. If you have any doubts or reservations about an applicant's ability to manage the role, always make these known.

## Fairness

This is always essential, but you need to be particularly aware of it when you are involved with internal applications or where you know one of the applicants personally. You should always make sure that other members of the selection team know of any professional relationship or friendship that you have with any of the applicants. To be fair to all applicants, you should give each application and each applicant equal attention – for example, at a formal interview, each will be asked the same questions.

## Objectivity

It is important that the person who fills the post is able to manage the workload and is genuinely the best person for the job, regardless of anything else. Be careful that your own attitudes and values do not colour your objectivity.

## Communication and interpersonal skills

Good interpersonal skills are an essential tool for people involved in the selection of staff. You will need to be able to express your opinion and assessments to others involved in the selection process, and to help put applicants at their ease, so that they can show you their strengths. You must also make sure that any information you supply in writing is clear and accurate, for example when asking for references or when writing to prospective candidates.

## Analysis

Selecting staff requires a level of analysis. You will need to consider whether the applicant really will fit the selection criteria and be able to manage the workload. You will also sometimes need to balance applicants' strengths against their weaknesses – few applicants will be absolutely perfect! You will need to read the selection criteria carefully and make sure that the prospective candidate matches these.

## Organisational and record-keeping skills

Whatever your role in the selection process, you will need to keep clear records and notes. If you are responsible for some of the administration of the process, you will need to be well organised, keeping files up to date and secure. You will also need to keep other members of the selection team, and in some cases other colleagues, informed of what you are doing.

Good organisation is also needed in relation to the applicants, as job descriptions and information about the post or the selection procedures will need to be given to them. The way in which you do this will contribute to applicants' impression of the setting, and if done well will help the selection process to run smoothly and fairly.

## Awareness of legal and organisational requirements

Throughout the selection process, you must be aware of legal and organisational requirements. For example, any details about applicants that are stored on computer will be covered by the Data Protection Act (see page 91). If you are unsure about any aspect of the selection process, seek advice from a senior person in your setting, or from organisations such as the Department of Trade and Industry or the Department for Education and Employment. Failure to follow selection procedures correctly could cause bad feeling in a setting, could damage the reputation of a setting, and could even create legal difficulties.

## Confidentiality

The ability to keep information confidential is of extreme importance, both during and after the selection process. You may have access to information which is highly confidential. The table below shows types of information that might form part of the selection process.

| Type of information | Purpose | Likely access arrangements |
|---|---|---|
| **Application forms** | Might be used as part of the selection process. Personal details will be provided by applicants, including experience, qualifications and employment history. | Blank application forms can be sent to anyone who enquires about the post. Completed application forms should only be seen by the personnel officer, and members of the selection team. |
| **Job descriptions** | Sent out with application forms to inform potential applicants about the nature of the post. | Some settings will allow any staff member to look at these. Other settings will restrict these only to people who express an interest in the post. All members of the selection team should see a copy of the job description. |
| **Curricula vitae** | Curricula vitae are produced by applicants to show their employment history, skills and experience. | Members of the selection team, and the personnel officer. |
| **List of applicants** | Put together when deciding on a shortlist. | Members of the selection team, the administration staff, and the personnel officer. |
| **References** | Applicants might be asked to write down the names of people who can vouch for them. References are then taken up by telephone, or more usually in writing. | The selection team, the administration staff, and the personnel officer |

| Type of information | Purpose | Likely access arrangements |
|---|---|---|
| **Rates and scales of pay** | Rates and scales of pay might be discussed to make sure that the remuneration for the post is fair. | The selection team, and the administration or finance staff. |
| **Reasons why applicants were not shortlisted or offered the post** | Notes are often made to help the team remember the basis for the decisions. These notes can be used later to provide feedback to applicants at their request. | The selection team. |
| **Opinions offered by the selection team about individual applicants' suitability** | Opinions might be expressed during the course of the decision-making. These opinions must be treated as confidential. | The selection team. |

The information provided in selection processes is so sensitive that most settings would take disciplinary measures against anyone involved in the process who breached confidentiality. Even one-off comments, inside or outside the setting, can cause extreme distress, anger and embarrassment, as the case study below shows.

## Case study

A committee member, whose setting is looking to recruit a part-time member of staff, meets an old friend who is working in another play setting. When asked about the advert in the paper, she says 'Yes, we are hoping to expand. Shaheen has applied, which is really brilliant.' Shaheen is a playworker at the friend's play setting. The diagram shows how this chance remark could cause enormous problems.

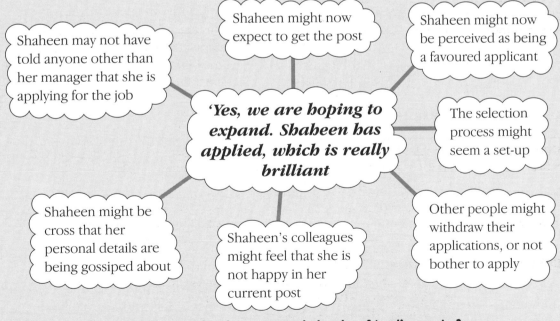

*How should the committee member have responded to her friend's enquiry?*

It is also important to be careful not to make any comments *inside* the setting, especially when an internal post is being advertised. Applicants might ask you if you have any news, or if you could help them with, for example, their application forms. If you are part of the selection process, your actions must be seen to be scrupulously fair. It is always best to avoid making any comments or discussing the selection process with anyone who is not directly involved.

## People who might be involved in selecting personnel

The people who might be involved in the selection of personnel will vary from setting to setting. Typically there will always be someone at the management level, along with some or all of the following:

- the personnel officer (usually found in larger organisations)
- the chair or vice chair of the management committee
- the manager or deputy of the setting
- the member of staff who will be directly managing the successful applicant
- a representative from another organisation which contributes funds to the setting
- recruitment specialists.

By involving several people in making the selection, the setting ensures that a balanced view is taken, and that the staffing needs of the organisation are met. It is also important that the selection process is *seen* to be fair – one single person making the selection alone could be seen as being biased.

## Selecting personnel

Various specific tasks and roles are important in appointing personnel. Carrying out these tasks effectively will allow the selection process to run smoothly. In some settings these tasks might be carried out by a personnel officer, while in a small setting they may be carried out by a small team. Where several people are involved, good communication must be maintained to prevent potential hitches, such as references not being taken up or unsuccessful candidates not being informed.

### Collecting applications

Once applications have been received, the selection team will sift through them and draw up a shortlist of applicants. These will be people who appear to have the right skills and experience. If you are responsible for collecting the application forms, you should photocopy them and make sure that each member of the selection team receives copies, in an envelope marked 'Confidential'. A date for a shortlisting meeting might also be made after the applications have been received.

### Shortlisting candidates

To do this well, those involved need to read through the job description or the personnel requirements already drawn up, and then read through each application carefully. It is a good idea to look at each one separately, and make notes about it. Most selectors find that they end up with three piles – one of strong applications, another of applications that are not suitable, and a middle pile of applications that have some strengths and some weaknesses.

The selection team will then meet to discuss the shortlist, and compare their choices for the shortlist. The team will often find that they have made similar choices, perhaps with slight differences of opinion. At this stage, the notes made earlier will be helpful in explaining why you have rejected an application or considered it to be a strong one.

At the shortlisting meeting, set a date for interviews and arrange a location. Time should be set aside to meet before and after the interviews, so that a decision can be made quickly.

## Responding to applicants

Once the shortlisting process has been completed, letters must be sent out to all applicants, either inviting them for interview (or other chosen selection method) or saying that their application has been unsuccessful on this occasion. It is good practice and professional for letters to be sent out promptly, so that applicants are kept informed of what is happening.

If you are responsible for this part of the selection process, you should file all the applications carefully: you might need to refer back to them later, in case of a future query. It can also be a good idea to hold applicants' details on file in case another vacancy occurs. If you intend to do this you must inform the applicants, so that they can object if necessary.

**NEWTOWN PLAY CLUB**
*Promoting play opportunities for children*

15–19 Market Road
Newtown, Hants PO22 1SR
Tel no: 01747 390101

12 July 2000

Ms Tara Peters
24 New Ridgeway Road
Bristol
BS4 2TR

Dear Ms Peters

Thank you for attending the recent interview. We regret to inform you that on this occasion we are not able to offer you this post.

We would, however, like to keep your details on file and will contact you if any further position becomes available.

Yours sincerely

Sarah Dawson
Play Club Co-ordinator

*A letter of rejection*

## Taking up references

Some settings decide to take up references *before* shortlisting candidates, while others wait until the successful candidate has been appointed. If you are responsible for taking up references, it is usual either to write to the named person or to telephone him or her. You should always ask for spoken references to be followed up with written references: these are often needed to meet registration and organisation requirements.

When asking for a reference, make sure that the person giving it understands the nature of the post that the applicant has applied for. It is usual to ask the referee the following types of questions:

- How long have you known the applicant?
- In what capacity have you known the applicant?
- Give the type of post applied for, would you be able to recommend the applicant?

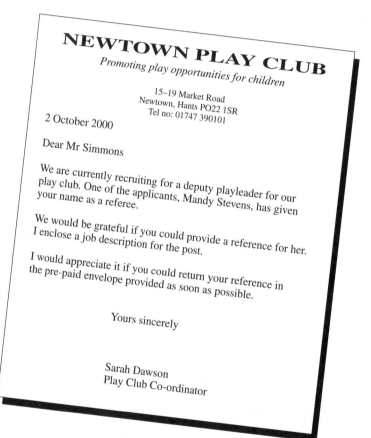

### NEWTOWN PLAY CLUB
*Promoting play opportunities for children*

15–19 Market Road
Newtown, Hants PO22 1SR
Tel no: 01747 390101

2 October 2000

Dear Mr Simmons

We are currently recruiting for a deputy playleader for our play club. One of the applicants, Mandy Stevens, has given your name as a referee.

We would be grateful if you could provide a reference for her. I enclose a job description for the post.

I would appreciate it if you could return your reference in the pre-paid envelope provided as soon as possible.

Yours sincerely

Sarah Dawson
Play Club Co-ordinator

*A letter asking for a reference*

## Preparing for interviews

Most settings organise an interview to meet the applicants. This needs to be carefully organised, to make the applicant feel at ease and also to make the setting look an attractive place in which to work. Staff in the setting must be informed of the date of the interview. Make sure that the timings of the interviews are realistic, as applicants are usually shown around the setting as well.

The selection team should meet beforehand and agree upon the questions to be asked and who will ask them. Questions should be carefully thought through to make sure that they cover many aspects of the role. They also need to be clear and fair.

## Interviewing

As an interviewer, you should be warm and courteous, and try to put each applicant at their ease. In a formal interview, it is good practice to keep to the prepared questions, so that all applicants have the *same* questions. Keep notes of applicants' replies, both to your own questions and to those posed by other members of the selection team.

If applicants have been asked to give a presentation, listen carefully to the information presented and observe the skills that are being shown. You should again make notes. This will allow you to discuss the strengths and weaknesses of applicants in depth and in definite terms.

## Making the decision

Once the interviews, observations of work or presentations are complete, most selection teams discuss applicants' suitability for the post straight away. At this point the notes that you have made will be important. You should put forward your point of view, as well as listening to others'. Keep in mind the job description and the personnel specification.

Once a decision has been made, it is usual to note down the reasons why the other applicants were *not* offered the post. This makes it easier if the decision is queried, or if feedback is required by the unsuccessful applicants.

## Informing applicants of the selection

It is usual to inform the successful applicant of the decision as soon as possible, and to check with them that they do still wish to accept the post. If they agree to take the post, a written offer should be made. Once this has happened, the other applicants need to be informed promptly that they have not been successful. This should be done in writing; but where there are internal applicants it is important to let them know personally.

It is a good idea to offer internal applicants some feedback, so that they understand why they were not successful. Some settings also offer unsuccessful internal applicants the opportunity to have an appraisal interview, to counteract feelings of rejection and demotivation (see Unit A55).

# Delays and postponements

The selection process does not always run as smoothly as everyone would wish. This can be very frustrating for everyone involved, and means that your plans must be flexible enough to cope with not recruiting a staff member straight away.

There are several reasons why selection might not result in an appointment.

## Shortage of time

Organising a selection process requires a lot of time. Job descriptions, selection methods and personnel requirements all have to be agreed, and an application form and an advertisement for the post produced. Where settings have no administrative back-up, this can be difficult to manage, and the process may be slower than expected.

## Changes in funding or the requirements of the setting

Sudden changes in funding or personnel requirements can mean that the selection process is delayed or postponed. Examples would be when another member of staff resigns, creating the opportunity for the whole structure of the setting to be reconsidered; or when funding is suddenly increased, which would allow the setting to recruit more than one member of staff.

## Labour market

The setting may find that although it is advertising widely, it is not receiving enough applications of the right calibre. Several attempts at advertising may be necessary, and in some cases the setting may reconsider its personnel requirements.

## Case study

Shirley, the playleader, has been authorised by the management committee to recruit two further members of staff for her summer playscheme, in response to social services' request to place two children with moderate learning difficulties.

1 *Who might Shirley ask to join her on the selection team?*
2 *What qualifications, qualities and skills will potential candidates need to have for these posts?*
3 *Write down three questions that might be used at interview to help selection.*
4 *Explain the reasons for your choice of questions.*

## A36 unit test

1 Why is it important to identify personnel requirements carefully?
2 Why is it important to think about the skills that are needed to carry out a job role?
3 List the type of information you might need to present in order to make a case for additional staffing.
4 Why is it essential that confidentiality is maintained during and after the selection process?
5 Why are good organisation and record-keeping skills important?
6 Describe three methods of selecting candidates.
7 Why is it important to take up written references for candidates?
8 Explain why the selection process may sometimes be delayed.
9 Who might be involved in the recruitment process?
10 Why is it important to keep prospective candidates informed during the selection process?

# Unit B211

# Contribute to marketing, developing and promoting services

All new services need to be planned carefully. This avoids costly and time-consuming mistakes, and ensures that any new services meet the needs of the people for whom they are being provided. In your playwork setting there are many reasons why you might need to develop new services – for example, you might be starting up a new playscheme or out-of-school club, or you might be considering extending the range of provision that you are offering.

This chapter looks at ways in which you might research, develop and promote new services.

The elements for this unit are:

B211.1  Contribute to researching the need for new services
B211.2  Contribute to developing new services
B211.3  Contribute to promoting new services
B211.4  Contribute to evaluating new services

## Element B211.1  Contribute to researching the need for new services

However pressing and obvious the need may seem to develop a new service, it is wise to carry out some research beforehand. Play settings need not only to meet local children's and their parents' or carers' needs but also to be financial sustainable. The diagram shows some of the new services that might be provided by organisations.

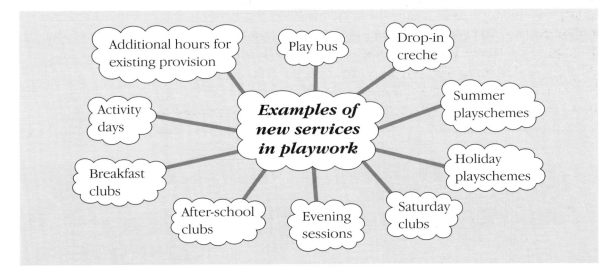

- Identifying the purpose of the research and continuing it with your responsible colleague
- Agreeing available resources and who the target groups are
- Using the most effective research methods to collect, record and analyse information
- Identifying possible new services and level of demand.

*A **play bus** is an example of a new service which could be offered by an organisation*

## Information that might be needed

Research is about collecting information. It is therefore important to know before starting any research what *type* of information is required. This will depend very much on the service you are hoping to provide. For example, if your organisation is considering opening a new out-of-school club, it will need to be sure that enough parents or carers and children are interested. Setting up a club on a hunch that it is needed could potentially be a very expensive mistake! Before drawing up detailed plans, therefore, most settings carry out some sort of research. This is often known as a feasibility study.

### Planning a new service

In carrying out a feasibility study most organisations are wanting to check that there is a level of demand to justify the service, and that it is possible to provide this service. The diagram below shows information that will need to be collected:

### Demand for the service

This is essential information. The following questions must be answered to make sure that the service will be successful.

- How many people are likely to use and support the service?
- How often would they use it, and what exactly would they like to be provided?

### Potential sources of funds

Some organisations may also want to find information about different sources of funding which might be available, to help them with the start-up costs of the project or in subsidising places. Local authorities, Early Years and child-care partnerships and funding councils might be approached for this information.

### Existing provision

An organisation new to an area might have to research what other provision already exists. This is important to avoid duplication of provision, unless there is enough demand to sustain two organisations doing similar work.

### Current costs

Many organisations need to ask for a contribution from parents or carers towards the places or services offered. It is therefore important to find out what the 'market' rate is for similar services, or to find out from potential service users how much they would be prepared to pay.

### Staffing

The number of staff required to carry out the service will also be an important factor: this will have a direct effect on the cost of the service.

### Availability of staff

In some areas of the country, it can be very difficult to recruit staff. There may be few appropriately qualified playworkers, or local rates of pay may be more than your setting can afford. Find out about the labour market in the area in which you wish to set up the service.

### Availability of premises

You may need to research the availability and cost of premises in the area where you are planning to set up, which might significantly affect the costs of the service.

### Start-up costs

On a practical level, the costs of furniture, equipment and resources also need to be researched. What exactly will be required?

### Registration and legal requirements

Are there any registration requirements or legal requirements that you need to understand which might affect your proposal? You could contact local social services or local authorities.

# Undertaking research

If you are responsible for undertaking the research for your organisation, make sure that you understand what type of information needs to be collected, and why. For example, if a bid for funds is being put together, your organisation might need some specific information that will support the bid. Being clear about the type and purpose of information needed is especially important if several people are working on the project, to prevent tasks from being duplicated or not finished on time.

## Agreeing resources and target groups

It is usually a good idea to draw up a research plan. This would indicate the type of information to be collected, how it is to be collected, and who will be responsible for collecting it. The plan should also make clear who will be approached for information, so that only one person from your organisation makes contact with them about the new service.

The group of people from whom you want to collect information is often referred to as the target group. Examples of potential target groups may include:

- parents and carers
- children
- local employers
- schools.

Any research that is carried out for your organisation should be agreed by your line manager or the person in charge of the project, as this person has overall responsibility for the smooth running of the project.

It is also a good idea to agree how much work time can be spent on the project, and a budget to cover travel costs, stationery and administration.

# Choosing research methods

There is a range of research methods that can be used to gather information. Each has its own advantages and drawbacks, so it is important to choose carefully. Factors that will affect the choice include time, cost, and ease of reaching the target group. If you are working on a large study or if you have not carried out any research before you might also need to seek some support or advice. It is also worth finding out whether other research has been carried out before, in case it used research methods that were not considered to have been successful.

## Questionnaires

Questionnaires have the advantage of being relatively easy and cheap. They can be sent out in the post, or handed out in the street or in places of work. The main difficulty with questionnaires is that not all of them will be returned, and you may gain information only from the people who have very strong views! The accuracy of the information can be variable, too; people sometimes tick the box or give the answer that they think the organisation will *want* to hear.

### Designing questionnaires

Questionnaires that are too long can put people off, while questionnaires that are too short will not give you enough information. There are two types of questions that can be used: closed questions and open questions.

- *Closed questions* give very clear-cut answers. For instance, 'Would you like your child to attend an out-of-school club?' 'Yes.' These are easy to process and collate, but may not give us a range of information.
- *Open questions*, such as 'What does your child enjoy most about the after-school club?', often generate more information, although people filling in questionnaires tend to give very short answers.

Most questionnaires use a mix of open and closed questions, and encourage people to provide more information by putting in a 'further comments' section. It is always a good idea to trial a questionnaire with a few people first, in case the questions you have chosen do not give you the depth or type of information that you were hoping for.

### Advantages
- Questionnaires are quick and easy for participants to use.
- Participants can complete them in private.

### Disadvantages
- The return rate for questionnaires is often poor.
- People who do return questionnaires may do so because they have strong opinions.
- It is harder to select a representative sample.
- People may become bored if questionnaires take too long to complete.
- Some people may have difficulty in filling them in.

## Active knowledge ✔

Try to find an example of a questionnaire that has been professionally designed. Do not worry about the subject matter.

1  How many questions are used?
2  Can you identify the open questions?
3  How long is the questionnaire?
4  What do you think of the overall design of the questionnaire?
5  What have you learnt about questionnaire design from seeing this one?

## Interviews

Face-to-face interviews can be more useful because the researcher can pick out a sample of participants and, if desirable, can follow up on their answers. There are two types of interviews, structured and unstructured. A *structured interview* has pre-set questions and the participant is led through the interview. This type of interview is often used where large numbers of people are involved, as analysing the data is more straightforward. *Unstructured interviews* allow the researcher to explore some answers in more depth.

In any interview situation, it is important that questions are chosen carefully so that participants do not feel that there is a 'right' answer. As with questionnaires, two types of questions can be used, closed and open.

### Advantages
- Interviews can provide detailed answers and information.
- Participants who do not enjoy writing down their opinions and thoughts are more likely to come forward.
- Unstructured interviews can help researchers find out more about a participant's thoughts.

### Disadvantages
- Interviews rely on the participants being truthful.
- Participants may feel that there is a 'correct' answer that they should give.
- Interviews can be expensive to conduct as they take time.

## Informal consultation

Informal consultation means talking to people in the target group and listening to their ideas and views. This can give you an 'on the ground' feel for local issues as well as some useful ideas. It is also a good way of communicating with people who might not feel comfortable about filling in questionnaires or having a face-to-face interview. The main disadvantage is that it is not a very objective way of carrying out research: you might only be hearing one side.

### Advantages
- Informal consultation provides detailed information.
- Participants might feel at ease with this method.

### Disadvantages
- Information given may not be representative of a target group's views.
- Information collected this way can be harder to collate.

## Focus groups

Focus groups are used to ask questions of a small group of people – usually around six to eight. Structured questions can be prepared, for the group to talk about; or a facilitator can allow the group to talk about specific issues. Focus groups are good ways of listening to several different points of view, although it is important that the facilitator is able to guide the group and make sure that everyone's opinions are heard.

*A focus group can produce interesting information from potential users of a service*

### Advantages
- Information can be gained from several people.
- No written skills are required.
- Ideas and comments can be interesting.
- This method involves potential users.

### Disadvantages
- Focus groups need to be carefully managed to avoid one person monopolising the conversation.
- Information gained this way can be hard to process.

## Studying existing information

Using existing information is extremely useful and can save you a lot of time. Existing information may include the numbers of children and families living in the local area, reports on setting up other provisions, as well as information already collected by other organisations. Possible sources of information include:

- the local authority
- local colleges of further education
- local schools
- early years' and childcare partnerships
- organisations such as the Kids Club Network

### Advantages

- This method saves time and money.
- It can be done from a desk.
- It creates networking situations.

### Disadvantages

- The information may be out of date.
- The information may be inaccurate.
- The information may be incomplete or not completely relevant.

## Making sure that information is representative

It is important when using methods such as questionnaires and interviews that the information that you gain is representative. To make sure that you are getting a cross-section of views, ideas and opinions, you might have to select from within your target group. This is called *sampling*. For example, from within a target group of children, you might decide that you need to speak to children of different ages, as well as to children who go to different schools. Sampling helps you to get a wider picture.

You will also need to make sure that you get *enough* views and ideas to form a representative picture. For example, if there are 300 children attending a local school, you will need to talk to enough of them to gain a fair sample – perhaps 25 per cent, or 75 children.

There are three different ways of sampling. The table below shows how they could be used if you had to collect information from a total of 75 children (assuming that you had permission to do so!).

| Type of sampling method | Method |
|---|---|
| **Random** | You might put the names of the 300 children in a box and then pull out the names of 75 at random. The main disadvantage of this method is that some of the children might not want to give you any information, or they might not be present. You might also find that they are all boys, or that a majority of them are in the same year group. |
| **Opportunity** | You could take information from the first 75 children that you met who wanted to help you. The main disadvantage of this method is that you would only get keen, willing children, whose views might not be representative. |
| **Quota** | This is one of the most-used techniques in commercial market research. If you wanted a balance of information between different age groups, you would firstly work out how many children there were in each of the age groups – for example, out of 300 children there might be 30 children who are 6 years old (10%) – and you would then make sure that around 10% of the children you asked were 6 years old (that is, seven or eight of the 75 children). |

## Collating, analysing and interpreting information

Once the information has been collected, it needs to be accurately collated and analysed. This is essential: it will otherwise be very hard to be able to draw accurate conclusions.

The extent of the analysis and the way in which it is presented will depend on the needs of the setting. A setting that is presenting its information formally might consider looking at visual ways of presenting information, such as graphs or charts; whereas a setting where information is to be used internally might ask for a short summary report and that you present your findings to them.

## Storing information

If any of the information you collect is sensitive, it should be kept in secure conditions. It is also a good idea to keep the *sources* of information, such as the completed questionnaires or your notes from interviews: if there is a query later about your findings, this will allow you to check that no mistakes have been made.

Any information that is stored on computer must comply with the Data Protection Act 1998. This Act allows people to check that details held about them on computer are accurate, and prohibits transfer of this information without their consent.

## Identifying conclusions

After collating the information, spend some time analysing it and then drawing some conclusions. It is important that you keep an open mind during the information-gathering stage – there is always a danger in research that people draw conclusions that reflect their hopes!

While analysing information you may sometimes feel that the technique chosen has not given you enough information, or that there are some gaps. If so, you will need to consider whether further time can and should be spent gaining more information.

When identifying conclusions, you may be able to identify whether or not there is enough interest in the new service – for example, you might see that a summer playscheme would be popular, but that an ongoing out-of-school club would not. Judging the level of demand is vital: once resources have been invested in a project, the project must remain sustainable. If demand appears to be short-term – for example, out-of-school care may be required only in the summer – the organisation may then consider other options, such as hiring a hall and hiring temporary rather than permanent staff.

It is not unusual for researchers once they have made some initial conclusions to design some more research to check that these conclusions are right. This is often done if the first piece of research was very wide.

## Presenting your findings

You need to present your findings clearly and accurately. Make sure that any conclusions that you reach are based on the evidence. When presenting your findings, explain briefly how the research was carried out and any drawbacks of the research method. The importance of accuracy cannot be over-emphasised: there is little point in carrying out research if you then disregard its findings.

In presenting your findings to others, you could use:

- graphs
- charts
- a presentation with slides
- a report with conclusions
- your complete study, written up and including your research data in an appendix.

## Element B211.2 Contributing to developing new services

Once some research has been carried out which indicates the level of demand for and interest in the proposed new service, more detailed plans will need to be drawn up to move the project forward. For any new service to work well, you need to spend time consulting everyone who will be involved, including staff and the potential users of the service.

### WHAT YOU NEED TO LEARN

- Consulting with the relevant people on proposed new services
- Seeking approval to develop and test new services
- Involving appropriate people in developing a specification for the services
- Testing the desirability of the services with representative groups
- Getting feedback
- Agreeing full implementation of the new services

## Consulting colleagues

Launching any new service should be seen as a co-operative project: it will then be more likely to succeed. Take time to consult colleagues about ways in which the new service might work, and then bring the information together. The many benefits of a co-operative approach are summarised in the diagram.

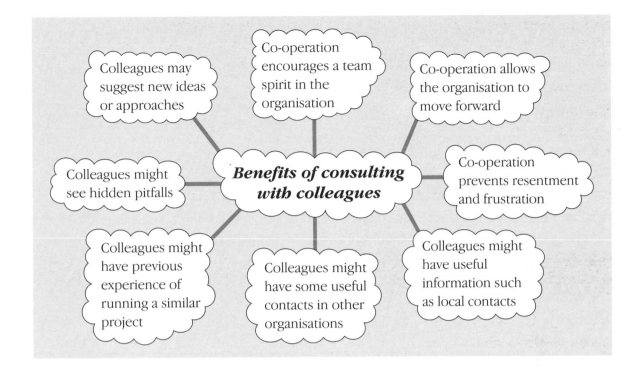

## Ways of consulting colleagues

How you consult colleagues will depend on the size of your organisation and the complexity of the service you are considering. In very large organisations, a core team will emerge who will be mainly responsible for working on the project; while in smaller organisations the project might involve nearly everyone, with one or two people taking direct responsibility. In large organisations, staff might be consulted using questionnaires, with other input being gained through interview or informal consultation; in small organisations, much of the consultation will be informal and the project may be discussed in staff or team meetings.

Try to ensure that the consultation process is seen as an open one, or staff might feel left out and be resentful. A communications board in the staff room might be used, so that if anyone has any comments about the service they can note them down.

Throughout the planning and implementing of the new service, keep consulting with colleagues. Their advice and input can be useful, and often they will contribute experience or ideas that will help the new service run more smoothly.

## Active knowledge ✔

*What are the most effective ways of consulting with colleagues in your own setting?*

## Developing and testing a new service

### Gaining approval

Once time has been spent consulting with colleagues, listening to their ideas and gathering information, an outline of how the new service is likely to be provided and funded will start to take shape. At this stage, it is important that key people in the organisation such as the manager or project officer agree with the proposal and are happy that the project is taken forward. This is not a decision to make lightly: once the go-ahead is given, time and resources will be needed.

## Developing a specification and a plan

When the outline proposal for the new service has gained approval from the key people in the organisation, it will be important to draw up a specification and a detailed plan of how the new service is to be developed.

A *specification* is a list of the requirements of the new service – for example, where it should be located, the times that it might be open, the type of equipment that will be needed. A specification could be thought of as the shopping list of requirements.

The *plan* should show how the service is to be developed. It is usually broken down into steps, with dates – for example, the date when the service is to be opened, and the date when marketing is to be started. Plans might also show who is responsible at each stage. Plans must be as detailed as possible, and realistic. Check that timescales are as accurate as possible, or the project might be delayed and people become frustrated because they are waiting for others to complete their part of the project.

## People who might contribute

A range of organisations or individuals might be asked for help in drawing up the plan because they have particular expertise or because their approval is needed. It is usually worth involving other organisations at an early stage, as their advice may affect the overall plan.

The table below shows the types of people who might be involved in drawing up a plan.

| Organisations or individual | Reason for contact |
|---|---|
| **Inspection unit** | For guidance about the registration requirements, and for staff clearance. |
| **Early-years and childcare partnerships** | For advice about funding arrangements, and help in advertising the service through the Child Information Service. Development workers will also be able to give advice as to how best to proceed. |
| **Architect** | (Where premises are being adapted, extended or built.) For planning, design, and advice about the timescale. |
| **Builder, electrician** | (Where premises need improving or adaptations must be made.) For a forecast of potential costs, the scale of the work, and the time that should be allowed. |
| **Solicitor** | For advice about any legal agreements, such as renting premises. |
| **Fire officer** | For advice on fire prevention and safety. |
| **Environmental officer** | For advice about the layout of kitchens, toilets and other areas. |
| **Planning officer** | For advice about planning regulations, and whether planning permission must be sought. |

## Working on the plan

If you are responsible for drawing up a plan and a specification, you need to be well organised. Everyone involved will need copies of the plan, and everyone will need to know exactly what their roles are and the timescales. For example, if leaflets are to be prepared as part of the plan, the person responsible for the design of the leaflets will need to know the date by which they should submit the designs.

If the plan needs to be adapted or the timings altered, it is essential that the key people and others who are working on the project are all kept informed. This means that the plan needs to be carefully monitored and progress checked.

## Inviting feedback

As well as consulting colleagues, and other organisations about the plan, it is important to keep in contact with the likely users of the service, the target group. They might include the children, schools, parents and carers, and employers.

As the plan progresses, seek their opinions about the way you envisage the service. The best way of consulting them will probably be to meet them and to ask them to consider specific points, such as the hours of opening and the cost, which tend to be major factors in whether or not the service is successful. Make sure that children are consulted, too, they are the core of the project! You might like to raise with them questions about the types of equipment and resources needed in the setting, and its layout and design.

The main reason why projects are delayed or cost more than expected is that plans are changed frequently. By involving the key users of the service while *devising* the plan, you are less likely to consider major changes later, when they might be expensive – especially if there is any building work involved.

The diagram below shows some of the benefits of consulting with potential users of the project.

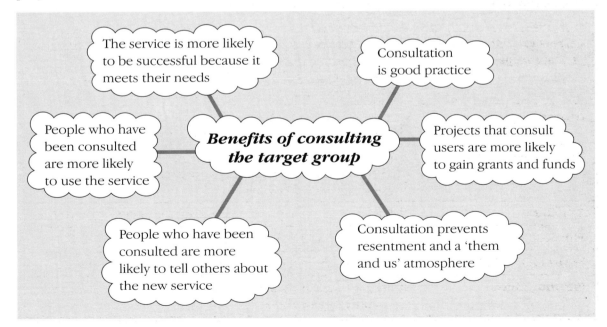

## Fully implementing the plan

At each key stage of the plan, get approval from the key people within your organisation, such as your line manager or the management committee. Keep them informed of any developments or setbacks as the plan progresses. In particular, they should be informed about, and their approval sought for, any adjustments to the plan. This is essential, as changes to the plan could have financial implications – for instance, increasing the hours of the service would have staffing and organisational implications. Wherever possible, research the cost and other implications of any changes, and make sure that these are accurate.

As the plan is implemented, you may need to call on the support and expertise of particular colleagues, or people outside the organisation such as personnel officers, treasurers, or health and safety officers. Very few new projects go ahead without some setbacks, so it is important to be patient and cheerful!

## Case study

Jamie has taken the lead responsibility for opening an out-of-school club to be attached to the nursery. The nursery management committee has agreed to refurbish a section of the nursery in order to create two separate rooms for the club.

During the project Jamie has been keen to make most of the decisions himself, but nearing the end of the project he invites a colleague into a room which is nearly finished. The colleague asks Jamie where the computer is to be installed, and Jamie then notices that there are no electrical sockets nearby. He asks the builder to install some more sockets and also a few extra storage cupboards, as these too were suggested by the colleague. Later that month, the builder's bill arrives and the manager is concerned to find that it is significantly higher than expected. The builder explains that the main cause was the installation of the extra sockets after the wiring had already been completed, as well as the additional materials and labour for the cupboards.

1 *In what way did Jamie act unprofessionally?*
2 *How could this situation have been avoided?*
3 *What further problems could this cause for the setting?*
4 *Why is it a good idea if more than one person is involved in planning new services?*

## Element B211.3 Contribute to promoting new services

Most new services need to be promoted, in order that the target group finds out about them and is attracted to the service. This is an important part of developing a service: both the 'right image' and information must be given to prospective users. This section looks at the range of common promotional methods, and the way in which they might be used.

- Making suggestions for promotional methods
- Discussing and agreeing the promotional methods
- Developing promotional materials and methods
- Finalising details
- Implementing promotional methods

## Promotional methods

There are several methods that organisations can use to promote a new service. As each one has its advantages and disadvantages, most organisations use a combination of methods. The table that follows outlines some common methods.

| Method | Advantages | Disadvantages |
|---|---|---|
| **Radio/TV commercial** | A local radio or television commercial can be a way of raising awareness of a new service. | Commercials are expensive. Several adverts may be required. There is no guarantee that the listeners or viewers will be potential users. |
| **Leaflets/flyers** | A cheap way of providing written information about a new service. They need to be carefully designed to contain plenty of information without looking overcrowded. | They need to look professional. The information must be accurate. Distribution can be time-consuming. |
| **Advertisement in local paper** | Adverts need to be large enough to be noticed, and the amount of information that can be included is limited. | Adverts are expensive. Several adverts may be required. |
| **Open day** | Effective in raising awareness of a new service within the local community. They are cheap, but require good organisation. | There are expensive staffing costs. Good administration skills are needed. A lot of preparation is required. |
| **Using the local media** | This is an excellent way of raising awareness without spending any money. Most local newspapers and radio stations are keen to have new stories which have local interest. | You need to make contact with a reporter or an editor. All the information you supply might not appear. Stories are not always accurate. |
| **Using other organisations** | Advising other organisations about a new service and giving them leaflets or flyers to distribute encourages greater networking and co-operation between organisations. | Other organisations might be too busy to distribute your leaflets. This relies on goodwill towards your setting. |

| Method | Advantages | Disadvantages |
|---|---|---|
| **Using word of mouth** | Considered to be one of the best forms of marketing. It is free, and recommendation from other people is often powerful. To encourage this, you need to make personal contact with as many existing users of the service as possible. | Information passed this way might not be 100% accurate. It requires good interpersonal skills. |
| **Posters** | Posters can be visually appealing. They can be put in local shops, and existing users might be prepared to display them at home. | Posters need to be attractive. Only a limited amount of information can be put on posters. |
| **Stands/displays** | Stands or displays are portable, and potential users can meet people from the organisation. Stands and displays can be put up in shopping centres, schools, and local community centres. | The people who man the stand need good interpersonal skills. Stands at exhibitions or commercial locations can be expensive. Display boards can be expensive. |

*Open days can be an effective promotional tool*

## Complying with the law

Any services or goods that are advertised come under laws designed to protect the consumer. When promoting your services, you must be careful to avoid exaggerating, or giving misleading information.

## Considering the audience

Most organisations use a range of methods, as in this way they are more likely to meet the varying needs of the target groups. Children, for example, are less likely than adults to read a local newspaper, but may notice a poster in a shop window. Be aware of those in your target group who may not have strong literacy skills in English, or who may have an impairment that will prevent them from reading or listening to the information: a word-of-mouth campaign or an open day can be effective in passing on information. Settings might also consider presenting information in a range of languages if they are aware of a potential language barrier, or using taped information for those with a visual impairment.

Remember that children and adults prefer different types of visual images. When creating literature or posters, consider involving children in their design, or at least encouraging them to comment on designs.

### Active knowledge ✔

Look at several advertisements or posters that are aimed at children.

1  *How do they differ from similar ones aimed at adults?*
2  *Ask a group of children to look at some adverts with you. What do they like or dislike about the adverts that you are showing them?*
3  *What can you learn about designing promotional materials aimed at children?*

## Consulting colleagues

Before going ahead with any form of promotion, consult with colleagues and seek the approval from the key people within your organisation. Their input and suggestions can make a difference, and they may also be able to see hidden drawbacks – such as noticing that a vital piece of information is missing!

Most promotional work has financial implications, including the costs of producing materials, photocopying, and postage. It is therefore sensible to agree a budget, making sure that it is realistic.

If you do not involve others fully, a situation may arise in which someone rings in about an advert, and the staff member who takes the call does not know what they are talking about!

## Developing promotional materials

Materials such as flyers, posters and adverts must be carefully thought out, so time must be allowed to develop them. Promotional materials should be shown to the 'key' people within your organisation for their approval. Poorly produced or inaccurate materials and information can reflect badly on the new service, and damage its reputation before it gets established.

Wherever possible, try to get posters and flyers professionally printed, to give a more 'professional' look to the service. Most printers are able to give advice on layout and style. It is also a good idea to look at similar organisations' materials, as this will help you decide what 'look' you wish to achieve.

## Active knowledge ✔

Collect four adverts from your local paper.

1 *Which advert is the most eye-catching?*
2 *Can you work out why this advert appeals to you?*
3 *Design an advert for an existing or a new service that you offer.*

## Posters

To be eye-catching, posters need to be on a minimum of A3 paper. They should be visually attractive and easy to understand. Lettering must be large and clear, and the minimum of information must be given. Make sure that contact details are easy to read.

Most organisations now use typeset lettering as this looks more professional. Professionally printed posters can give you a 'glossy' look, and if ordered in large numbers can be quite economical. If you are careful about making sure that the information is general rather than specific, the posters can be used to promote your setting for a period of time.

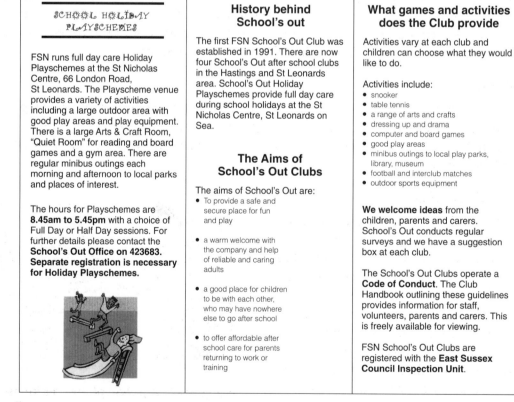

### SCHOOL HOLIDAY PLAYSCHEMES

FSN runs full day care Holiday Playschemes at the St Nicholas Centre, 66 London Road, St Leonards. The Playscheme venue provides a variety of activities including a large outdoor area with good play areas and play equipment. There is a large Arts & Craft Room, "Quiet Room" for reading and board games and a gym area. There are regular minibus outings each morning and afternoon to local parks and places of interest.

The hours for Playschemes are **8.45am to 5.45pm** with a choice of Full Day or Half Day sessions. For further details please contact the **School's Out Office on 423683. Separate registration is necessary for Holiday Playschemes.**

### History behind School's out

The first FSN School's Out Club was established in 1991. There are now four School's Out after school clubs in the Hastings and St Leonards area. School's Out Holiday Playschemes provide full day care during school holidays at the St Nicholas Centre, St Leonards on Sea.

### The Aims of School's Out Clubs

The aims of School's Out are:
- To provide a safe and secure place for fun and play
- a warm welcome with the company and help of reliable and caring adults
- a good place for children to be with each other, who may have nowhere else to go after school
- to offer affordable after school care for parents returning to work or training

### What games and activities does the Club provide

Activities vary at each club and children can choose what they would like to do.

Activities include:
- snooker
- table tennis
- a range of arts and crafts
- dressing up and drama
- computer and board games
- good play areas
- minibus outings to local play parks, library, museum
- football and interclub matches
- outdoor sports equipment

**We welcome ideas** from the children, parents and carers. School's Out conducts regular surveys and we have a suggestion box at each club.

The School's Out Clubs operate a **Code of Conduct**. The Club Handbook outlining these guidelines provides information for staff, volunteers, parents and carers. This is freely available for viewing.

FSN School's Out Clubs are registered with the **East Sussex Council Inspection Unit.**

*A leaflet*

## Flyers

A flyer is like a miniposter, so it has similar characteristics, such as being easy to read, and visually effective. Using coloured paper makes the flyer stand out. Flyers can be delivered with the local newspaper, for a small cost or distributed by hand. The flyer should give some general information about the setting, with contact details for further information.

## Leaflets

A leaflet can be made by folding a piece of A4 into thirds. Leaflets can give much more information than posters or flyers, but still need to be visually pleasing. Leaflets can be distributed on request by post, or left out in public places such as libraries and schools. Leaflets should be typewritten, though not necessarily professionally printed.

## Adverts

Adverts which appear in the local newspaper need to be typeset, and carefully worded so as to maximise their impact and keep down the cost. This means being very selective about the information to be presented. Look at other adverts and the way in which they are laid out, and use them as a guide.

# Other promotional ideas

### Contacting local media

To gain some free publicity about your new service, it is a good idea to speak to the editor of the local newspaper or radio station, and then follow up with a short piece in writing about your new service. If you send some details in writing, the report that appears is more likely to be accurate. It is helpful if you can make a 'story' out of the development of the new service, for example by linking it with a recent news story.

## Open days

Open days can be used to launch the new service and can be a good way of involving many members of the organisation. A lot of preparation is required, including flyers, invitations, and basics such as food and drinks. An open day can also be used as a way of attracting local media attention.

## Stands and displays

A stand or a display in a public place can be an ideal way of promoting a new service. It allows passers-by to stop and pick up leaflets and ask questions about the service. Stands require some organisation, and need to be manned by people who are knowledgeable about the new service. Stands at shows, conferences and exhibitions can be quite expensive, and you will need to be sure that your potential users will be present. Some schools, employers or even shopping centres

*A display in a public place can be an ideal way of promoting a new service*

may allow you to put up a stand free of charge. The display materials on the stand must be of a high standard.

## Promotional products

Some organisations use promotional products such as pens, bookmarks and carrier bags in order to raise awareness of a new service. These need to be carefully chosen, and ordered well in advance of being needed. The amount of information about the new service that can be included is extremely limited. Promotional products can be combined with other types of activities, such as open days and stands.

## Scheduling promotions

Once the different promotional activities have been prepared, check that the key people in your organisation have been informed. You may wish to stagger promotional activities over a couple of weeks, so that prospective users of the service hear about it several times. It is usual to develop a promotional plan, which shows what activities are taking place when.

Timing is an important factor when carrying out promotional activities: it is usually a good idea to avoid promoting a new service around holiday times, such as Easter or May Day. To make this plan realistic, you will need to find out the timescales to which printers, newspapers and other organisations work – for example, the latest deadline for receiving adverts in the local paper might be 2 p.m. on a Thursday.

## Evaluating promotions

It is also a good idea to carry out some evaluation to find out how successful different methods have been. If further promotion is necessary, you can then repeat the methods that have been most successful.

One effective way of evaluating the success of promotional activities is to ask each person who contacts the organisation about the new service how they heard about it. To do this effectively, you will need to brief the people who answer the telephone to ask this question, and keep a note of what is said.

### Consolidation

Reflect on how you have helped contribute to the promotion of a new service in your setting.

◆ *What methods did you use?*
◆ *Why were these chosen?*
◆ *What sort of response did you get from the promotional activities?*

# Element B211.4  Contribute to evaluating new services

In order to check that the new services you provide are working well and meeting the needs of the users, it is essential that you evaluate the service. Developing strategies for such an evaluation is therefore an important part of managing any new service.

## WHAT YOU NEED TO LEARN

■ Suggesting evaluation methods and criteria

■ Discussing and agreeing evaluation methods and criteria

■ Developing detail of how evaluation will take place

■ Collecting, storing, recording, analysing and interpreting information accurately

■ Reporting the evaluation results

## Evaluations

Ongoing evaluations of any service that you are providing will help to maintain its quality and effectiveness. Organisations that do not carry out regular evaluations of their work tend gradually to lose touch with the needs of their clients. A system of regular evaluation will prevent this.

### Methods of carrying out evaluations

Evaluations are ways of collecting and analysing information. Some of the methods used in research, such as interviews and questionnaires, are also used to help evaluate a service. The methods used can be divided into two categories: quantitative and qualitative. Both have advantages and disadvantages, so where possible it is good to design an evaluation process that has a combination of both types.

#### *Quantitative methods of evaluation*

*Quantitative* methods of evaluation often rely on information-gathering techniques such as questionnaires, whereby many people can be asked the same question and their replies then analysed. Quantitative methods of evaluation often produce statistics such as '81% of people replied that they were happy with the service'. The advantage of quantitative methods is that analysis is quick.

Common methods include:

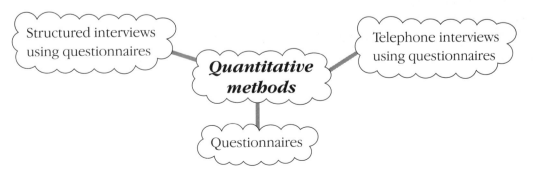

### Qualitative methods of evaluation

*Qualitative* methods of evaluation use smaller numbers but produce more in-depth information. A good example of a qualitative method is a focus group, in which a small group of users is asked in detail about the service. The disadvantage of qualitative methods is that they tend to be more time-consuming, and the information, though interesting, can be harder to process.

Common methods include:

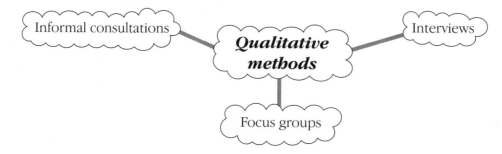

## Planning an evaluation

### Deciding what to evaluate

At an early stage, think what you wish to gain feedback about. This will affect the questions that you wish to ask, and the issues that you wish to raise with your users and colleagues. There is not much point in gathering information and then finding that you do not have the time to process it, or that it will be impossible for the organisation to act upon it. Wide-ranging, in-depth evaluations often seem appealing at the outset, but unfortunately are usually hard to carry on. They are time-consuming to analyse, and they tend to result in very long questionnaires or lengthy interviews. Users may begin to cut down on the amount of information that they give, simply in order to finish!

Most settings tackle this problem by developing evaluations that cover many aspects of the service, and then carry out further, more detailed, evaluations if any area is highlighted as needing investigation.

### Sources of information

The main starting point when evaluating a service is the users: it is they who have first-hand knowledge of the service and who can tell you whether their needs are being met. The main users of a service based in playwork are likely to be:

* children
* parents and carers
* employers
* local outreach and development workers.

It is also worth gaining information from the staff who are working on the new project. They may wish to give feedback about internal difficulties, which will be important to settle quickly so that the service can run smoothly. Most new services find in the early stages that there are a few administrative, building or staffing problems that need to be resolved.

## Type of information that might be needed

You will be interested to learn more about:

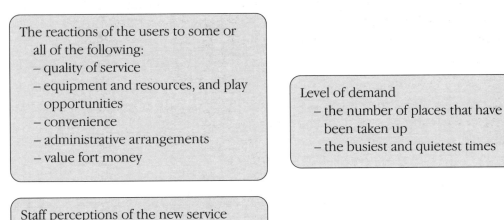

The reactions of the users to some or
all of the following:
- quality of service
- equipment and resources, and play
  opportunities
- convenience
- administrative arrangements
- value fort money

Level of demand
- the number of places that have
  been taken up
- the busiest and quietest times

Staff perceptions of the new service

## Timing and frequency of evaluation

When designing an evaluation process, think about the frequency of the evaluations. It is generally thought to be good practice to have regular evaluations, so that the service can be monitored, changes made, and then the changes themselves monitored. How frequently should the service be monitored? Most organisations use annual monitoring and evaluations, but in the first few months of a new project more evaluations might be required.

It is also worth thinking about the timing of evaluations, as this can affect people's views. People will often feel positive about any new service initially, but then become more critical once it has been established for a few months. Also, some organisations may find that at certain times of the year, staffing and resources are tight, so the evaluation process would create too much pressure.

## Agreeing the evaluation process

Once you have considered information-gathering methods and the timing and frequency of the evaluations, seek approval from the key people in your organisation. They will be concerned with the cost to the organisation in terms of staff time and resources. Your line manager or other key people in your setting may also wish you to gain specific information. This often happens when a setting has been given some funding – for example, all European-funded projects need to provide in-depth evaluations which include some analysis of the participants who have benefited from the service.

## Developing the evaluation process

Once an outline evaluation process has been agreed, it must be developed in detail, according to the methods chosen. The type of preparation required for the three most-used methods are outlined below.

### Questionnaires

Most settings use some form of questionnaires as part of their evaluation process. These need to be carefully designed and also trialled (see page 281). Details of how the questionnaires are to be distributed and collected also needs to be thought through. Getting replies back from questionnaires can be quite hard – response rates are normally only around 30–40 per cent, which may be improved if the setting provides an incentive such as a prize draw.

There are advantages if users fill in questionnaires at home – they are more likely to be honest, and they are more likely to take their time and give fuller answers. Where questionnaires are being filled in at a setting, try to provide a quiet area, with pens, where users can fill them in privately. To ensure that users do not feel under pressure to give imagined 'right' answers, you can provide envelopes and allow users to be anonymous.

### Interviews

Play settings usually use a structured interview that combines a questionnaire with some follow-up questions. The interviewer might ask a secondary question to gain more detail, if for example a user says that she would not be able to recommend the service to others. Interviews generally last about 15–25 minutes, and should take place in a quiet, comfortable area where the participant will not be distracted.

### Focus groups

A list of questions or topics should be prepared in advance, so that the facilitator knows in what direction to steer the group. At least an hour should be set aside for a focus group, and a comfortable, quiet room should be found. It is important to create an atmosphere in which participants feel that they can air their real views.

## Collating, analysing and storing information

There is no point in collecting information if it is not then analysed and acted upon. Information once gathered should be carefully collated so that it is easy to refer to. The next step is to look out for any patterns or trends, which might indicate potential problem areas – for example, that the overall level of demand seemed to be falling. You should also consider whether the evaluations are representative, and have given you a good overview of the service.

Once you have analysed the data, you need to store it carefully. All personal details held on computer will be covered by the Data Protection Act 1998 (see page 285). You may also wish to dispose of the original questionnaires; once they have been collated, you will no longer need them. Disposing of documents should be done sensitively, and they might need to be shredded.

The findings of your evaluation should remain confidential until you have discussed them with the key people in your organisation, such as your line manager or the management committee.

## Evaluating the evaluation!

Whilst working on analysing the evaluations, you should also reflect on the evaluation process itself. How effective has it been? Do any changes need to be made to it in the future?

When thinking about the success of the evaluation process, you should consider these questions.

- What was the response rate like, if questionnaires were a chosen method?
- Do you feel that the evaluation process was representative of the users' views?
- Did you gain the amount of information that you had hoped for?
- Were there any questions that were not understood by participants?
- Did the evaluation method allow users to make positive as well as negative comments?
- How time-consuming has the process been?

---

Q1 What time would you like the holiday scheme to open from?

| | |
|---|---|
| 7.00 am | 6 responses |
| 7.30 am | 6 responses |
| 8.00 am | 17 responses |
| 8.30 am | 19 responses |
| 9.00 am | 5 responses |
| Other | 1 × 7.45 am   1 × 9.30 am |

Q2 What time would you like to pick up your child from the holiday scheme?

| | |
|---|---|
| 4.00 pm | 2 responses |
| 4.30 pm | 14 responses |
| 5.00 pm | 17 responses |
| 5.30 pm | 14 responses |
| 6.00 pm | 8 responses |
| Other | 2 × 6.30 pm   1 × 3.30 pm |

Q3 How many days in the week would you use the holiday scheme?

| | |
|---|---|
| 1 | 4 × responses |
| 2 | 9 × responses |
| 3 | 15 × responses |
| 4 | 23 × responses |
| 5 | 10 responses |
| Other | 5 × unable to say at this stage |

Q4 What ages of children would use the playscheme

| | |
|---|---|
| 4–6 years | 11 |
| 6–8 years | 14 |
| 8–10 years | 19 |
| 10-12 years | 13 |
| 12 years + | 6 |

**Collated information following a questionnaire**

## Reporting of evaluation results

The results of the evaluation should be presented to your line manager or other key people, as they are directly responsible for the quality of the service. The way the information is presented will depend on the needs of the setting. Some settings may require only an overall summary, while others will need a longer report. Settings that receive funds for other organisations such as the European Social Fund (ESF) or the New Opportunities Fund (NOF) may need to produce more detailed evaluation reports. It is usual to say what types of evaluation methods have been chosen, and the response rate. If there have been any difficulties in carrying out the evaluation process, these also should be stated.

If you have some responsibility for the running of the new service, try to make some suggestions as to how to improve the service, based on the findings. In some cases, you might suggest that further information is needed in order to shed light on these findings – for example, contacting all users who are no longer using the service, to find out why.

When looking at the findings of the evaluations, it is important to remain professional and not to blame individuals if the results are not as positive as hoped.

## Agreeing changes

Once the key people in the organisation have seen the findings of the evaluation, it is often a good idea to discuss the findings with colleagues involved with the new service. They may have changes to the service to suggest, or they may have explanations as to why certain comments have been made. This approach tends to work better than simply making changes without consultation. It is also essential to share any *positive* comments and feedback – concentrating only on ways to improve the service can feel very demoralising.

---

### Consolidation

Look at one area of work in your setting.

◆ **Work out a process by which you might be able to evaluate it.**
◆ **Which methods would you use, and why?**
◆ **What type of information would you hope to gain?**
◆ **Why is it important that settings often carry out evaluations to monitor their work?**

---

## B211 unit test

1 Why is it important to carry out research before going ahead with a new project?
2 Explain what is meant by sampling.
3 What are the main advantages of using questionnaires?
4 Why is it important to analyse information carefully before drawing conclusions?
5 What are the advantages of consulting widely with colleagues?
6 List three types of organisations that might be involved with you during the planning.
7 Why is it important that the potential users of the service are asked for feedback?
8 Why is it essential for 'key people' within organisations to be fully informed about the implementation of the plan?
9 Give three examples of ways in which you might be able to promote a new service.
10 Why can it be helpful to draw up a plan for promoting a new service?
11 Why should new services undergo an evaluation process?
12 What is meant by a qualitative method of evaluation?
13 Who might be approached for information which will help towards evaluating the service?
14 Why is it important to evaluate the effectiveness of the evaluation methods chosen?
15 Why can it be helpful for colleagues to look at the findings of the evaluation?

# Unit PC 21

# Contribute to children's health and well being

While looking after children, we are responsible for their health and safety. In some settings this will include providing food, snacks and drinks during sessions, as well as taking responsibility for children's personal hygiene.

The elements for this unit are:

PC21.1  Provide food and drinks for children
PC21.2  Contribute to the maintenance of children's personal hygiene

## Element PC21.1  Provide food and drinks for children

Preparing and providing food and drinks carries major responsibilities. Not only do playworkers need to meet children's nutritional requirements, they also have to be certain that their own food preparation and hygiene skills are of a high standard. Outbreaks of food poisoning can be potentially fatal, so playworkers who regularly prepare food and drink should consider taking a Basic Food Hygiene course alongside this unit.

### WHAT YOU NEED TO LEARN

- Taking account of nutritional needs, and special dietary requirements
- Observing cultural requirements and parents' wishes
- Handling food safely and hygienically
- Encouraging children to be aware of health issues when choosing food

## The importance of food and drink

Food and drink are necessities for the human body to survive. The body requires a balance of nutrients in order to have energy, grow, repair itself, and fight infection.

There are five categories of nutrients:

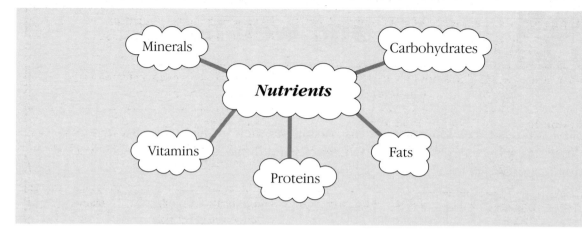

To gain all the nutrients the body needs, we have to eat a *range* of foods. This is because although most foods and drinks contain one or more kinds of nutrients, few foods and drinks will contain everything that a body needs. A varied diet is therefore needed to balance the body's needs – hence the term 'balanced' or 'nutritious' diet. In addition to the five categories of nutrients, the body also needs water; although this is essential, it is not strictly considered a nutrient.

In order to be able to check that you are offering a balanced diet, it is useful to understand the role of the nutrients, and also which foods and drinks they are found in. The table below shows the nutrients in common foods, and why these nutrients are needed.

| Nutrient | Benefits to the body | Examples of foods |
| --- | --- | --- |
| **Carbohydrate** | Gives energy. | Bread, pasta, flour, potatoes, yams, bananas, plantains, vegetables, sweet potatoes. |
| **Protein** | Helps the body to grow and repair cells. In children, protein is linked to growth. | Meat, eggs, fish, milk and dairy products, soya. Wheat, corn, oats, pulses (beans and peas). These proteins need to be eaten with other foods, to work well (as with beans on toast). |
| **Fat** | Gives energy and helps the body to absorb vitamins A and D. | Butter, margarine, and vegetable oil; as well as hidden fats in meat, fish and dairy products. |
| **Vitamin A** | Improves eyes and eyesight. | Carrots, milk, apricots, fatty fish, margarine. |
| **Vitamin B** (there are a number of vitamins in the vitamin B group) | Needed for the nervous system; and helps release energy from other foods. | Bread, meat, yeast, pasta, flour, rice, noodles. |

| Nutrient | Benefits to the body | Examples of foods |
|----------|---------------------|-------------------|
| Vitamin C | Needed for the skin and gums. | Oranges, lemons, grapefruit, blackcurrant, potatoes, kiwis. |
| Vitamin E | It is not fully understood how this vitamin is used. | Vegetable oils, green leafy vegetables, milk, nuts, wheatgerm. |
| Vitamin K | Helps blood to clot. | Most vegetables. |
| Vitamin D | Needed for the teeth and bones. | Milk, margarine, cheese, yoghurts, and other dairy products. |
| Iron | Helps the blood to carry oxygen. | Red meat, broccoli, spinach, plain chocolate, egg yolk. |
| Calcium and phosphorus | Needed for the bones and teeth. | Milk, cheese, butter, yoghurts, and other dairy products. |
| Fluoride | Needed for the teeth and bones. | Water, sea fish. |

## Meeting the dietary needs of children

As children's bodies are growing, they need foods that will give them plenty of nutrients and sufficient energy. The dietary needs of younger children and older children vary slightly. Younger children are not able to eat in large quantities: they need nutritious snacks provided for them, alongside main meals, in order that they can take in enough nutrients. Older children need plenty of protein to support their growth, with adolescent girls also needing to take in plenty of iron and calcium.

Children also have increasing energy requirements as they get older. The energy that food provides is measured in kilocalories or kilojoules. Some foods that are high in energy and favoured by children, such as crisps and sweets, are however low in other nutrients. This can mean that by filling up on these foods, children lose out on other essential nutrients. The energy requirements of children are shown in the table below.

### Types of food, snacks and drinks

Wherever possible you should try to provide children with food, snacks and drinks that contain several nutrients. There are no 'set' rules as to what children can or cannot eat; the secret of a balanced diet is to eat a variety of foods that are high in nutrients. Foods that are highly processed tend to have fewer nutrients, as the manufacturing process tends to reduce the vitamin content – a frozen pizza with peppers, for example, will have fewer nutrients in it than a home-made one, as the vitamins in the peppers will have been affected by the freezing process. This means that wherever possible you should aim to give children *freshly prepared foods* that contain a *range of nutrients*.

### Meals

As well as making sure that meals are nutritious and contain a balance of nutrients, you also need to make sure that they are tasty and attractive to children. Some foods are more popular than others – for example pizzas, pasta, burgers and curries are all currently popular foods with children. Although many of these foods are often shop-bought, they can be made in settings with fresh and nutritious ingredients.

| Main meals | Accompaniments | Desserts |
|---|---|---|
| Home-made pizza | Mixed green salad | Cheese and biscuits |
| Vegetable curry | Tomato salad | Fruit yoghurt |
| Lasagne | Rice, pepper and sweetcorn salad | Fresh fruit salad |
| Chicken drumsticks | Mixed bean salad | Strawberries and cream |
| Quiche | Grated carrot salad | Pineapple and kiwi salad |
| Spaghetti bolognaise | Pitta bread | Baked apples |
| Breaded fish | Naan bread | Rice pudding |
| Home-made beefburgers | Brown rice | Banana custard |
| Moussaka | Basmati rice | Home-made icecream |
| Sausage casserole | Pasta with cheese | Fromage frais and fruit |
| Cauliflower and broccoli bake | New potatoes | Blackcurrant mousse |
| Nut roast | Mashed potatoes | Lemon mousse |
| Vegetarian 'meatballs' | Sweetcorn | |
| | Beans, peas, broccoli, carrots, cauliflower | |
| | Yams | |
| | Sweet potato | |

## Snacks

Most children need some snacks during the day: their energy requirements are quite high and they become hungry. Snacks can lead to children developing poor eating habits, however, if they are often offered foods that are high in fat, salt and sugar. Crisps, chocolates and biscuits are tasty and high in energy, but are low in nutrients. If children fill up on these type of snacks they may not be so hungry for the foods that will provide the nutrients. Gaining the taste for high-energy, low-nutrient foods may also cause children to become overweight when they are adults: once they reach the age of about 17, the body is no longer growing and extra energy will be turned into fat. A healthy snack is therefore one that does not spoil children's appetite for their meals and that gives children some nutrients.

Examples of nutritious snacks:

- fresh fruits and vegetables, such as banana, apple, oranges, kiwis, carrots
- nuts
- sandwiches
- popcorn
- yoghurt
- soups
- home-made ice creams and sorbets
- cheese and biscuits
- celery sticks filled with cheese
- cheese and pineapple sticks
- vegetables and dips.

*Healthy snacks provide nutrients and don't spoil children's appetites*

## Drinks

As well as food, the body also needs water. Water is used in the body to support many vital functions, including digestion, flow of blood, temperature control, and chemical balances. Alongside food and snacks, therefore, you should also be offering drinks. The best drink is water, although milk is also considered to be a good drink as it contains water and other nutrients such as calcium and vitamins. Fruit juices can also be provided for children, although these may be high in natural sugars.

Sugary drinks are not considered to be as useful: they give children the taste for sweetness, and filling up on sugary drinks may reduce children's appetites for main meals. Sugary drinks and some fruit juices can also cause dental decay, as the sugar in them coats the teeth, and turns into a weak acid.

Here are some ways of encouraging children to drink water and milk:

- make sure that water is always available at mealtimes
- make sure that water is cool and fresh
- consider serving water with ice cubes
- consider serving water with thin slices of lemon or orange
- make fruit milkshakes with children
- make yoghurt drinks with children
- make hot or cold chocolate drinks.

### Active knowledge ✔

You have been asked to plan a picnic lunch for children going on an outing.

1. Write down the types of food that you would choose.
2. Explain how the foods you have chosen would provide children with a nutritious meal, whilst being easy and practical to eat.
3. What type of drinks would you provide?

## Special dietary requirements

While planning food, snacks and drinks for children, you also need to be aware of any specific dietary requirements that they may have. Dietary requirements can vary considerably, so it is essential that you find out as much as possible from the parents or carers and the children. If you are unsure whether or not a food should be given to a child, *always ask* – in some cases of food allergies, exposure to the allergen can be *fatal*. Information about children's dietary requirements should be carefully recorded, usually as each child first enters the setting, and those who prepare or give out food should be made aware of any restrictions or requirements. A notice may be put up in the kitchen to act as a constant reminder.

Dietary requirements can be put into five categories, although in some cases you might find that a child has more than one requirement – for example, a child may be diabetic and also vegetarian.

### Medical

Some children may be on a specific diet or have particular requirements because of a medical condition such as diabetes.

### Allergic

Some children have allergies to specific foods, which means that they need to avoid them and any foods that might contain them. Common allergies include nuts, dairy products, and strawberries. Some children may also be gluten-intolerant, which means that they have to avoid many products with cereals in them, such as wheat, barley and oats.

### Religious

Many religions have requirements about what food can be eaten and the way it is prepared. For example, pork and shellfish are not eaten by Jews and Muslims, and many Hindus are vegetarian.

### Cultural

Children and their families may have food preferences based on their culture. This may also affect the way that food is served or eaten.

### Ethical

Increasingly, people are becoming aware of how food is being produced. This means, for example, that some families will only eat organically grown food, or meat that has been 'ethically' raised and slaughtered.

## Meeting religious, cultural and ethical dietary requirements

Meeting children's religious, cultural and ethical dietary requirements is of huge importance, as it is about respect. If playworkers are not prepared to meet a child's dietary requirements they are sending out a hidden message that they do not respect the child's family. You need to listen carefully to the feelings of parents, and make sure that you try your utmost to meet their requirements. In cases where this might not be possible, or where you are unsure about how best to meet the requirements, you should always refer back to the parents or carers. For example, Muslims and Jews normally only use meat that has been slaughtered in a particular way, and buying in this might pose a problem for some settings. Parents or carers might therefore prefer to bring in meals for their children.

It is also important that we do not make *assumptions* about dietary requirements. Some families follow some but not all of a religion's practices – for example, they may not fast, or they may not be completely vegetarian.

| Food | Muslim | Jew | Sikh | Hindu (mainly vegetarian) | Rastafarian (mainly vegetarian, although take milk products) |
|------|--------|-----|------|---------------------------|-------------------------------------------------------------|
| **Lamb** | Halal | Kosher | Yes | Some | Some |
| **Pork** | **No** | **No** | Rarely | Rarely | **No** |
| **Beef** | Halal | Kosher | **No** | **No** | Some |
| **Chicken** | Halal | Kosher | Some | Some | Some |
| **Cheese** | Some | Not with meat | Some | Some | Yes |
| **Milk/yoghurt** | Not with rennet | Not with meat; separate cooking dishes used for dairy products | Yes | Not with rennet | Yes |
| **Eggs** | Yes | No blood spots | Yes | Some | Yes |
| **Fish** | Halal | With fins, scales and backbones | Some | With fins and scales | Yes |
| **Shellfish** | Halal | **No** | Some | Some | **No** |
| **Cocoa/tea/coffee** | Yes | Yes | Yes | Yes | Yes |
| **Fast periods** | Ramadan | Yom Kippur | | | |

## Sources of information about dietary requirements

There are many excellent sources of information about children's dietary requirements. If you are working with a child who has particular dietary requirements, it might be a good idea to find out more about these requirements, which might also mean getting ideas for recipes. Below is a list of possible sources of information:

- local library
- health promotion unit
- health visitors and dieticians
- cookbooks
- videos
- parents, carers and community leaders
- specialist grocers
- local restaurants
- support groups and organisations – for example, the Diabetic Association.

# Keys to good practice

## Meeting children's dietary requirements

✎ Find out from parents or carers exactly what children can and cannot eat.

✎ Check the labels of any food products, to make sure that the ingredients are suitable.

✎ Make sure that other staff are aware of particular children's dietary requirements.

✎ If you are unsure how to prepare food to meet religious requirements, always ask.

✎ Adapt recipes to meet dietary requirements whenever possible, so that children do not always feel that they are 'different'.

✎ Do not make any assumptions about dietary requirements.

# Preparing, serving and storing food

Anyone who handles food carries a lot of responsibility: food poisoning is a real threat to health. It is estimated that 40 people die of food poisoning each year, and children and young people are a vulnerable group.

The threat to public health posed by food poisoning means that legislation relating to food handling is very strict. Settings should make sure that their practice conforms to the 1995 Regulations under the Food Safety Act 1990. The regulations specify that anyone handling food should be supervised, trained or instructed in the handling of food, at a level appropriate to the task they are carrying out. The level of food hygiene in a play setting that provides food should be similar to that of a restaurant: settings that do not comply with the Regulations can be closed by the environmental health team.

## Food poisoning

Food poisoning occurs when the body takes in certain bacteria in the food. Food poisoning cases are usually the result of poor hygiene practices, which have either allowed bacteria to reach the food, or the bacteria already in the food to spread. The most common symptoms of food poisoning are vomiting and diarrhoea.

## Principles of good food hygiene

There are three principles of food hygiene:

- prevent bacteria from reaching the food
- stop the bacteria in the food from spreading and multiplying
- destroy the bacteria.

### Preventing bacteria from reaching food

Bacteria are all around us and on us! This means that very good standards of hygiene are required if we are to stop the bacteria from reaching the food. The commonest way that bacteria reaches food is on our hands. The diagram below shows ways in which we can prevent bacteria from reaching the food.

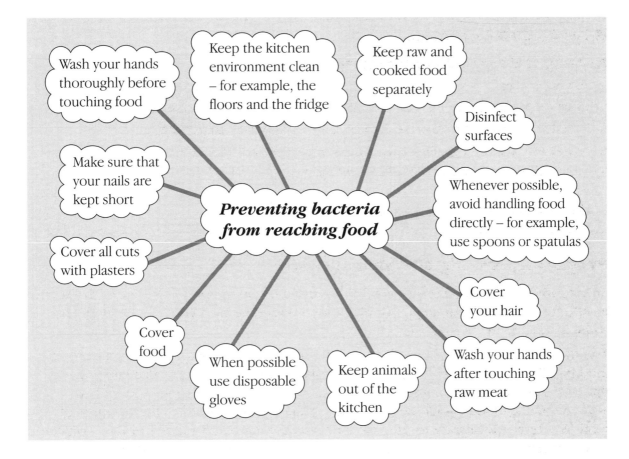

Wash your hands thoroughly before touching food

Keep the kitchen environment clean – for example, the floors and the fridge

Keep raw and cooked food separately

Disinfect surfaces

Make sure that your nails are kept short

**Preventing bacteria from reaching food**

Whenever possible, avoid handling food directly – for example, use spoons or spatulas

Cover all cuts with plasters

Cover your hair

Cover food

When possible use disposable gloves

Keep animals out of the kitchen

Wash your hands after touching raw meat

## Preventing the spread of bacteria

One factor in preventing the spread of infection is storing food safely. Fridges and freezers help this by keeping food cold. This does not completely stop bacteria from multiplying, but it does slow this down. Fridges and freezers should be regularly checked to make sure that they are at the correct temperature – fridges should be kept at 1–4 °C whilst freezers should be kept at −18 to −23 °C.

Bacteria grow quickly at room temperature or in a warm area, such as in the sun. The 'danger zone' is 5–63 °C: between these temperatures bacteria multiply very rapidly.

Many raw foods – for example, chicken, meat, eggs and dairy produce – already contain bacteria when they come into the kitchen. This is why separating raw foods from cooked foods is essential. It is also important to use foods by the date recommended, and to store them as instructed.

The table below shows how to store food.

| Food group | Examples of food | Storage |
|---|---|---|
| **Dry foods** | Rice, flour, pulses, baby milk, couscous | Do not allow them to become damp. Bacteria cannot grow while these foods are dry. |
| **Perishables** | Meats (raw and cooked), dairy products (such as cheese, milk, and butter), eggs, fish | Keep in the fridge. The fridge temperature must not rise above 4 °C. Cooked foods must be covered, and kept in a separate place in the fridge. |
| **Vegetables and fruit** | Root vegetables, carrots, sweet potatoes, yams, apples, plums, plantains, tomatoes, etc. | These should be kept as cool as possible, and off the floor. Root vegetables such as potatoes need to be stored in the dark. Do not eat green potatoes. Fruit and vegetables lose their vitamin C if they are not eaten while fresh. |

### *Destroying bacteria on food*

The main way in which we can destroy bacteria is to heat food up to a temperature of at least 72 °C. The food needs to remain at this temperature for several minutes to kill off the bacteria. If food is only slightly warmed through, bacteria will flourish; when reheating any food, make sure that it is piping hot.

When using microwaves to cook or heat food, follow manufacturer's instructions, as well as stirring the food to ensure that all of the food has reached 72 °C.

## Serving food and washing up

As well as making that there is good food hygiene in the kitchen, there also needs to be good hygiene when serving food and washing up. Before setting tables or handling plates and cutlery, you should always wash your hands. Children should be encouraged to wash their hands before eating.

The washing up of the dishes is also important: bacteria on cups and cutlery, for example, can spread infection. All plates, cups, glasses and the rest should be washed with hot water and washing-up liquid, and rinsed thoroughly.

## Monitoring hygiene in the kitchen

As part of their health and safety policy, most settings will have a procedure for monitoring hygiene in the kitchen. Many settings prepare checklists to make sure that the cleanliness of the setting is checked, for example on a weekly task sheet.

## Monthly Cleaning Checklist

**Month:** .....................................

The following areas must be thoroughly cleaned and checked **AT LEAST** once a month, **IN ADDITION TO** the normal daily and weekly cleaning check.

Please date and tick the box when the check or clean has been completed:

| | Completed/ checked | Date |
|---|---|---|
| 1. Tops of cupboards and cupboard doors | ☐ | ..................... |
| 2. All windowsills/doors | ☐ | ..................... |
| 3. Insides of all cupboards | ☐ | ..................... |
| 4. Fridge(s) | ☐ | ..................... |
| 5. Defrost freezer (when appropriate) | ☐ | ..................... |
| 6. Cooker | ☐ | ..................... |
| 7. Cooker hood (check filter and replace every 6 months if required) | ☐ | ..................... |
| 8. Vegetable rack | ☐ | ..................... |
| 9. Dishwasher | ☐ | ..................... |
| 10. Ensure that there is a supply of paper towels and liquid soap at the handwash sink | ☐ | ..................... |
| 11. Ensure that the First-Aid box contains Blue waterproof plasters | ☐ | ..................... |
| 12. Check deep-fat fryer and contents | ☐ | ..................... |
| 13. Microwave oven | ☐ | ..................... |
| 14. Toaster | ☐ | ..................... |

**Signature:** ..............................................................

*A monthly task sheet*

## Active knowledge ✔

1 *Who in your setting is responsible for hygiene in the kitchen?*
2 *What types of food are prepared in your setting?*
3 *How do you make sure that food is stored appropriately?*

## Encouraging children to learn about food and healthy eating

It is important that all children and young people develop healthy attitudes towards food and eating habits, as these play such an essential part in keeping us healthy. Playworkers can help in the following ways.

## Being a positive role model

Children are influenced by the actions and behaviour of the adults around them. If they see *you* eating a balanced diet, they are more likely to do the same.

Children also need to develop a positive attitude towards food. This means enjoying food, yet eating in moderation. It is therefore not a good idea for children to see adults who alternate between crash diets and indulgent eating. Positive role models are particularly important when working with slightly older children, who are becoming more conscious of their body shape.

## Cooking with children

One of the best ways in which we can help children learn about food is through planning or cooking meals. Involving children in planning meals means that they can learn about what makes a balanced meal, whilst actually cooking foods allows them to learn about the process of cooking. For children to learn, it is important that some explanation is given during the cooking process – for example, 'Did you know that chalk is added to white flour to make sure that people take in enough calcium?'

*Cooking is one of the best ways of teaching children about food*

## Helping children to read food labels

Food labels contain a lot of information. Helping children to read food labels can be turned into fun games – for example, labels can be taken off foods and then the children can guess which label goes with which food!

## Encouraging children to taste different types of food

One way in which children can learn about foods is by tasting new foods and meals. This allows children to try out new foods which they might not otherwise have as part of their ordinary diet. It is also a lovely way of involving parents and carers in settings, as they can donate 'favourite' recipes. One play setting compiled a recipe book which they then sold to raise funds.

# Involving children in the preparation and serving of foods

It is good practice to involve children in the preparation and serving of foods. This helps them to learn about cooking, food hygiene, and healthy diets. It also encourages them to feel part of a group, as mealtimes should be group and social occasions.

To make sure that hygiene is maintained, it is important you supervise children carefully, and the reasons for this should be explained to children. This helps them to learn about food preparation and hygiene.

Learning how to cook is also a practical life skill, and as such should be offered to all children. It is important to make sure that tasks within a kitchen do not get divided in a stereotypical way – for example, girls always washing and clearing away.

## Three recipes children might enjoy preparing

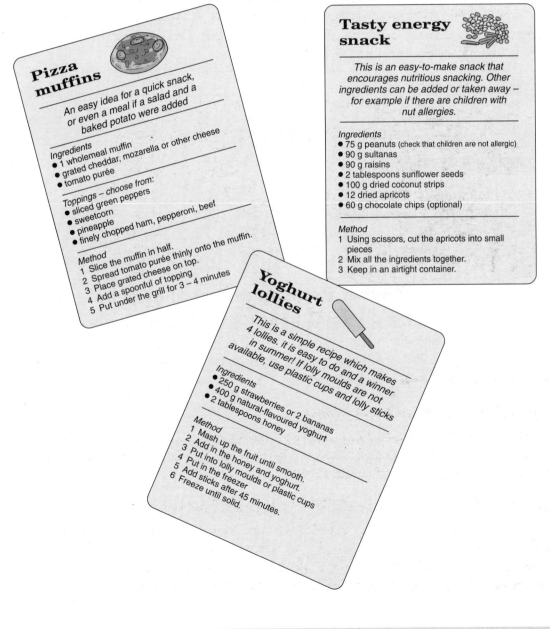

### Pizza muffins

An easy idea for a quick snack, or even a meal if a salad and a baked potato were added

**Ingredients**
- 1 wholemeal muffin
- grated cheddar, mozarella or other cheese
- tomato purée

Toppings – choose from:
- sliced green peppers
- sweetcorn
- pineapple
- finely chopped ham, pepperoni, beef

**Method**
1 Slice the muffin in half.
2 Spread tomato purée thinly onto the muffin.
3 Place grated cheese on top.
4 Add a spoonful of topping
5 Put under the grill for 3 – 4 minutes

### Tasty energy snack

This is an easy-to-make snack that encourages nutritious snacking. Other ingredients can be added or taken away – for example if there are children with nut allergies.

**Ingredients**
- 75 g peanuts (check that children are not allergic)
- 90 g sultanas
- 90 g raisins
- 2 tablespoons sunflower seeds
- 100 g dried coconut strips
- 12 dried apricots
- 60 g chocolate chips (optional)

**Method**
1 Using scissors, cut the apricots into small pieces
2 Mix all the ingredients together.
3 Keep in an airtight container.

### Yoghurt lollies

This is a simple recipe which makes 4 lollies. it is easy to do and a winner in summer! If lolly moulds are not available, use plastic cups and lolly sticks

**Ingredients**
- 250 g strawberries or 2 bananas
- 400 g natural-flavoured yoghurt
- 2 tablespoons honey

**Method**
1 Mash up the fruit until smooth.
2 Add in the honey and yoghurt.
3 Put into lolly moulds or plastic cups
4 Put in the freezer
5 Add sticks after 45 minutes.
6 Freeze until solid.

## Element PC21.1 Contribute to the maintenance of children's personal hygiene

Personal hygiene is an important factor in keeping healthy. In order to make sure that children remain healthy, therefore, you can look for ways to help children maintain their personal hygiene. Personal hygiene covers many areas, including care of hair, teeth and skin, as well as hand-washing.

### WHAT YOU NEED TO LEARN

- Observing cultural requirements and parents' wishes
- Providing suitable toilet and washing areas
- Encouraging children's personal hygiene
- Promoting self-care skills

## Respecting different expectations of personal hygiene

In some play settings, staff may have a very strong role in maintaining children's personal hygiene: they may be working with children with special needs, for example, running residential play schemes. In other settings, where children are with the staff only for shorter periods of time, the role will be more limited.

Whatever the role of the staff, it is important to make sure that playworkers respect the wishes of parents and children, as personal hygiene can be a sensitive issue. There are often variations between families in the levels and expectations of personal hygiene, as well as between different cultures. Some families might shower rather than bathe, to meet religious requirements; while others might insist that their children wash their hair every day. It is important not to make any general assumptions about personal hygiene requirements: instead, you need to talk directly with parents or carers and with children.

The table below shows some of the common variations in personal hygiene.

| Aspect of hygiene | Variations |
|---|---|
| **Frequency of bathing or taking showers** | This can vary enormously, with some children and families taking daily baths or showers. |
| **Showers** | Showers are becoming an increasingly popular way of washing for many people; but washing under running water has been a traditional method for many cultures and religions. |
| **Baths** | Baths were the traditional method of washing in Anglo-Saxon countries, and many people still prefer taking a bath to having a shower. |
| **Care of hair** | The way in which hair is looked after and cleaned varies considerably, with some families using oils rather than washing with shampoo. The frequency of hair washing also varies considerably, and depends in some circumstances on the actual hair type. |
| **Using handkerchiefs** | Some families prefer their children to use paper handkerchiefs and tissues, as this can prevent a spread of infection. |
| **Toileting** | This is a very personal and sensitive area: do not make any assumptions about children's requirements. Common variations include using the left hand only when toileting; and washing the genital areas after toileting, rather than using toilet paper. Most families understand the importance of washing both hands after toileting, and most practices are based on the need to avoid cross-infection. You may need to provide jugs of water to allow children to wash themselves in the toilet cubicles. |
| **Washing hands** | Many people prefer to wash their hands under running water. Some people also use nailbrushes. |
| **Using flannels and facecloths** | These are not used by every family; some families wash themselves using their hands. |
| **Soaps, shampoos and oils** | For a variety of reasons, not everyone will use soaps or shampoos. Some children may have skin allergies and may avoid using anything on their skin, while others might wash with oils. |

## Gaining information from parents and carers

These variations in personal hygiene routines and requirements make it essential that you gain information from parents, and maybe also from children. This will allow you to find out what types of toiletries are needed (such as soap, shampoos or oils), and what equipment or resources must be provided.

Playworkers need good interpersonal skills in approaching the subject of personal hygiene. It may be a difficult issue to raise later, and it is much easier to ask the parents or carers and children about it at the beginning, when you are showing them around the setting. Make a careful note of their requirements, and inform all staff who might be working with the child of any particular requirements. Addressing the issue directly at the outset will help you avoid potentially embarrassing and difficult situations in which staff have made incorrect assumptions about the needs of children, as the case study below demonstrates.

## Case study

Rayan is about to join a new holiday playscheme. The staff at the playscheme are keen to meet children's needs, and are secretly delighted as they have not worked with a Muslim family before. One of the members of staff decides to read up about Muslims and comes into the setting and tells everyone that Muslims wash themselves after going to the toilet, and that they will need to put a jug of water in the toilet for Rayan.

When Rayan and his family look around the setting, the manager of the setting points to a toilet cubicle and tells Rayan that this one will be prepared for him. Rayan is acutely embarrassed and later his father telephones the setting to cancel his place. It emerges later that Rayan was put off coming to the setting because the staff had made him feel different, and that he did not have particular toileting requirements.

1 *Explain how the staff at this setting did not handle this situation well.*
2 *Suggest the steps they could have taken to handle it more sensitively.*
3 *Why is it important not to make any assumptions about children's personal hygiene routines?*

## Maintaining toilet and washing areas within the setting

The areas in a setting that are used for washing and toileting have to be kept extremely clean. This prevents cross-infection, and also encourages children to use them. The toileting and washing areas in a setting can be inspected as part of the registration process, both by social services and by environmental health officers. Settings that fail to show that they are keeping these areas hygienically may lose their registration, or in extreme cases be forced to shut down.

A smelly toilet or wash area will be unattractive, so children are more likely to skip washing their hands in order to leave as quickly as possible. Maintaining the toilet and washing areas should be seen as a priority. Make regular checks throughout the sessions, and clean the areas thoroughly at the end of the day. Whoever cleans these areas should always wear either disposable or rubber gloves, as well as protective aprons or overalls: this is essential, to avoid infections. Follow carefully the manufacturer's instructions when using any cleaning product such as bleach or disinfectant, as the wrong use of some chemicals can produce side-effects. Cleaning products must be stored away out of children's reach, to avoid accidents.

Supplies of toiletries need also to be checked – children are unlikely to wash their hands if, for example, the paper towels have run out. It is a good idea to work hard at making the toilets and wash areas attractive to children: this will encourage them to take responsibility for flushing toilets and keeping this area pleasant. This can be done by putting up posters, buying pleasant and reasonable toiletries, and even by putting some pot-pourri baskets around.

*Clean washing and toilet areas prevent cross-infection and encourage children to use them*

## Keys to good practice

### Maintaining the hygiene of toilets and washing areas

- Check the toilet and wash areas regularly during sessions.
- Always wear rubber or disposable gloves and protective aprons or overalls when cleaning these areas.
- Follow manufacturers' instructions on cleaning products.
- Store cleaning products safely, and away from children.
- Warn children of wet floors, as these can be slippery.
- Clean the handles on toilets and doors, as these are places which may be overlooked.

### Checklist for checking the washing and toilet areas

Is there sufficient toilet paper? ☐

Are there bags for sanitary towels and tampons? ☐

Do the bins need to be emptied? ☐

Is the floor area clean? ☐

Are the toilets clean? ☐

Is the hot water at a reasonable and safe temperature? ☐

Are there enough soap, towels and other toiletries? ☐

Do the locks on the cubicles work? ☐

Is there sufficient ventilation? ☐

# Encouraging children's awareness of personal hygiene

It is sometimes hard for children to understand the need for good standards of personal hygiene as they cannot *see* germs. During a game, the temptation to run to the toilet and back without washing their hands is high: children do not want to 'waste' time washing their hands! It is vital that children do learn about personal hygiene, however, as this is part of developing respect for themselves and taking care of themselves.

There are several ways in which playworkers can help children learn about the importance of personal hygiene.

## Being a positive role model

Children need to see you washing your hands thoroughly, and taking care of your appearance. This helps them to see that this is 'adult and mature' behaviour, and they are therefore more likely to copy it.

## Activities that promote awareness of personal hygiene

It is possible to plan some activities that will help children to be aware of personal hygiene. Activities might include making perfumes and oils, or 'smell-testing' different toiletries and products. Visitors can also be invited in – a popular session with older children is a visit from beauty and skin-care advisers, who often bring free samples with them.

The use of disclosing tablets, which show where plaque is concentrated on teeth, can also be a fun activity, providing permission has been sought from parents or carers. You can also join in activities, quizzes and the like organised by your local health promotion unit. Some manufacturers of body-care products, such as the Body Shop, offer guided tours around their factories: this can be a fun way for children to learn about personal hygiene.

## Promoting independent self-care skills

As well as learning to respect and take care of their bodies, tasks in managing personal hygiene also help children to feel independent. This can boost children's self-esteem. To help children become independent, it is important that you encourage children to do as much for themselves as possible. This is important for all ages of children; but it is particularly important when working with older children who have special needs that mean that they require adult assistance, for example children who are incontinent, who have severe learning difficulties, or who have foreshortened limbs. If you work with special-needs children who have specific toileting needs, you might ask them what help they would like, or find out from their parents how much you should be doing for them.

The key to helping children gain independence is to look at their specific needs and then tailor your approach to these. Children will often need different types of encouragement and support, depending on their age or stage of development. Most children in the 5–8 age group will need reminders and supervision about washing hands and faces, while children in the 9–13 age group are generally quite independent and self-reliant. They may however need to be reminded about washing their hands before certain activities, such as cooking.

Most children in the 13–15 age group are capable of managing their personal hygiene, and will resent any reminders, but you might notice that some of them have become too relaxed in their hygiene, and for example are not washing their hands. A good tactic is to ask them if they could help with the supervision of younger children, or to design posters that will help all children remember to wash their hands.

The diagram below shows why it is important for playworkers to encourage children's self-care skills.

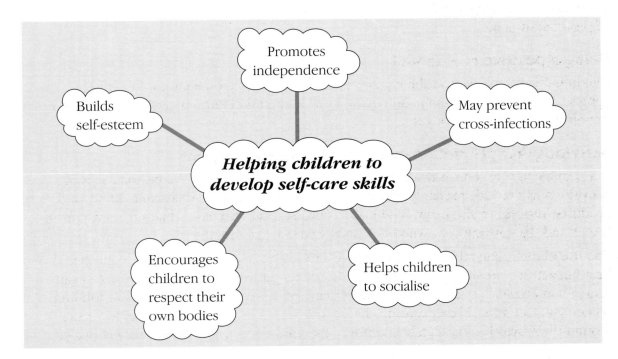

## Consolidation

Design a play activity that will encourage children to learn more about personal hygiene.

◆ **What age group could take part in this activity?**
◆ **What aspect of personal hygiene would it help children to learn about?**
◆ **Why would this activity appeal to children?**
◆ **If you are able to carry out this activity with a group of children, write about what they enjoyed doing.**

# PC21 unit test

1 Why is it important for children to learn about food?
2 List three ways in which bacteria might reach food.
3 Describe ways in which you could prevent bacteria in food from spreading.
4 What temperature must food reach in order for bacteria to be destroyed?
5 Why is it important to be aware of children's dietary needs?
6 Why is it important to make sure that the toilets and wash areas in settings are kept clean and attractive?
7 Why is it essential for playworkers to gain information about personal hygiene needs directly from parents and children?
8 Why should disposable gloves and protective clothing be worn when carrying out any cleaning in toilet and washing areas?
9 Give an example of an activity that would help children to learn about one aspect of personal hygiene.
10 Explain why playworkers should help encourage children to develop their self-help skills.

# Glossary of terms

**Anti-discriminatory practice:** – being aware of and removing potential barriers that might cause discrimination either intentionally or unintentionally.

**Applicants:** – people who are interested in working in a setting.

**Child-centred play environment:** – a place where children can play freely and in safety.

**Collating information:** – bringing different sources of information together.

**Conflict:** – times when children disagree during their play.

**Constructive criticism:** – feedback given in a positive way designed to improve performance.

**Disclosure:** – a term sometimes used when children report or indicate that they are being abused.

**Feedback:** – information given by others.

**Financial transaction:** – when money is transferred from one person or organisation to another.

**Formal feedback:** – information given in an organised way.

**Ground rules:** – clear guidance on behaviour and responsibilities agreed by and understood by children and adults.

**Informal feedback:** – information given in a spontaneous way.

**Joint initiatives:** – working together with other organisations, often to promote or organise new services.

**Marketing:** – a way of collecting information and also giving out information.

**Mentoring:** – support and advice given by another to a less experienced team member.

**Nutrients:** – substances found in food and drink that the body needs.

**Organisational policies and practices:** – policies and procedures that are used in settings.

**Organisational requirements:** – the needs of the setting.

**Personal development plan:** – a plan that helps people to organise their career development.

**Personal hygiene:** – practices relating to the care of the body such as handwashing, bathing, using the toilet.

**Personnel:** – adults who work in a setting.

**Play opportunity:** – a starting point from which children can develop their play.

**Positive images:** – ways of accurately challenging stereotypes that may lead to discrimination.

**Presenting recommendations:** – explaining to others the reasons behind your request for resources.

**Promotional materials:** – items to raise people's awareness of a setting or new service.

**Questionnaires:** – a way of collecting information from others by using written questions.

**Receipt:** – a record of how money has been spent.

**Reinforcing positive behaviour:** – a method to promote wanted behaviour.

**Researching new services:** – finding out about the need for a service i.e. longer hours or expanding the size of a setting.

**Resources:** – any asset including equipment that is used to help a play setting run smoothly.

**Reviewing the play environment:** – considering ways of improving the play opportunities/ equipment.

**Self-reliance:** – being able to take the initiative and show independence.

**Staff appraisal:** – procedures for looking at employees capabilities and career development.

**Supervision:** – using observation as a way of checking that children remain safe.

**Supporting play:** – looking for ways to help children during their play without taking control.

**Teamwork:** – working alongside others to provide a service.

**Work responsibilities:** – duties that a person does as part of their role.

# Useful addresses

The following addresses will prove to be useful, ether because the contacts are directly relevant to Playwork or because they have helpful background information.

British Red Cross Society
9 Grosvenor Crescent
London
SW1X 7EJ
Tel: 020 7235 5454
(Runs First Aid courses)

CACHE
8 Chequer Street
St. Albans
Herts
AL1 3XZ
**www.cache.org.uk**

Child Accident Prevention Trust
18–20 Farringdon Lane
London
EC1R 3AU
Tel: 020 7608 3828
(Advice on safety and prevention
of accidents)

Childline
Royal Mail Building
Studd Street
London
N1 0QW
Tel: 020 7239 1000

Citizen's Advice Bureau
National Association of Citizen's
Advice Bureaux
Myddleton House
115–123 Pentonville Road
London
N1 9LZ

DfEE
Sanctuary Buildings
Great Smith Street
London
SW1 3BT
**www.dfee.gov.uk**

Equal Opportunities Commission
Overseas House
Quay Street
Manchester
Tel: 0161 833 9244

Health Education Authority
Trevelyan House
30 Great Peters Street
London
SW1P 2HW
Tel: 020 7222 5300

Health and Safety Executive
Broad Lane
Sheffield
S3 7HQ
Tel: 0541 545500
**www.open.gov.uk/hse/hsehome.htm**

Individual Learning Account Helpline
Tel: 0800 072 5678
(For details about Individual Learning
Accounts)

KIDSCAPE
2 Grosvenor Gardens,
London
SW1W ODH
Tel: 020 7730 3300
Fax: 020 7730 7081
**www.kidscape.org.uk**
(Provides training and advice about child
protection. Also runs helplines for children)

Kids Club Network
Bellerive House
3 Muirfield Crescent
London
E14 9SZ
Tel: 020 7512 2112

Learning Direct
Tel: 0800 100 900
(Government-funded careers and
education helpline)

NSPCC
National Centre
42 Curtain Road
London
EC2A 3NH
Tel: 020 7267 1361

Parent Network
Room 2
Winchester House
11 Cranmer Road
London
SW9 6EJ
(Runs parent link groups which offer
support and advice)

Parents Anonymous
6–9 Manor Gardens
London
N7 6LA
Tel: 020 7263 8918
(Support for parents who feel that
they cannot cope or might abuse
their children)

Planit4kids.com
Information about activities and clubs for
children throughout the UK
**www.planit4kids.com**

SPRITO
24 Stephenson Way
London
NW1 2HD
Tel: 020 7388 7755
Fax: 020 7388 9733
**www.sprito.org.uk**

St John's Ambulance
1 Grosvenor Crescent
London
SW1X 7EF
Tel: 020 7235 5231
(Runs First Aid courses)

# Index